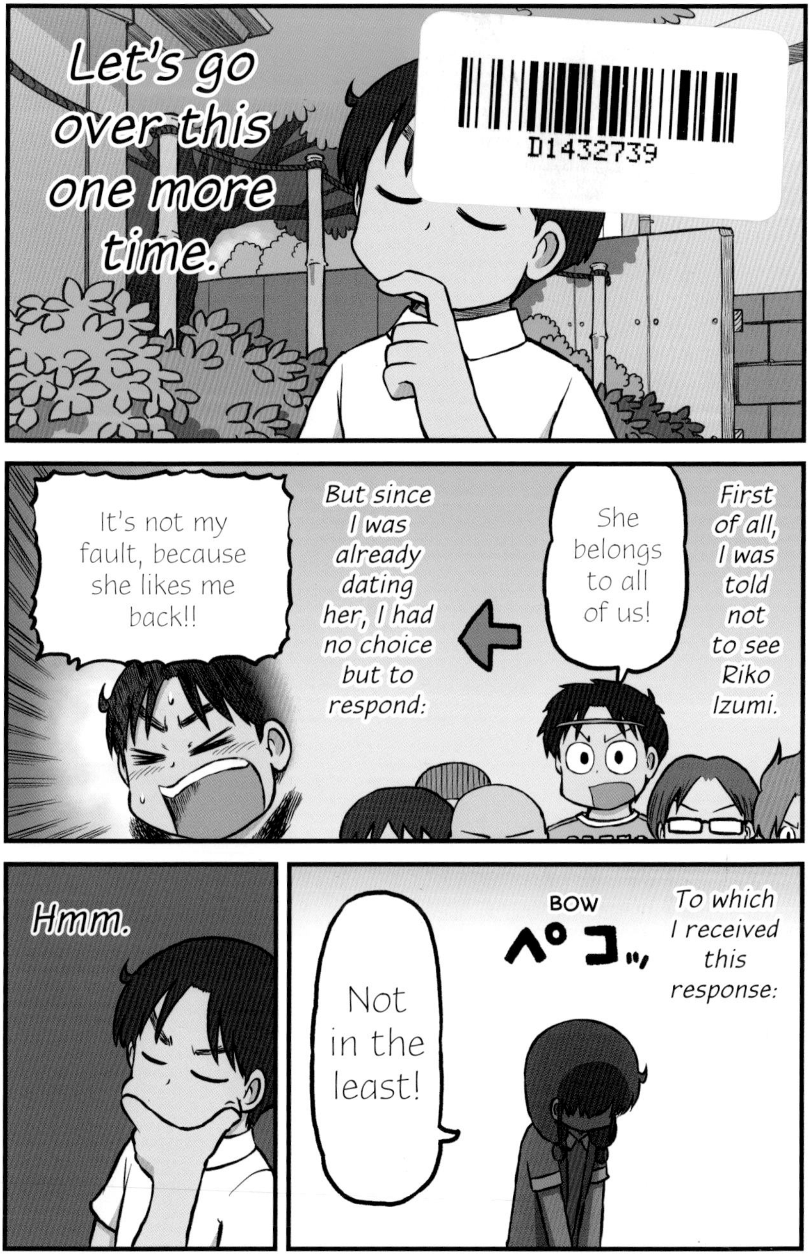
Let's go over this one more time.
First of all, I was told not to see Riko Izumi.
She belongs to all of us!
But since I was already dating her, I had no choice but to respond:
It's not my fault, because she likes me back!!
To which I received this response:
BOW
ペコッ
Not in the least!
Hmm.

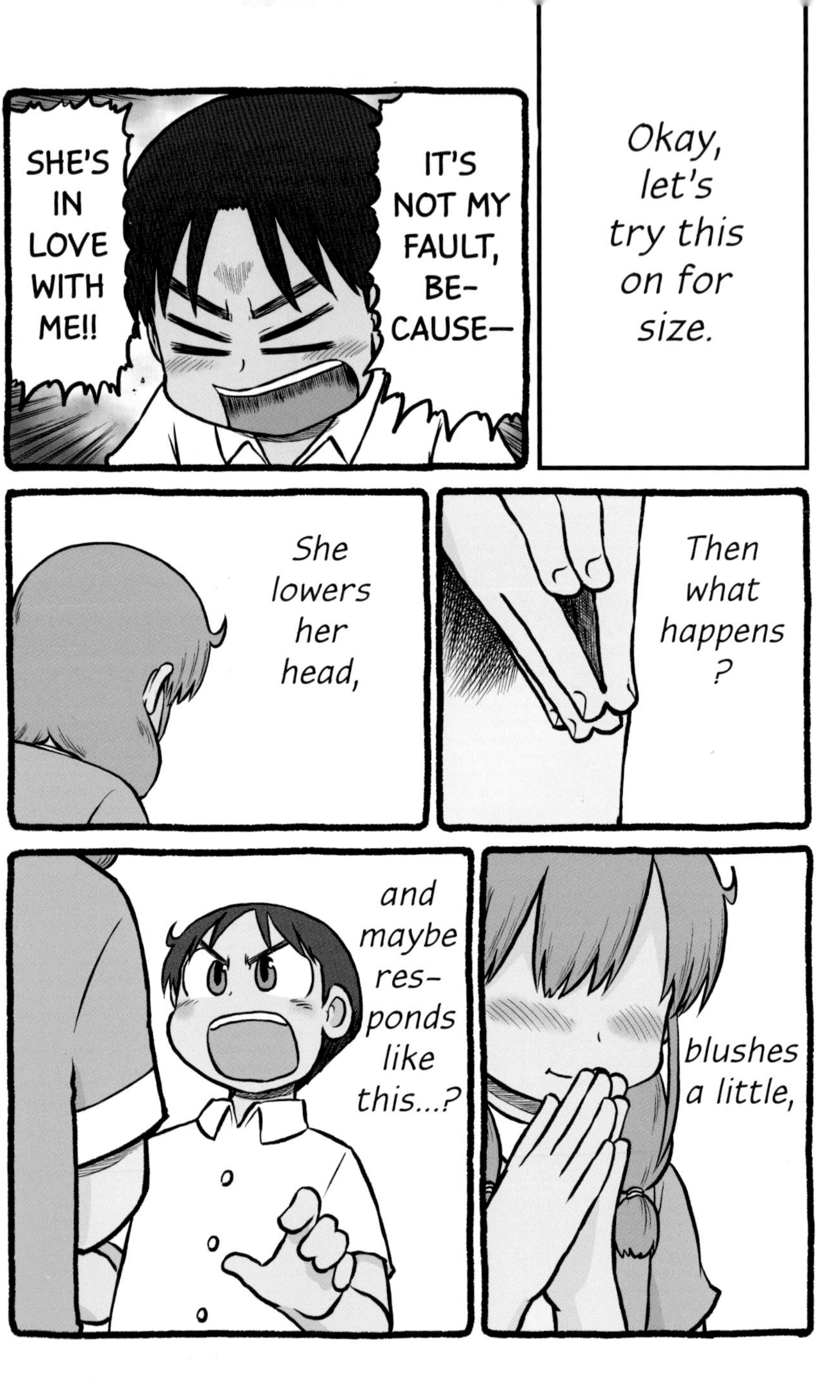
Okay, let's try this on for size.
IT'S NOT MY FAULT, BE-CAUSE—
SHE'S IN LOVE WITH ME!!
Then what happens?
She lowers her head,
blushes a little,
and maybe res-ponds like this...?

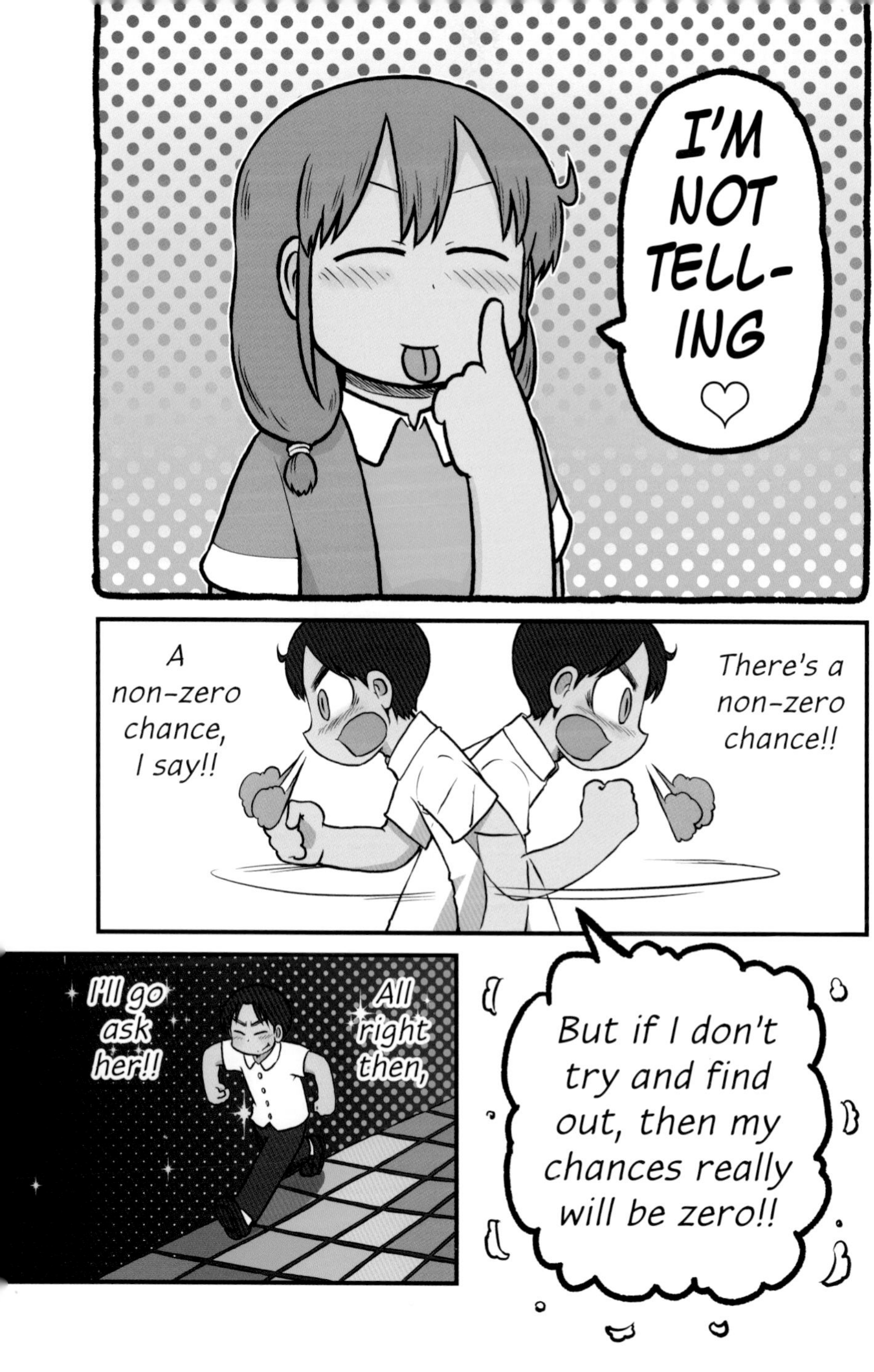
I'M NOT TELL-ING ♡
There's a non-zero chance!!
A non-zero chance, I say!!
But if I don't try and find out, then my chances really will be zero!!
All right then,
I'll go ask her!!

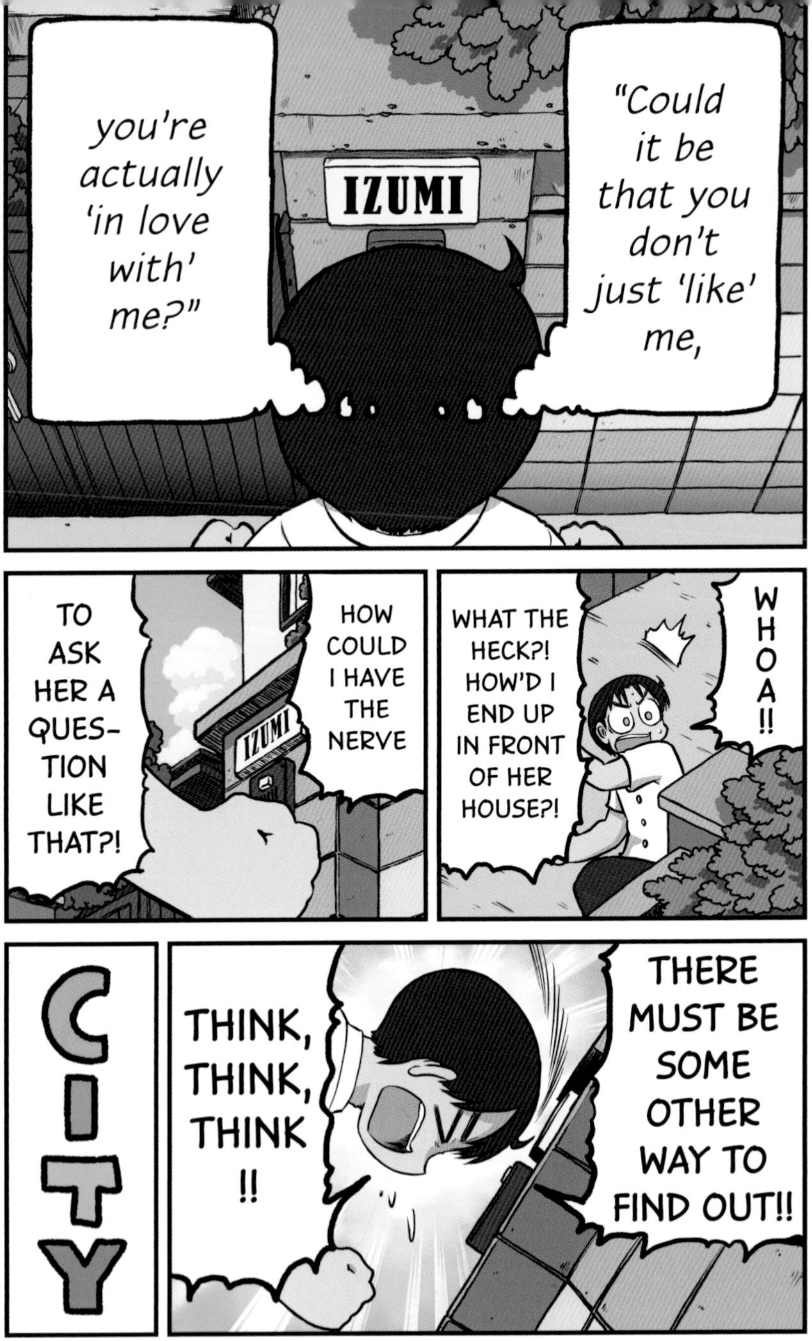
"Could it be that you don't just 'like' me,
you're actually 'in love with' me?"
IZUMI
WHOA!!
WHAT THE HECK?! HOW'D I END UP IN FRONT OF HER HOUSE?!
HOW COULD I HAVE THE NERVE
TO ASK HER A QUES-TION LIKE THAT?!
IZUMI
THERE MUST BE SOME OTHER WAY TO FIND OUT!!
THINK, THINK, THINK!!
CITY

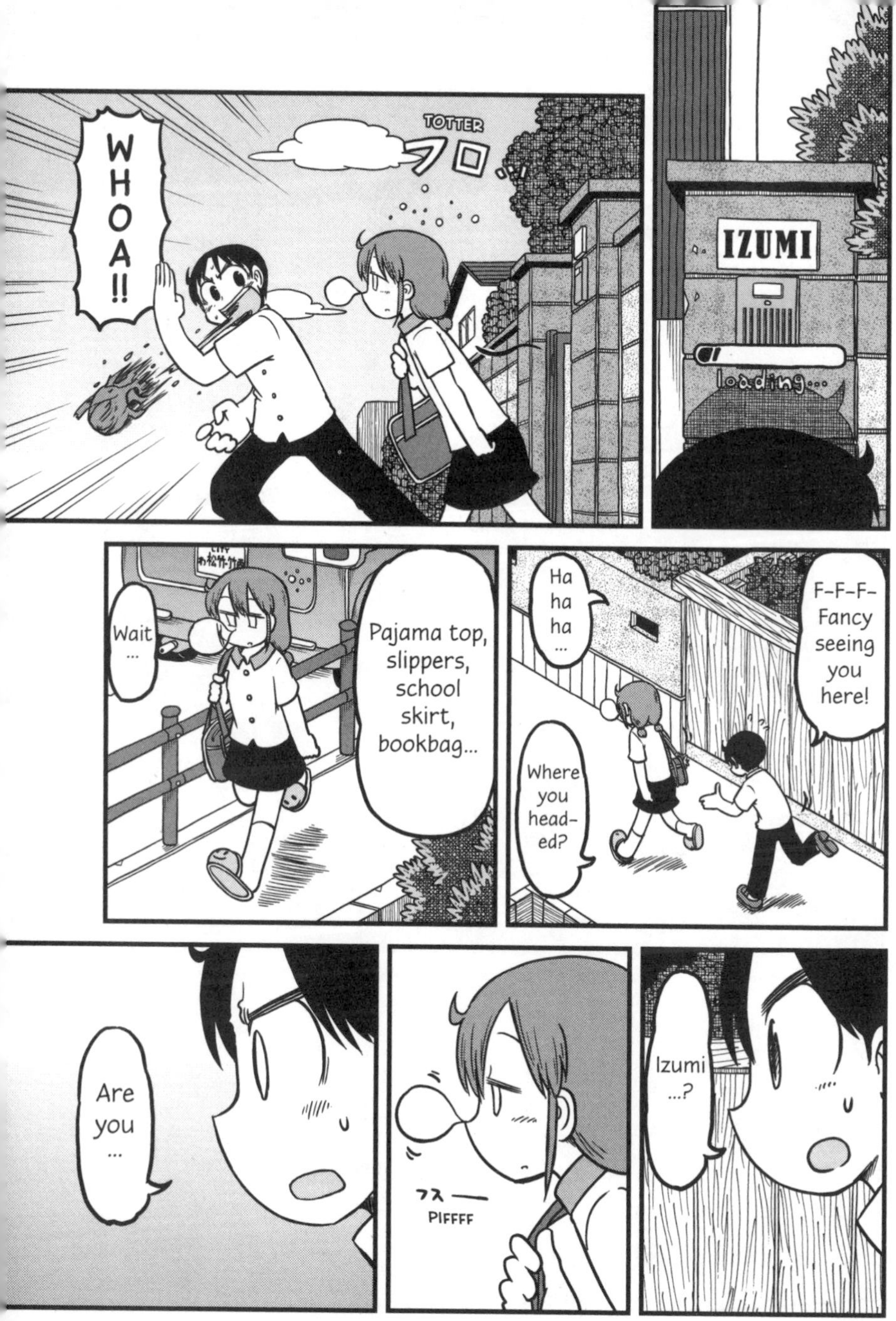
IZUMI
loading...
TOTTER
フロ
WHOA!!
F-F-F-Fancy seeing you here!
Ha ha ha...
Where you headed?
Pajama top, slippers, school skirt, bookbag...
Wait...
Izumi ...?
フスー
PIFFFF
Are you ...

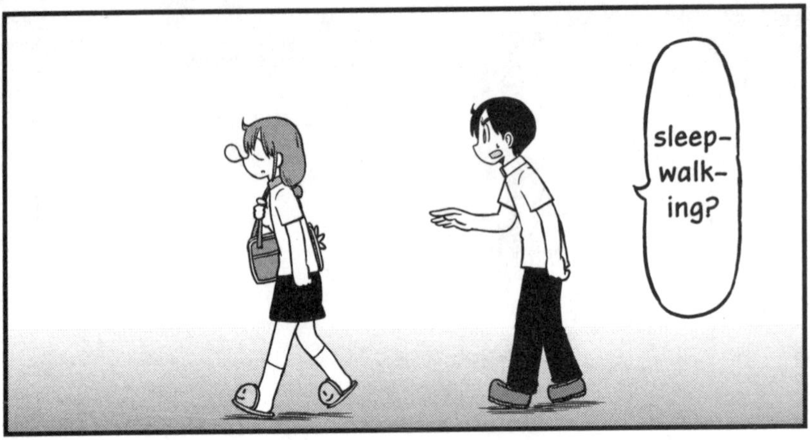
sleep-
walk-
ing?

Chapter 137 Riko Izumi Goes Sleepwalking

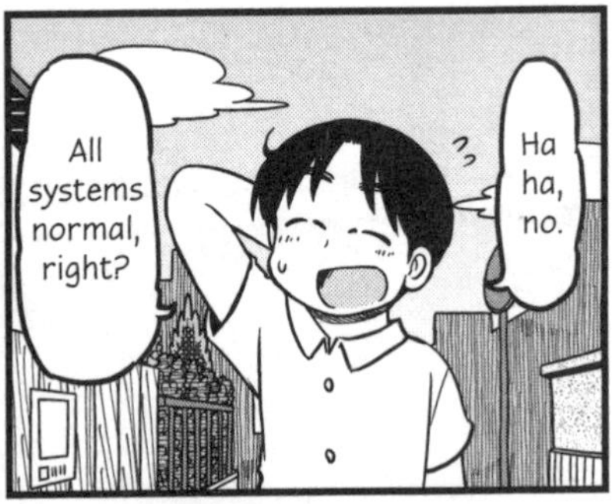
All systems normal, right?
Ha ha, no.

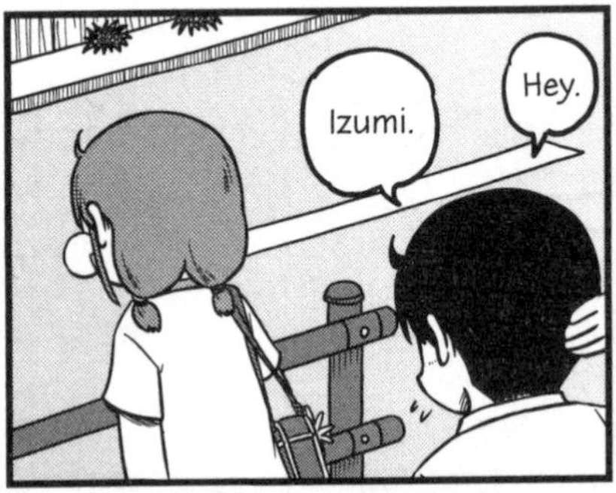
Hey.
Izumi.

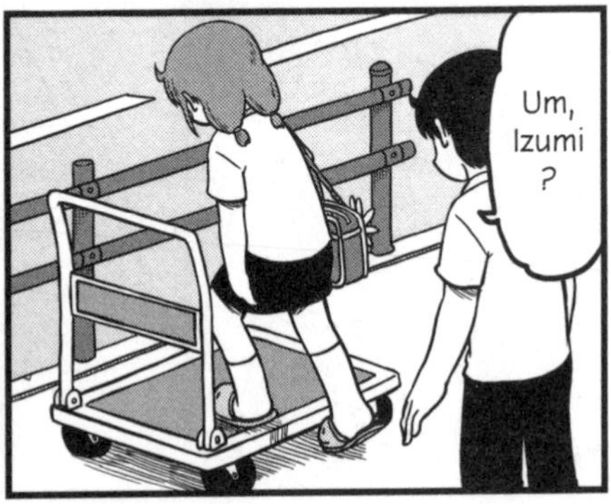
Um, Izumi ?

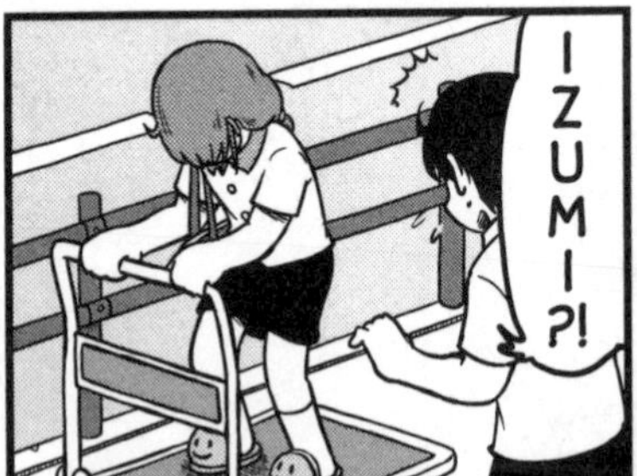
IZUMI?!

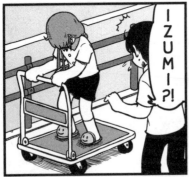

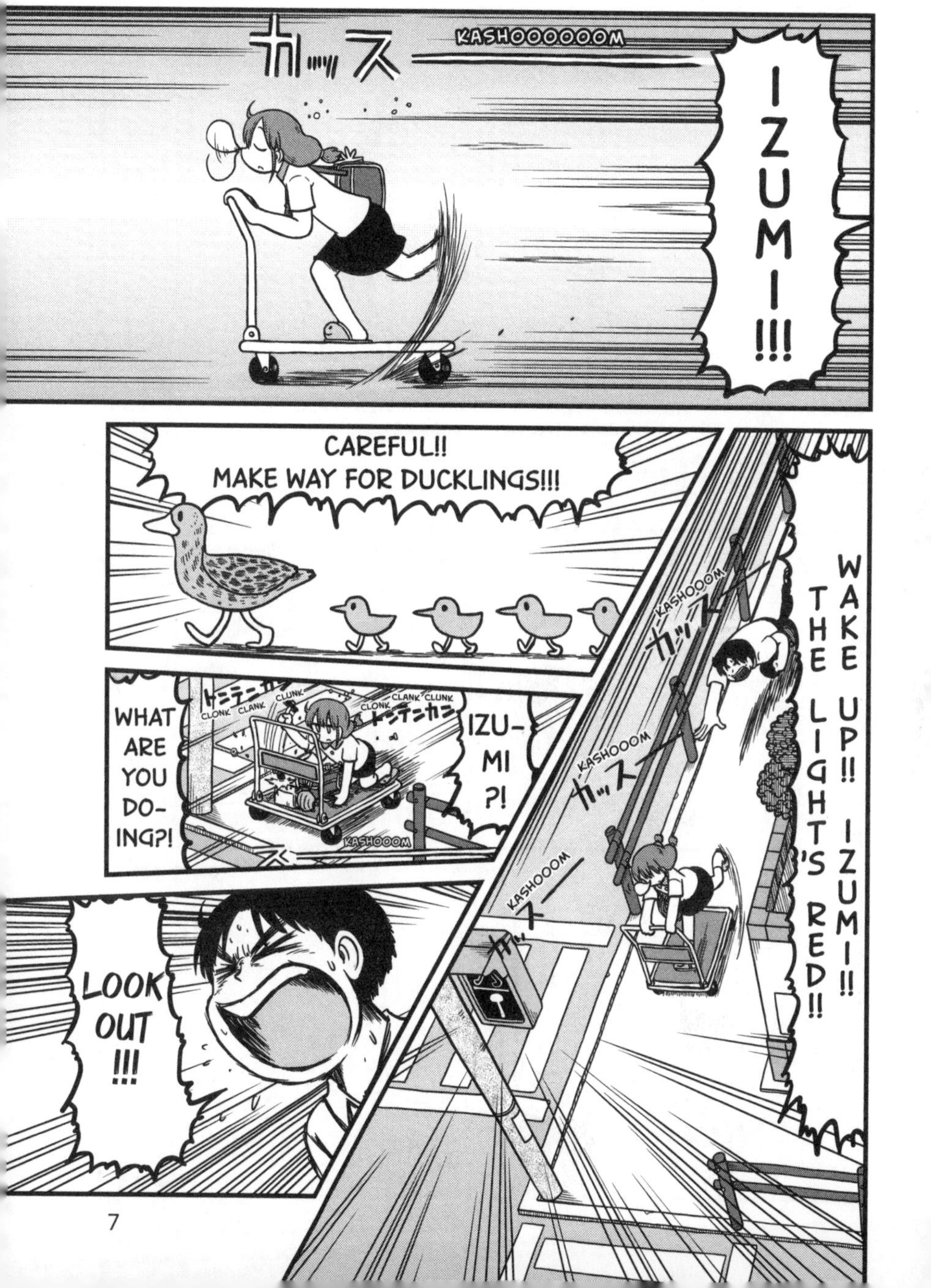

IZUMI!!!!
KASHOOOOOOOM
カッス
WAKE UP!! IZUMI!!
THE LIGHT'S RED!!
KASHOOOM
カッス
KASHOOOM
カッス
KASHOOOM
カッス
CAREFUL!!
MAKE WAY FOR DUCKLINGS!!!
IZUMI?!
WHAT ARE YOU DOING?!
CLONK CLONK CLONK
トンテンカン
CLONK CLONK CLONK
トンテンカン
KASHOOOM
LOOK OUT!!!

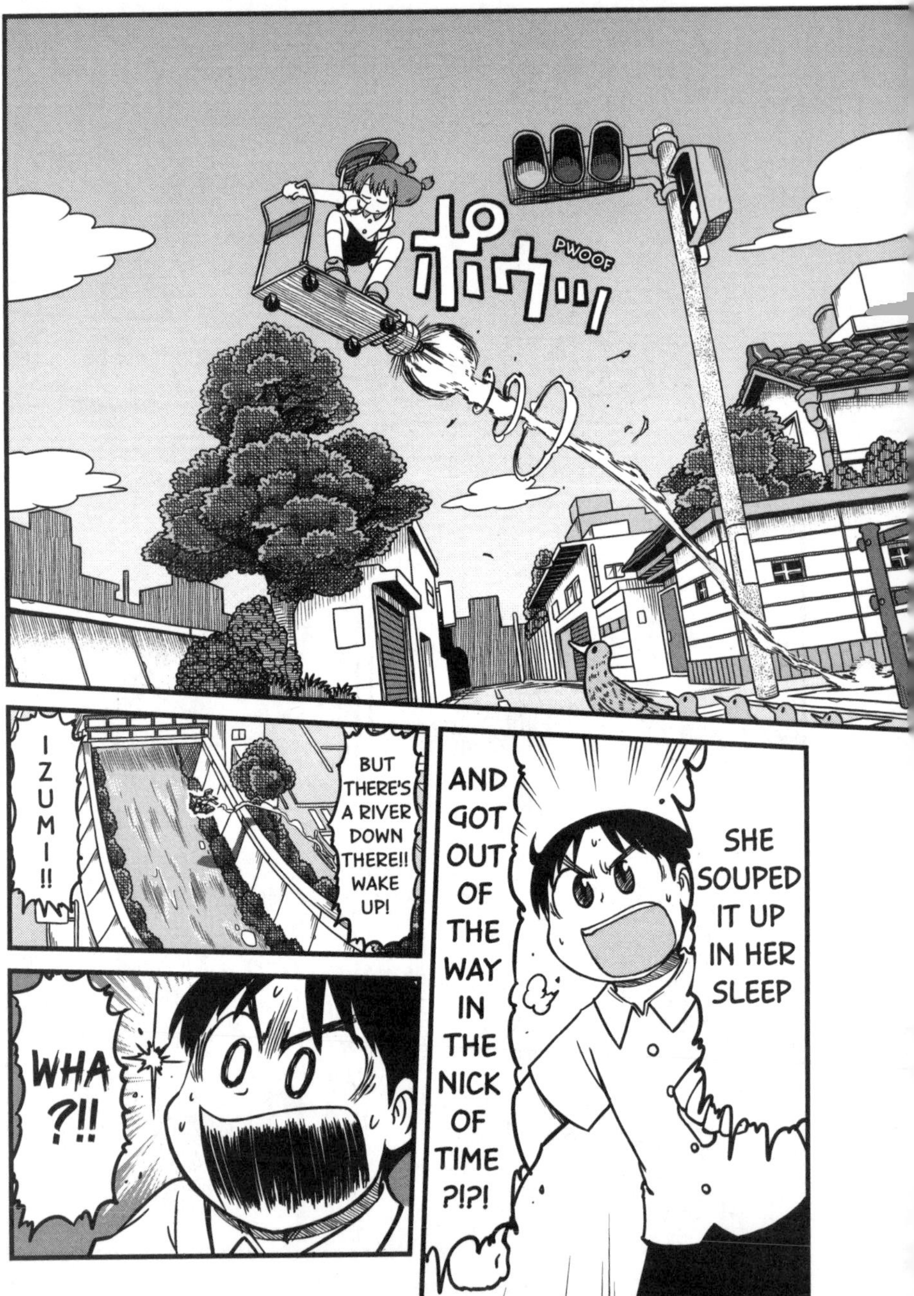
ポウッ
PWOOF
SHE SOUPED IT UP IN HER SLEEP
AND GOT OUT OF THE WAY IN THE NICK OF TIME ?!?!
BUT THERE'S A RIVER DOWN THERE!! WAKE UP!
IZUMI!!
WHA ?!!

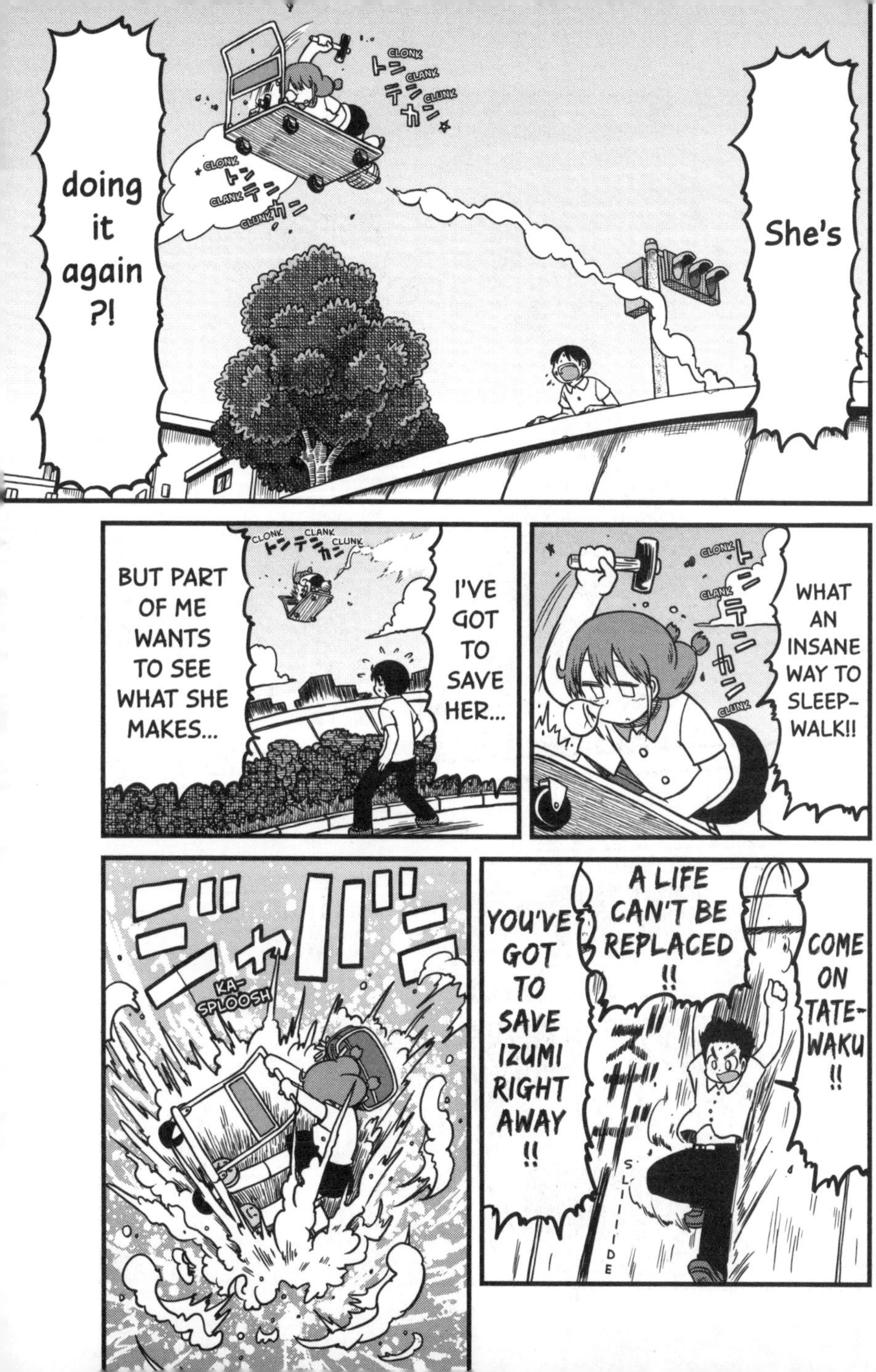
She's
doing it again?!
CLONK CLANK CLUNK
BUT PART OF ME WANTS TO SEE WHAT SHE MAKES...
CLONK
CLANK
CLUNK
WHAT AN INSANE WAY TO SLEEP-WALK!!
I'VE GOT TO SAVE HER...
CLONK CLANK CLUNK
COME ON TATE-WAKU!!
A LIFE CAN'T BE REPLACED!!
YOU'VE GOT TO SAVE IZUMI RIGHT AWAY!!
SLIIIIDE
KA-SPLOOSH

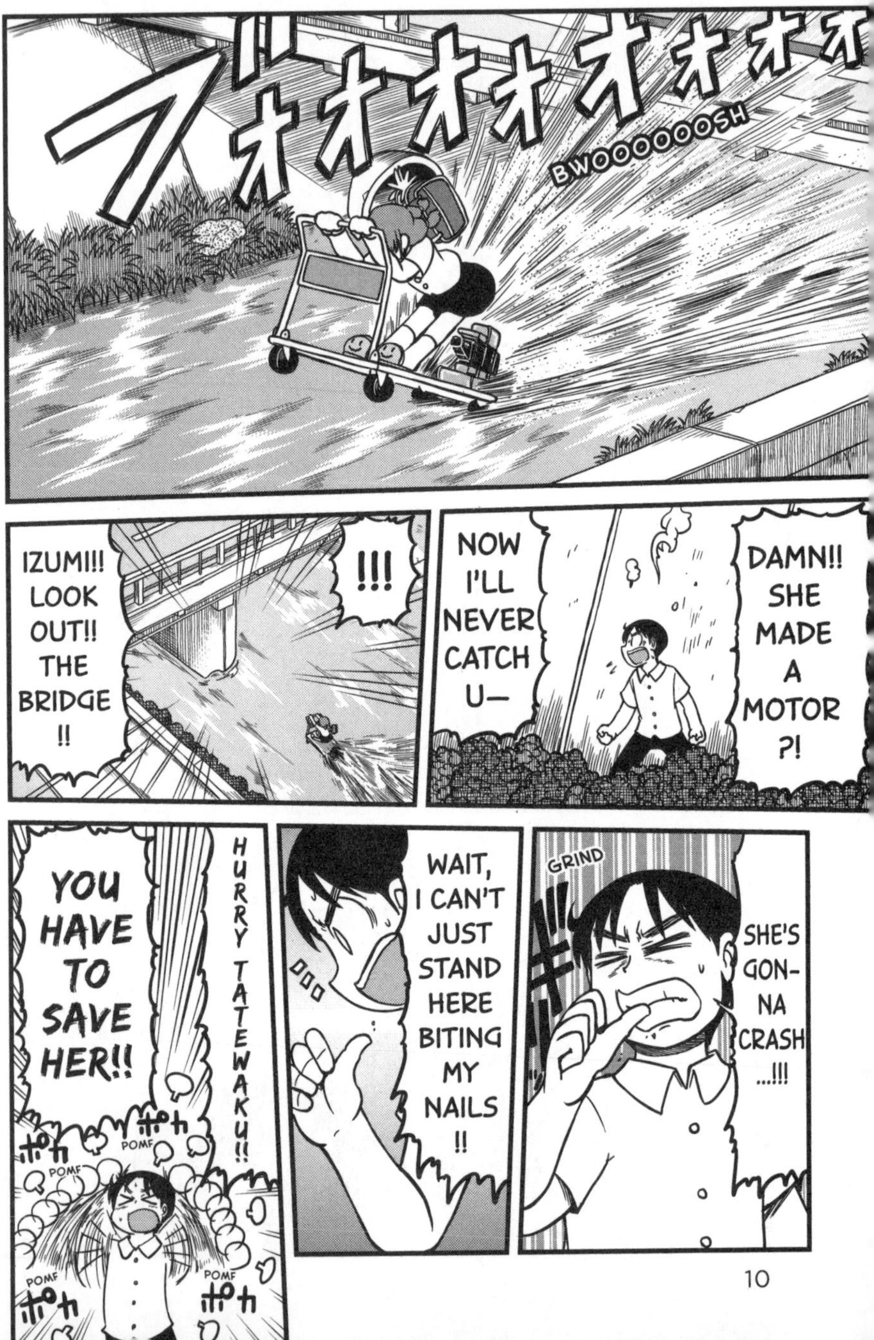
ブオオオオオオオ
BWOOOOOOOSH
DAMN!! SHE MADE A MOTOR ?!
NOW I'LL NEVER CATCH U—
!!!
IZUMI!! LOOK OUT!! THE BRIDGE !!
GRIND
SHE'S GON-NA CRASH ...!!!
WAIT, I CAN'T JUST STAND HERE BITING MY NAILS !!
HURRY TATEWAKU!!
YOU HAVE TO SAVE HER!!
ポカ
POMF
ポカ
POMF
ポカ
POMF
ポカ
POMF

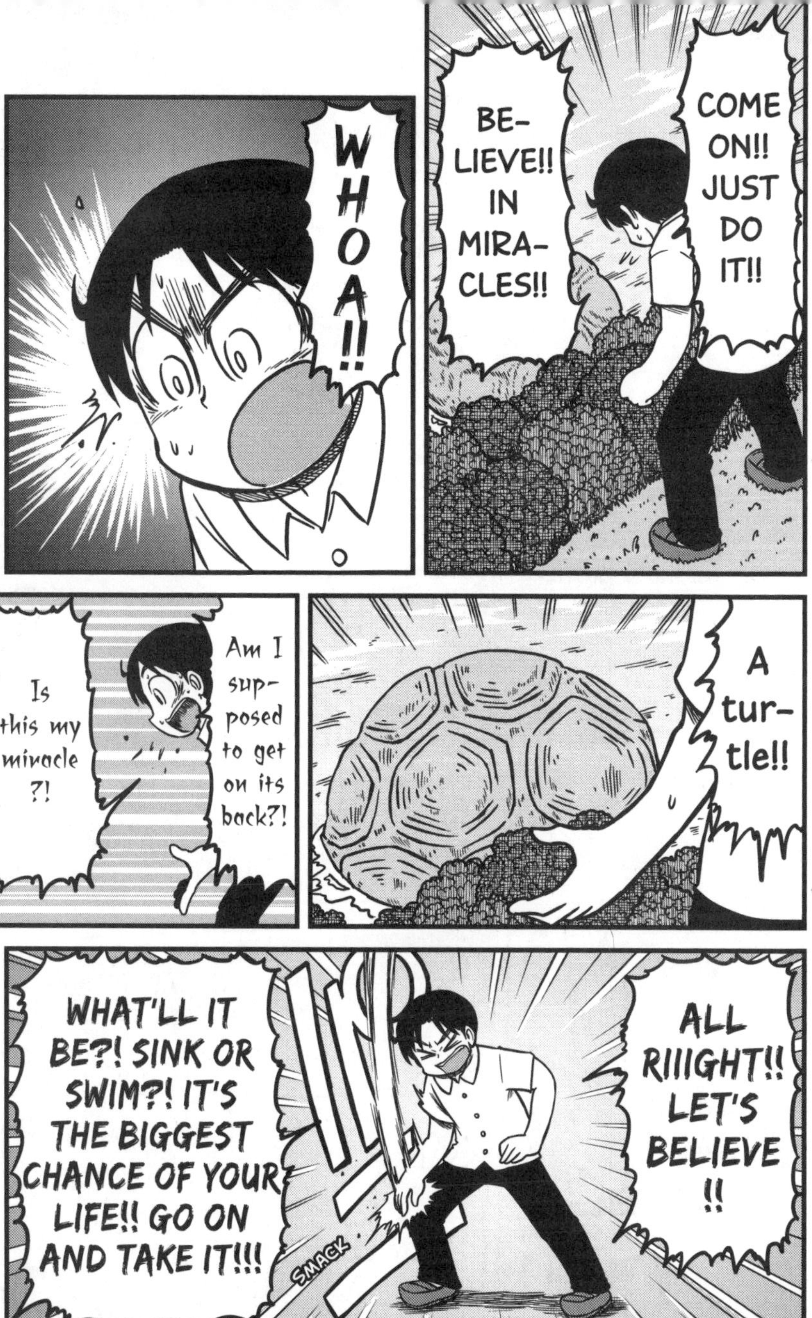
COME ON!! JUST DO IT!!
BE-LIEVE!! IN MIRA-CLES!!
WHOA!!
A tur-tle!!
Am I sup-posed to get on its back?!
Is this my miracle?!
ALL RIIIGHT!! LET'S BELIEVE!!
WHAT'LL IT BE?! SINK OR SWIM?! IT'S THE BIGGEST CHANCE OF YOUR LIFE!! GO ON AND TAKE IT!!!
SMACK

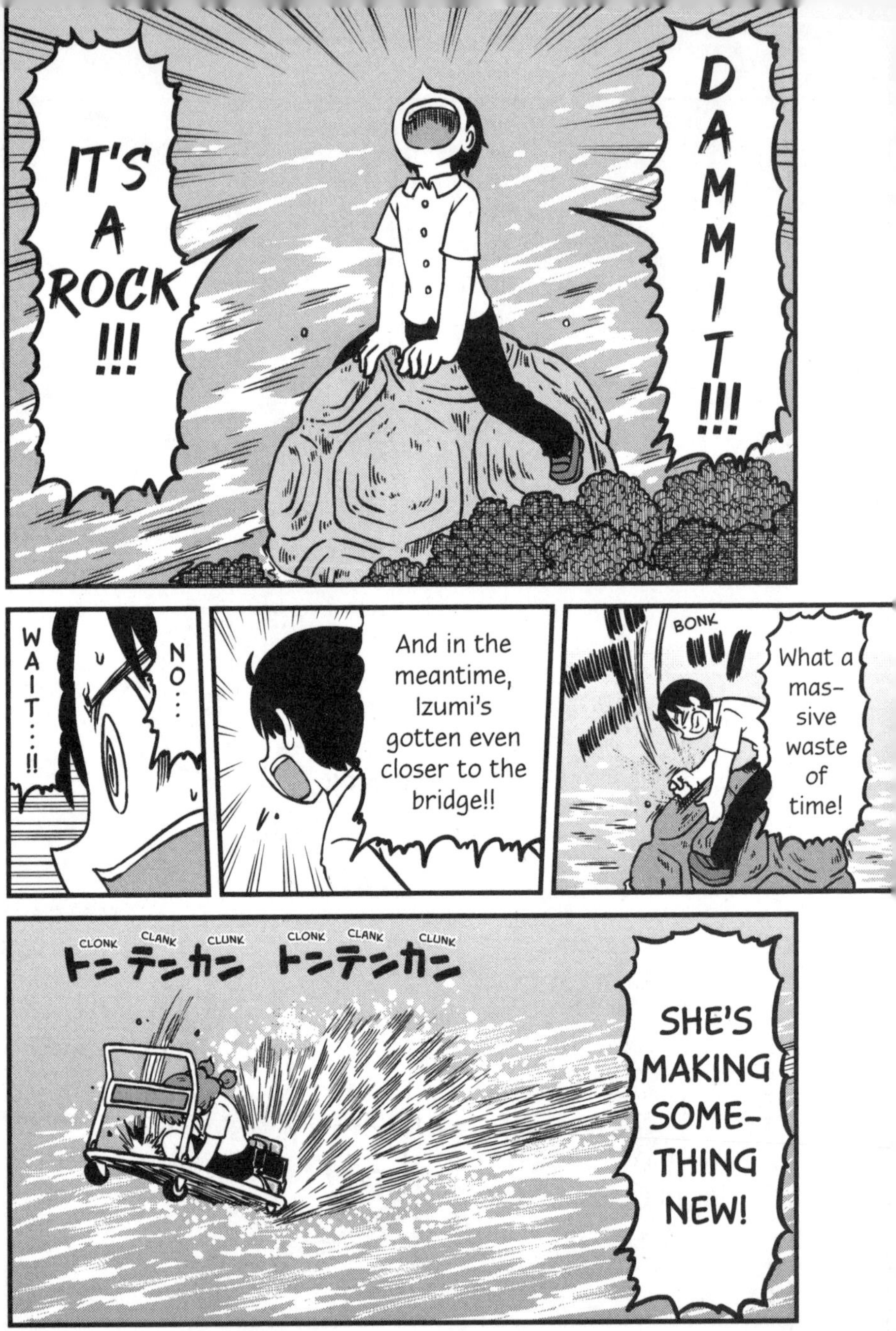
DAMMIT!!!
IT'S A ROCK!!!
BONK
What a mas-sive waste of time!
And in the meantime, Izumi's gotten even closer to the bridge!!
NO…
WAIT…!!
SHE'S MAKING SOME-THING NEW!
CLONK CLANK CLUNK
トンテンカン
CLONK CLANK CLUNK
トンテンカン

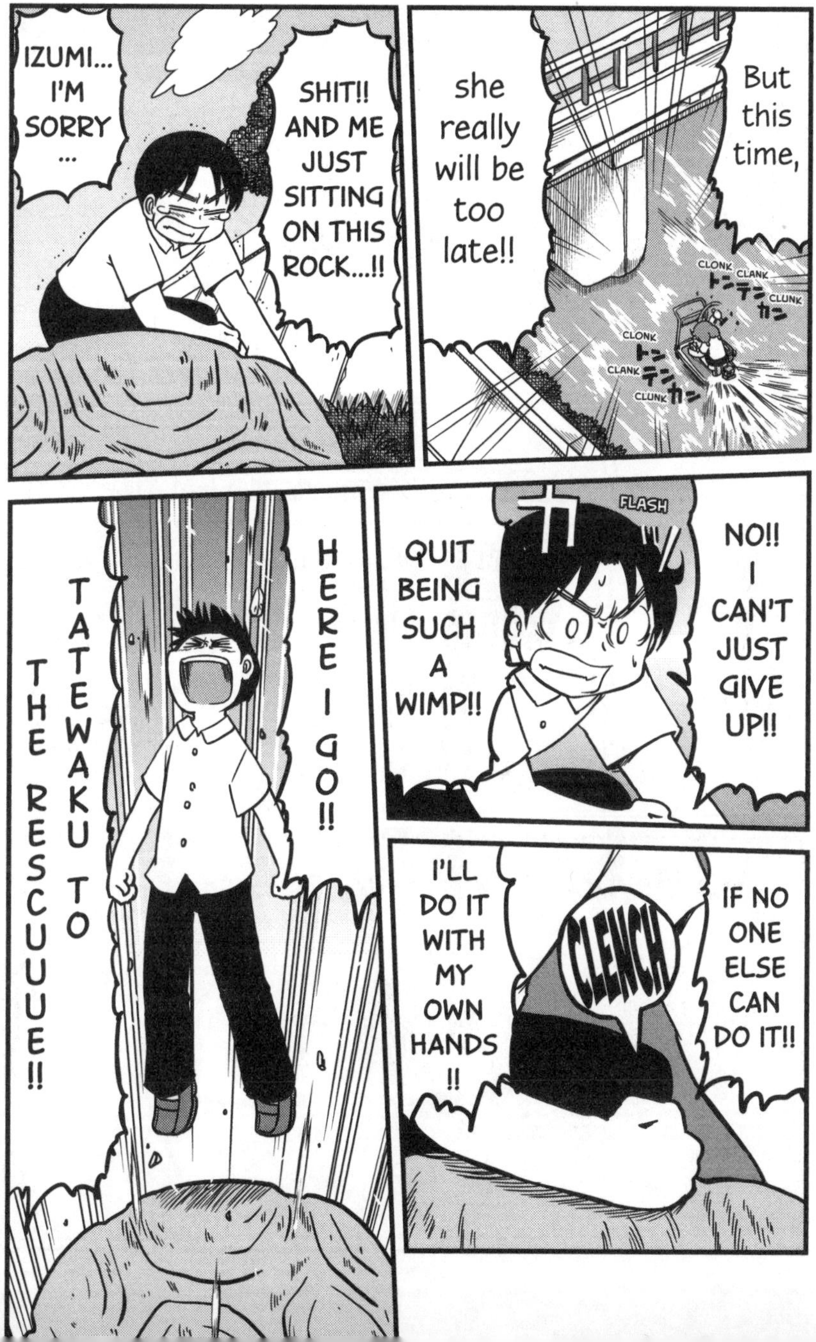
But this time,
she really will be too late!!
CLONK CLANK トンテン CLUNK カン
CLONK トン CLANK テン CLUNK カン
SHIT!! AND ME JUST SITTING ON THIS ROCK...!!
IZUMI... I'M SORRY...
FLASH
NO!! I CAN'T JUST GIVE UP!!
QUIT BEING SUCH A WIMP!!
IF NO ONE ELSE CAN DO IT!!
CLENCH
I'LL DO IT WITH MY OWN HANDS!!
HERE I GO!!
TATEWAKU TO THE RESCUUUUE!!

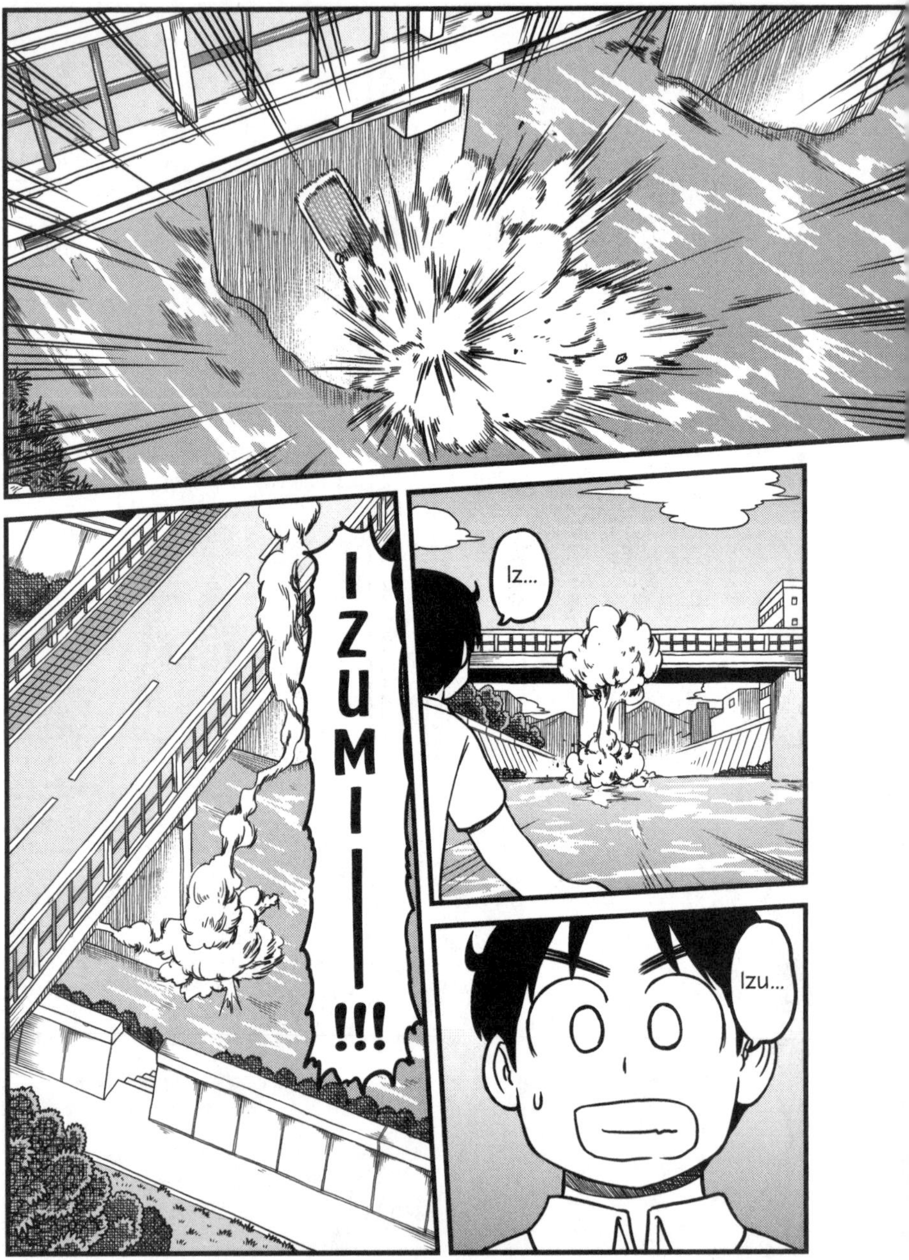
Iz...
Izu...
IZUMI———!!!

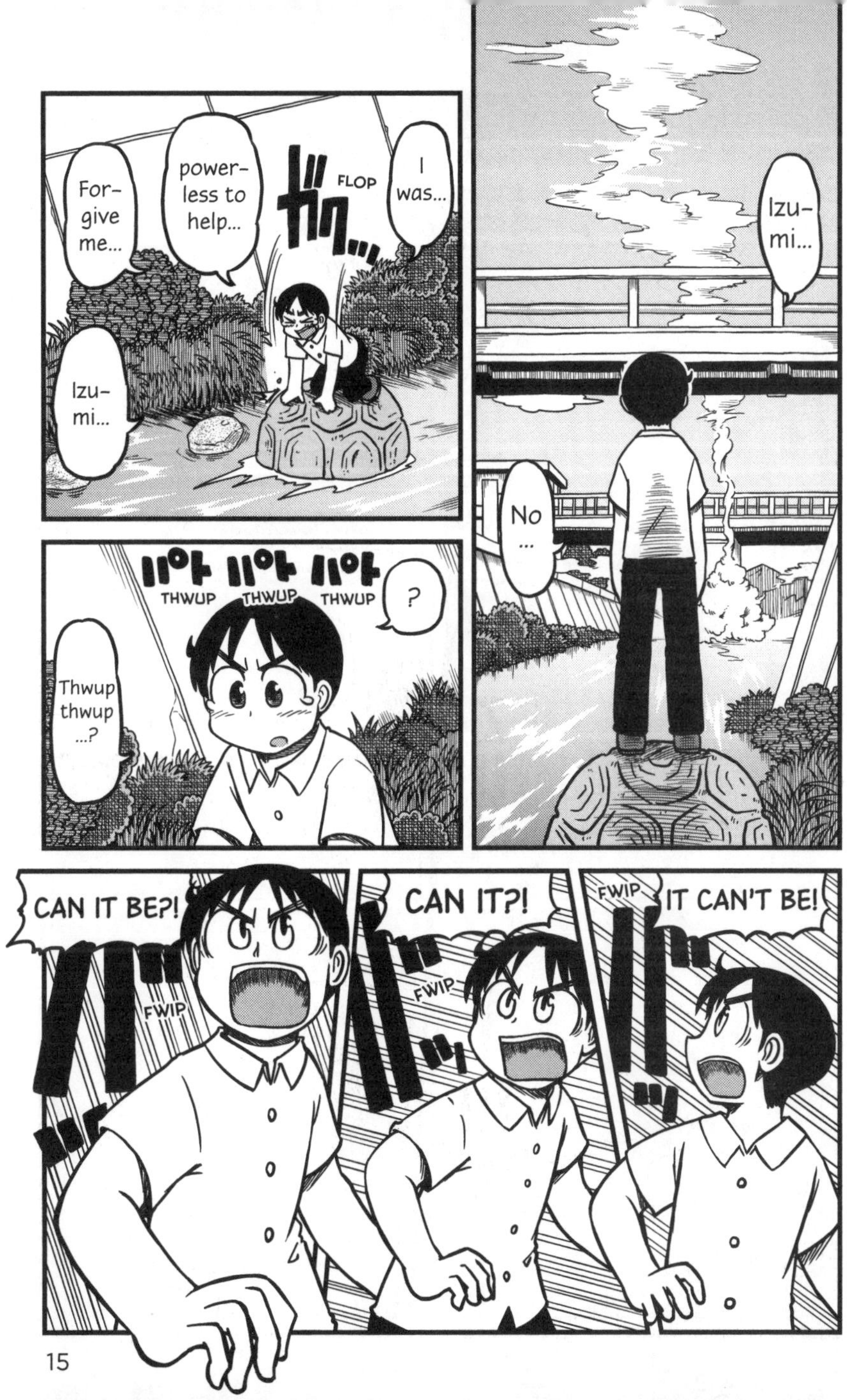
Izu-mi...
No ...
I was...
FLOP
power-less to help...
For-give me...
Izu-mi...
THWUP THWUP THWUP
?
Thwup thwup ...?
FWIP
IT CAN'T BE!
CAN IT?!
FWIP
CAN IT BE?!
FWIP

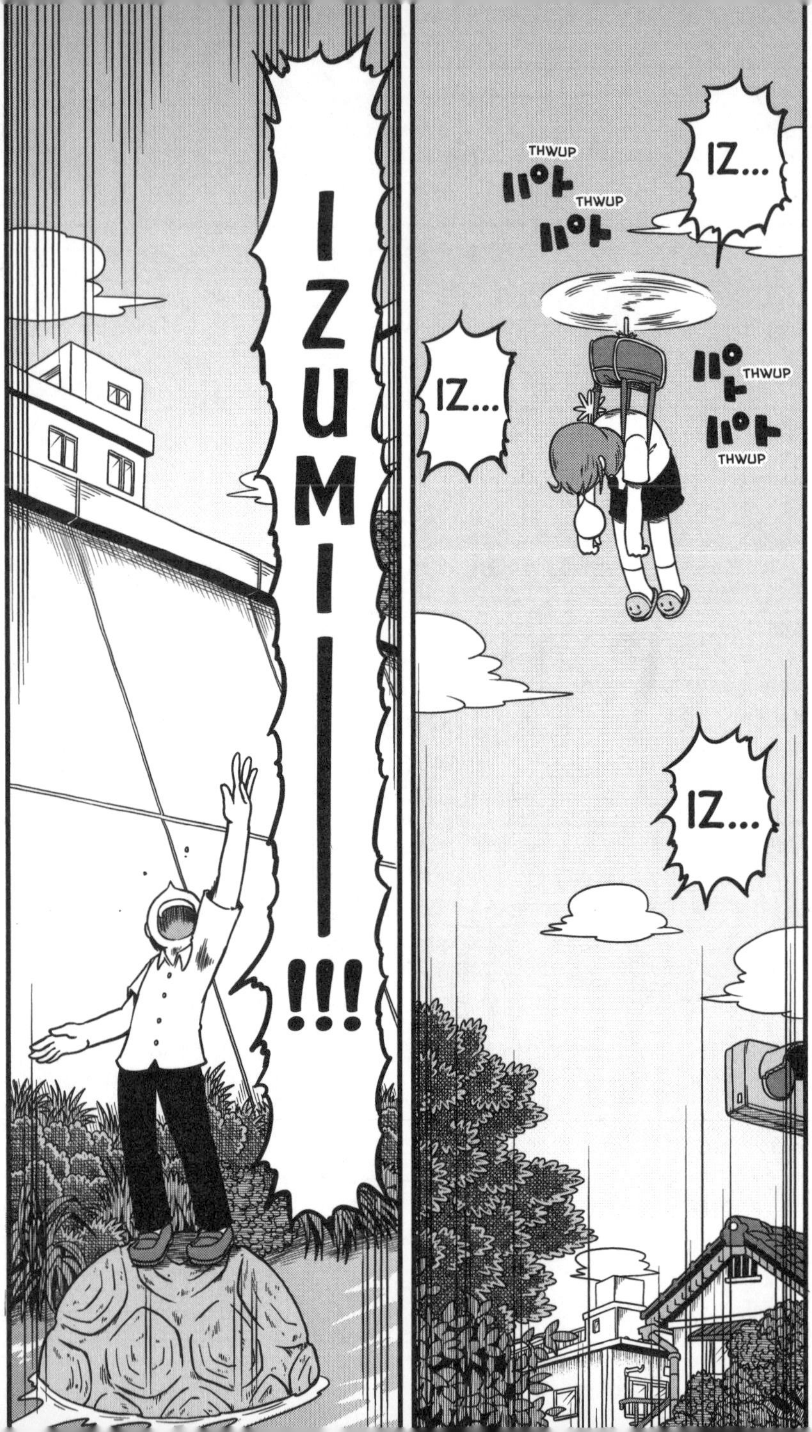
IZ...
THWUP
THWUP
IZ...
THWUP
THWUP
IZ...
IZUMI—!!!

BAM

Chapter 138 Riko Izumi Goes Sleepwalking 2

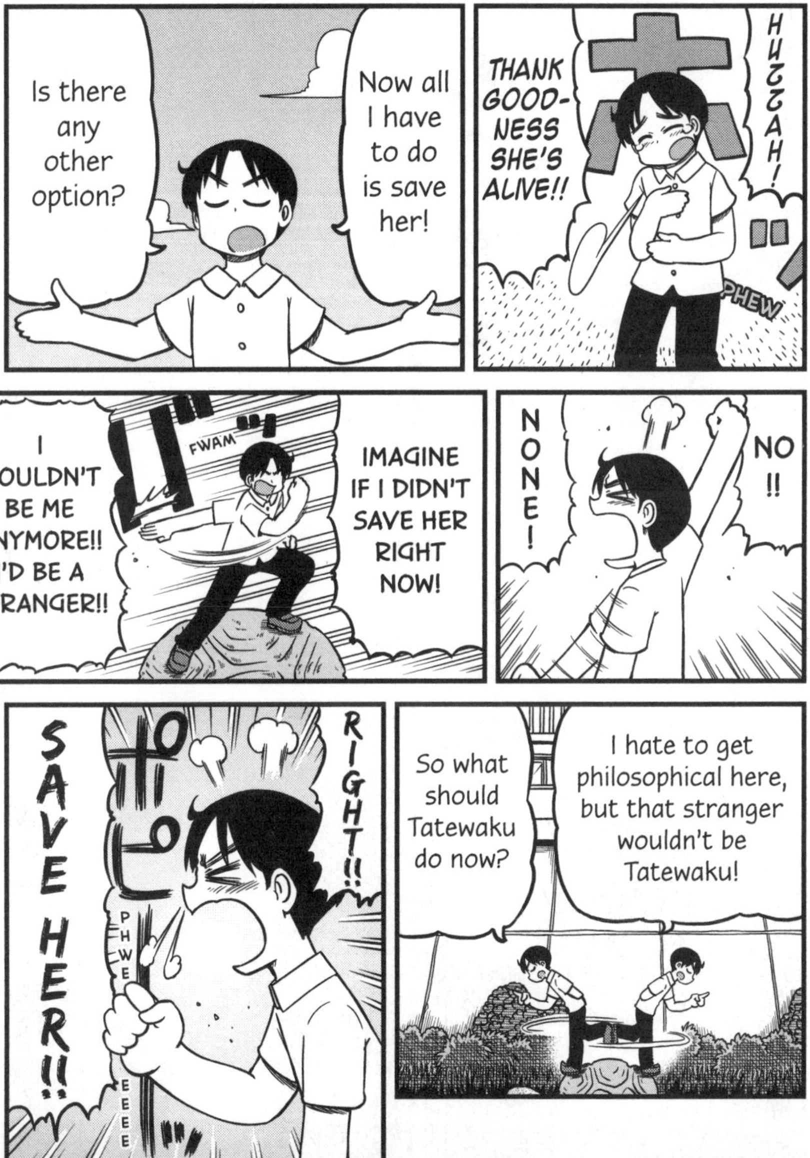
HUZZAH!
THANK GOODNESS SHE'S ALIVE!!
PHEW
Now all I have to do is save her!
Is there any other option?
NO!!
NONE!
IMAGINE IF I DIDN'T SAVE HER RIGHT NOW!
FWAM
I WOULDN'T BE ME ANYMORE!! I'D BE A STRANGER!!
I hate to get philosophical here, but that stranger wouldn't be Tatewaku!
So what should Tatewaku do now?
RIGHT!!
SAVE HER!!
PHWEEEEE

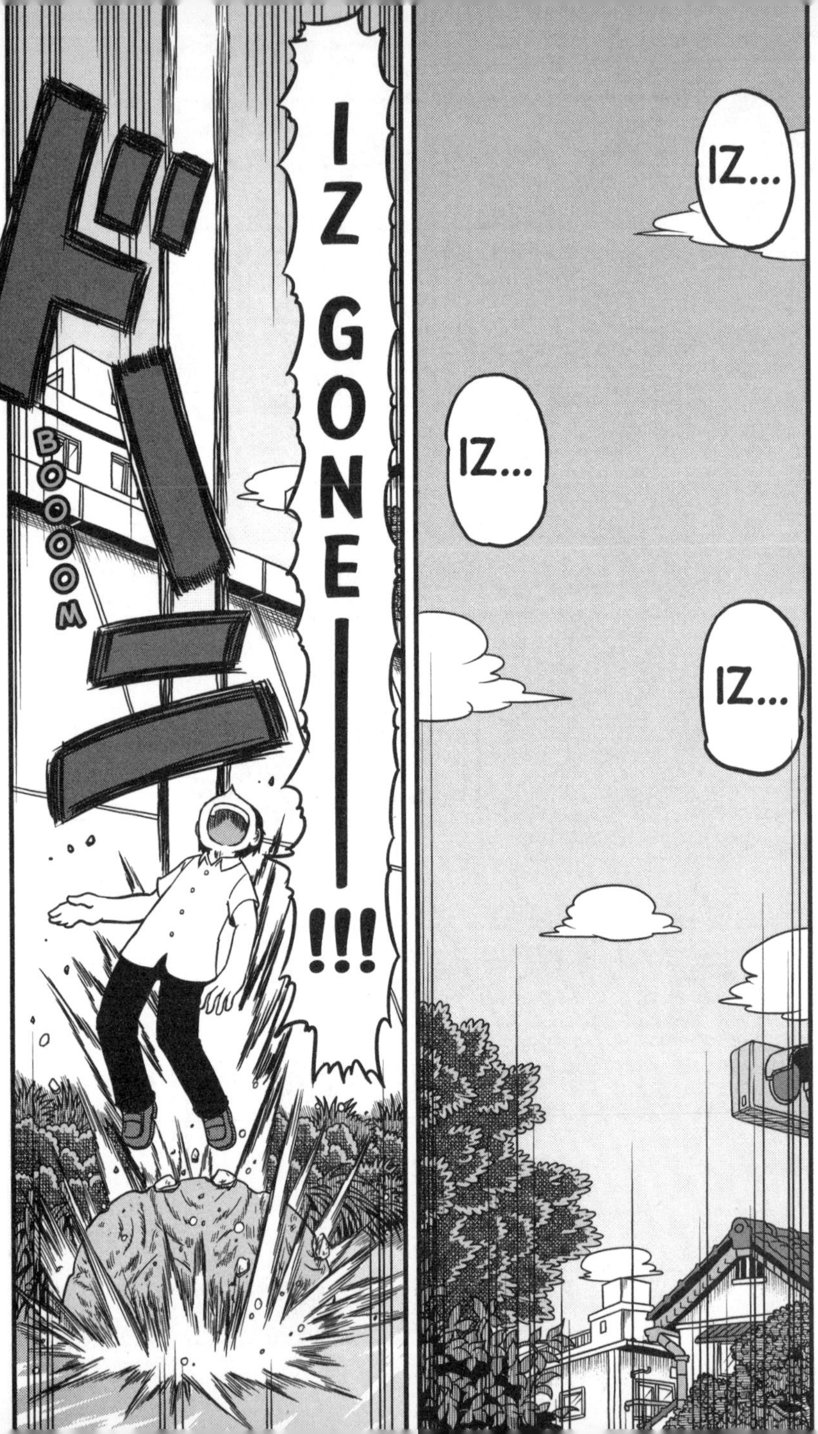
IZ...
IZ...
IZ...
IZ GONE—!!!
ドーン
BOOOOOM

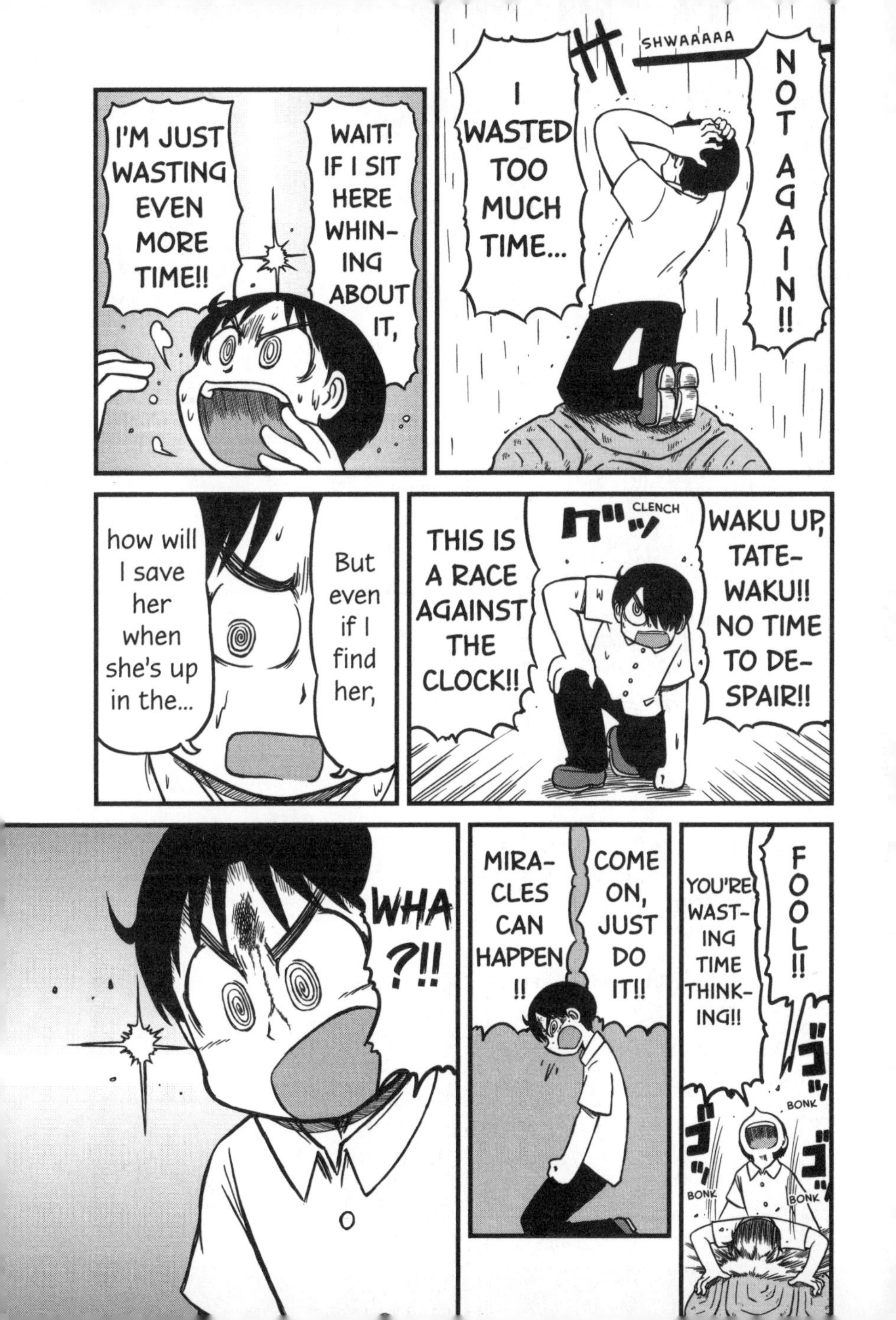

SHWAAAAA
NOT AGAIN!!
I WASTED TOO MUCH TIME...
WAIT! IF I SIT HERE WHINING ABOUT IT,
I'M JUST WASTING EVEN MORE TIME!!
CLENCH
WAKU UP, TATEWAKU!! NO TIME TO DESPAIR!!
THIS IS A RACE AGAINST THE CLOCK!!
But even if I find her,
how will I save her when she's up in the...
FOOL!!
YOU'RE WASTING TIME THINKING!!
BONK
BONK
BONK
COME ON, JUST DO IT!!
MIRACLES CAN HAPPEN!!
WHA?!!

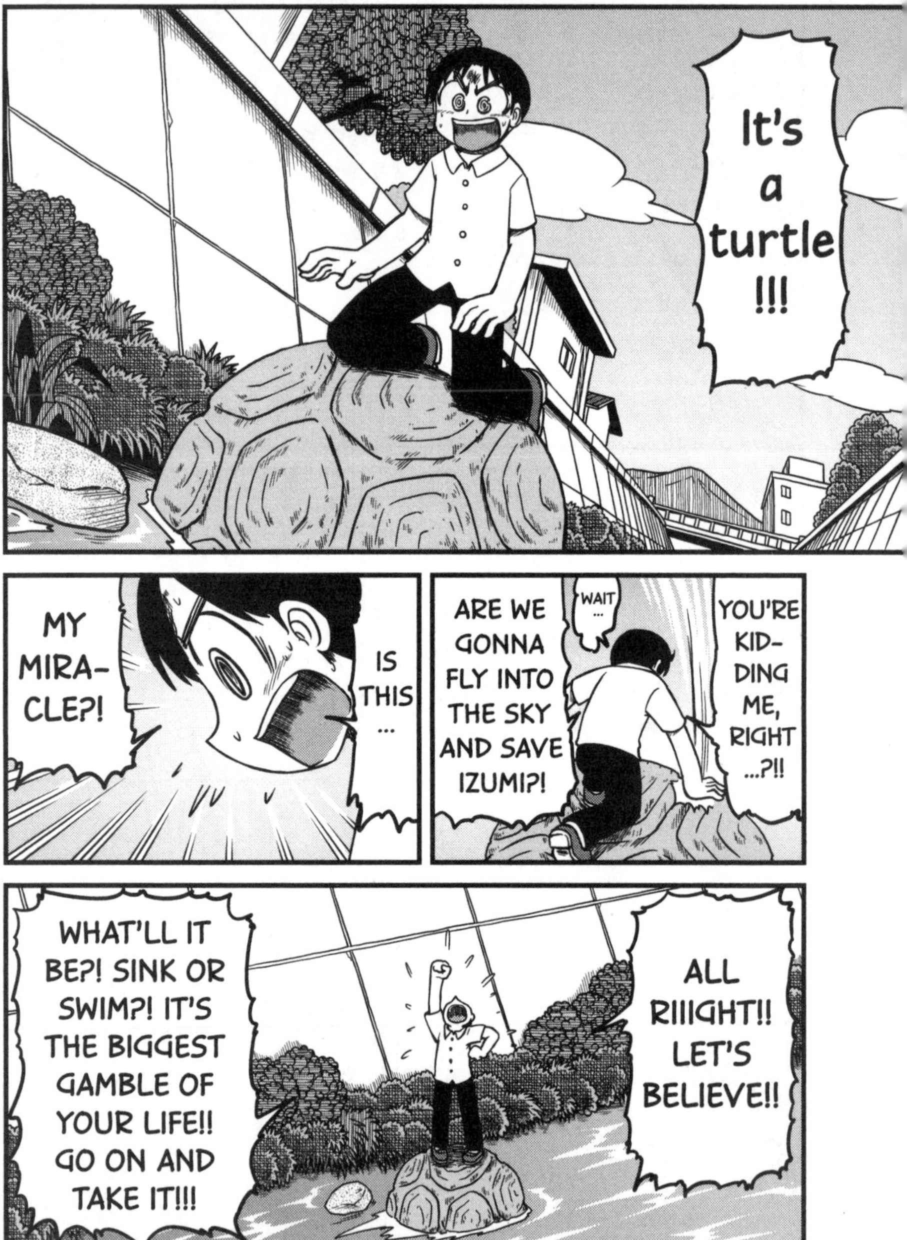
It's a turtle!!!
YOU'RE KIDDING ME, RIGHT...?!!
WAIT...
ARE WE GONNA FLY INTO THE SKY AND SAVE IZUMI?!
IS THIS...
MY MIRACLE?!
ALL RIIIGHT!! LET'S BELIEVE!!
WHAT'LL IT BE?! SINK OR SWIM?! IT'S THE BIGGEST GAMBLE OF YOUR LIFE!! GO ON AND TAKE IT!!!

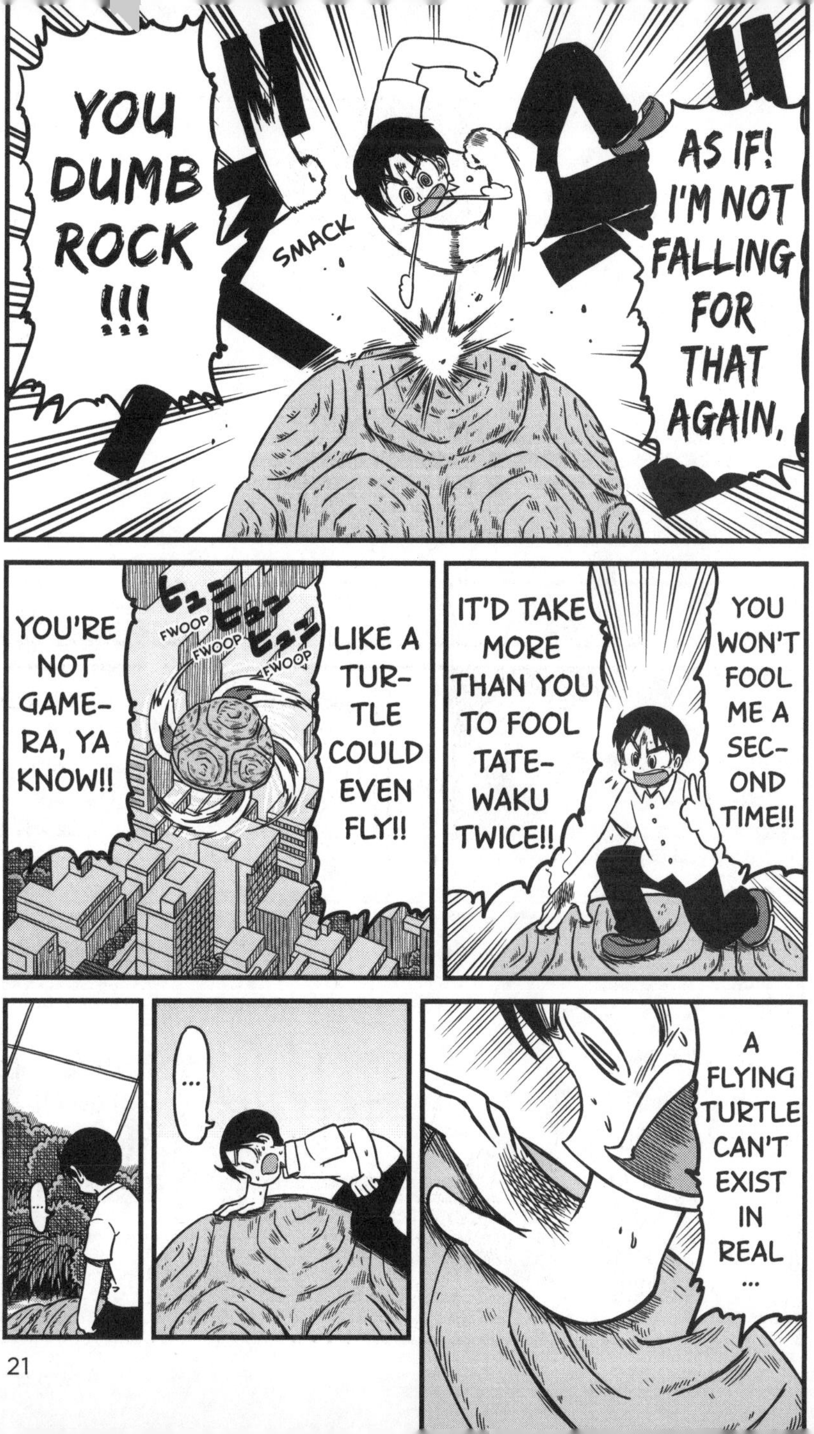
AS IF! I'M NOT FALLING FOR THAT AGAIN,
YOU DUMB ROCK!!!
SMACK
YOU WON'T FOOL ME A SEC-OND TIME!!
IT'D TAKE MORE THAN YOU TO FOOL TATE-WAKU TWICE!!
LIKE A TUR-TLE COULD EVEN FLY!!
YOU'RE NOT GAME-RA, YA KNOW!!
FWOOP
FWOOP
FWOOP
A FLYING TURTLE CAN'T EXIST IN REAL ...
...
...

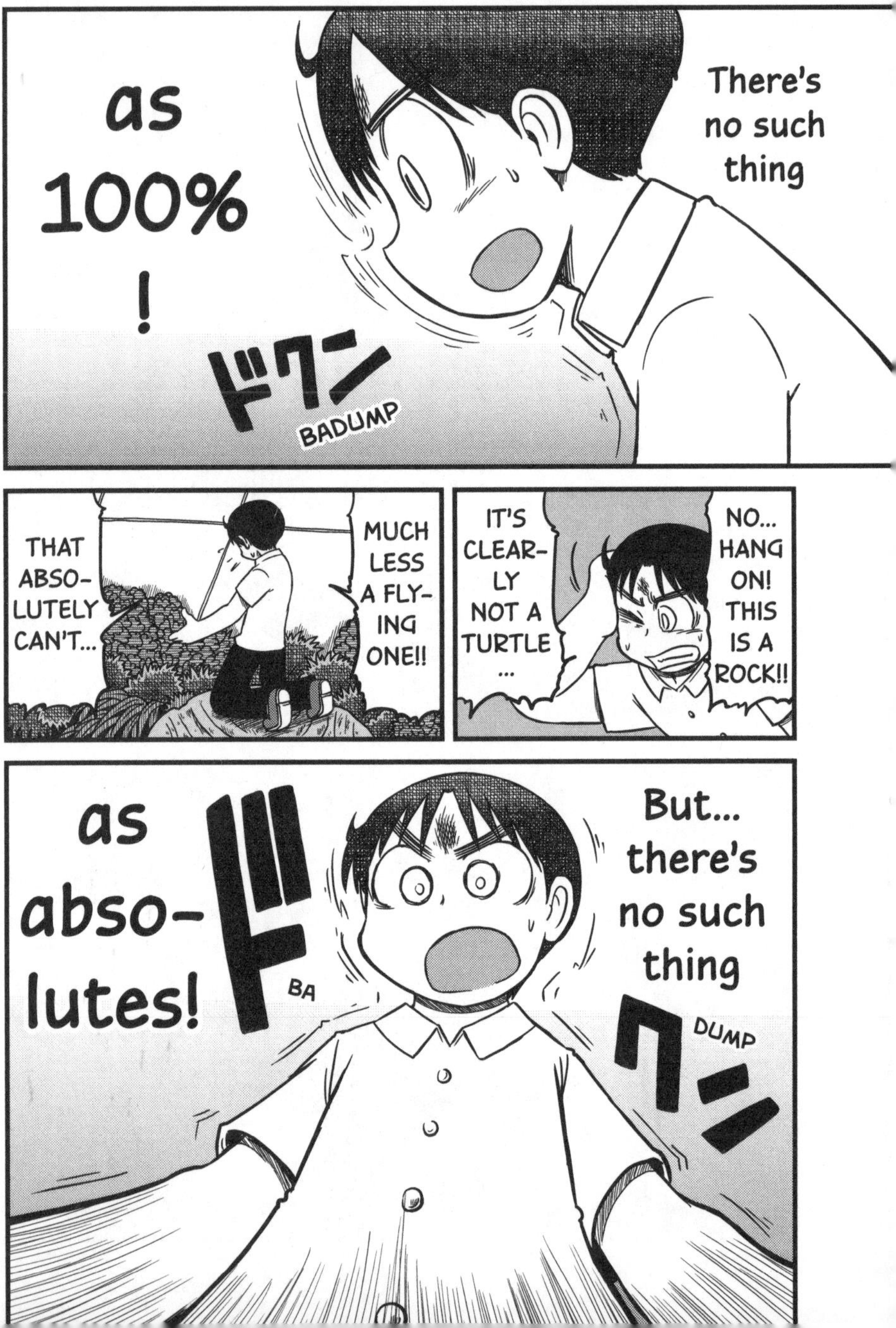
There's no such thing
as 100% !
ドクン
BADUMP
NO... HANG ON! THIS IS A ROCK!!
IT'S CLEAR-LY NOT A TURTLE ...
MUCH LESS A FLY-ING ONE!!
THAT ABSO-LUTELY CAN'T...
But... there's no such thing
as abso-lutes!
ド
BA
クン
DUMP

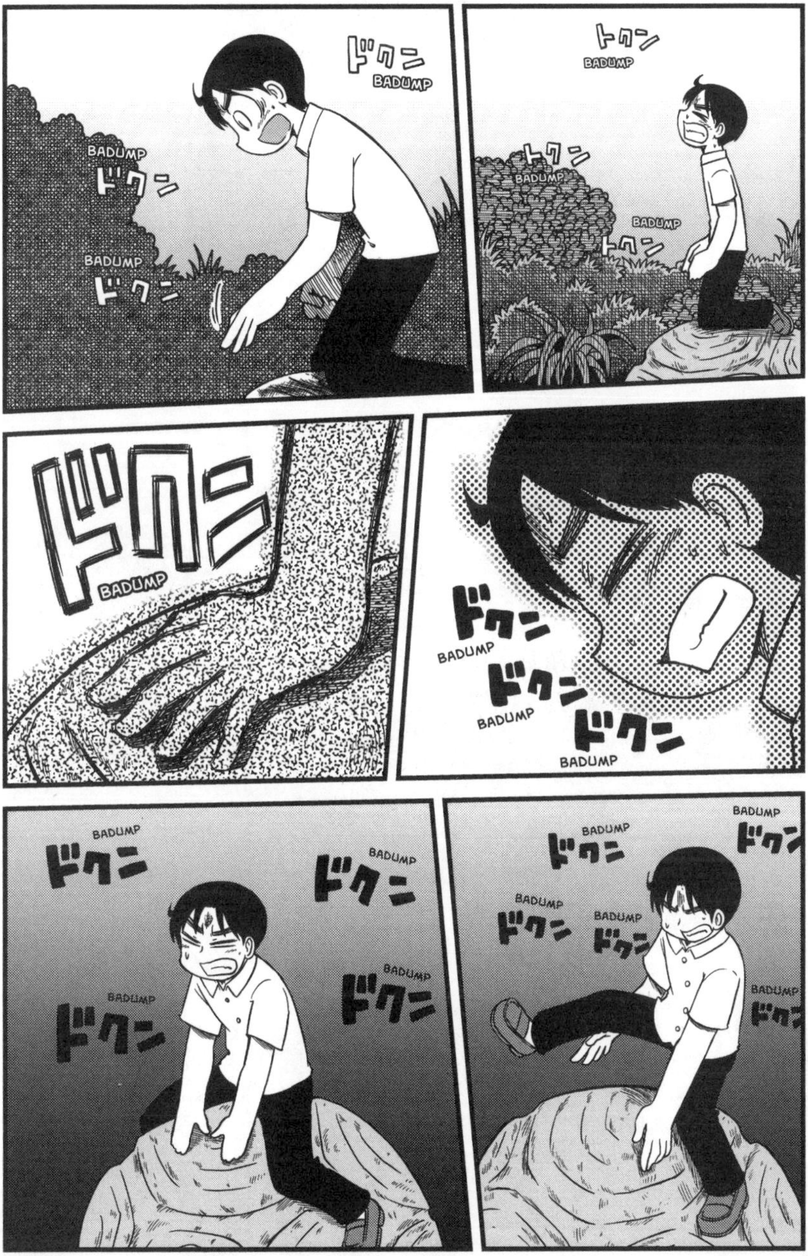
トクン
BADUMP
トクン
BADUMP
BADUMP
トクン
ドクン
BADUMP
BADUMP
ドクン
BADUMP
ドクン
ドクン
BADUMP
ドクン
BADUMP
ドクン
BADUMP
ドクン
BADUMP
BADUMP
ドクン
BADUMP
ドクン
BADUMP
ドクン
BADUMP
ドクン
BADUMP
ドクン
BADUMP
ドクン
BADUMP
ドクン
BADUMP
ドクン
BADUMP
ドクン

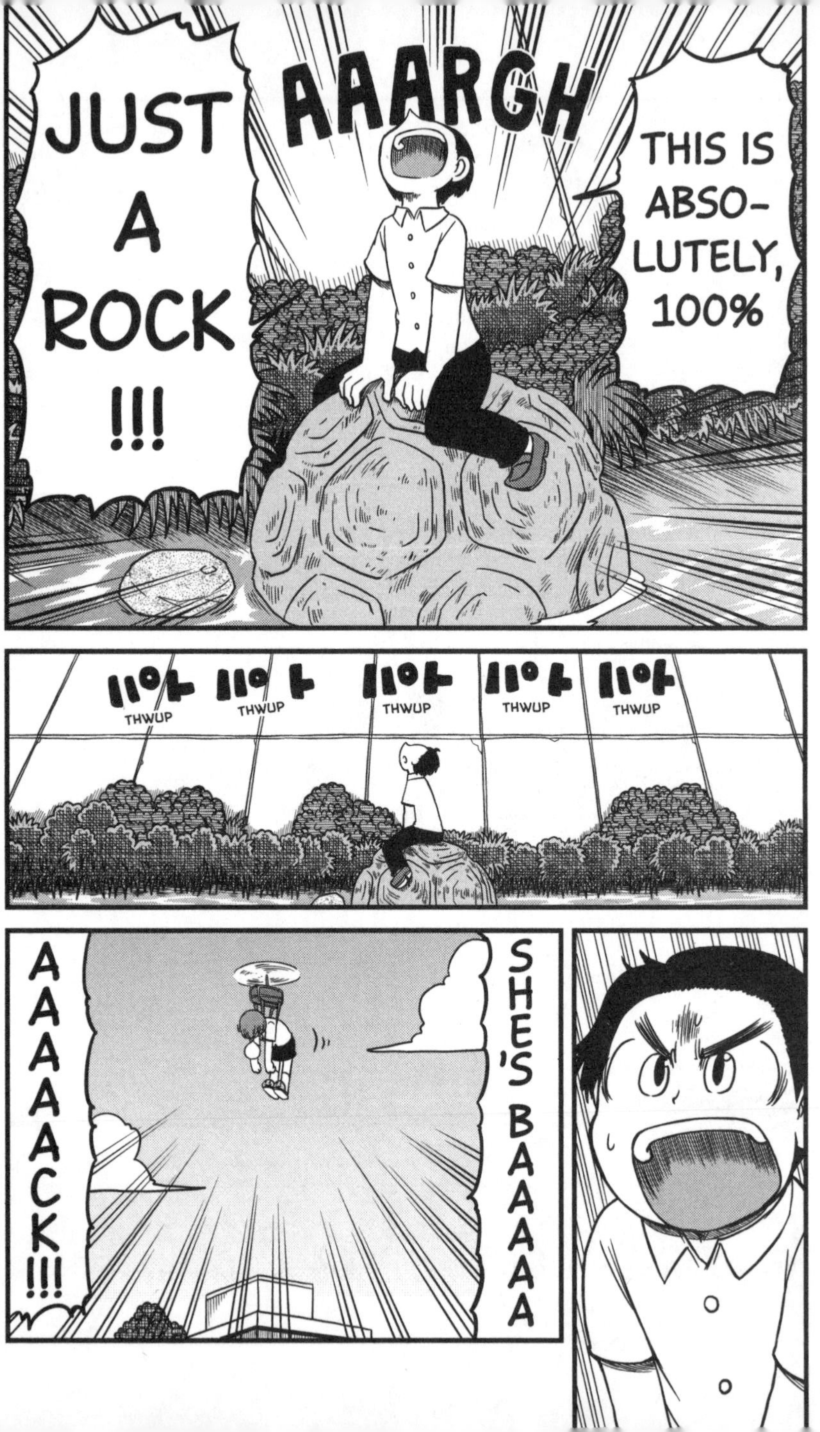
THIS IS ABSO-LUTELY, 100%
AAARGH
JUST A ROCK!!!
THWUP
THWUP
THWUP
THWUP
THWUP
SHE'S BAAAAA
AAAAAACK!!!

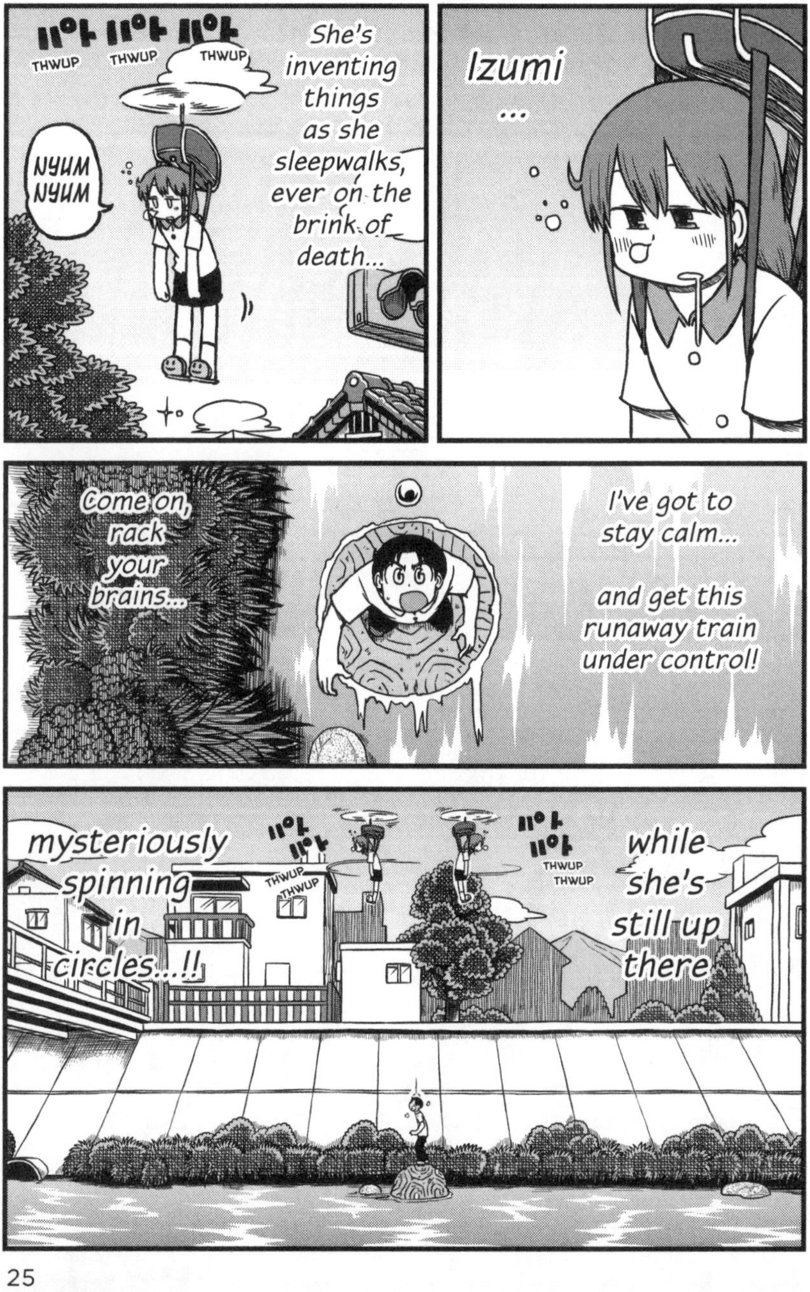

Izumi ...
She's inventing things as she sleepwalks, ever on the brink of death...
THWUP THWUP THWUP
NYUM NYUM
I've got to stay calm...
and get this runaway train under control!
Come on, rack your brains...
while she's still up there
THWUP THWUP
THWUP THWUP
mysteriously spinning in circles...!!

Chapter 139 ◇ Riko Izumi Goes Sleepwalking 3

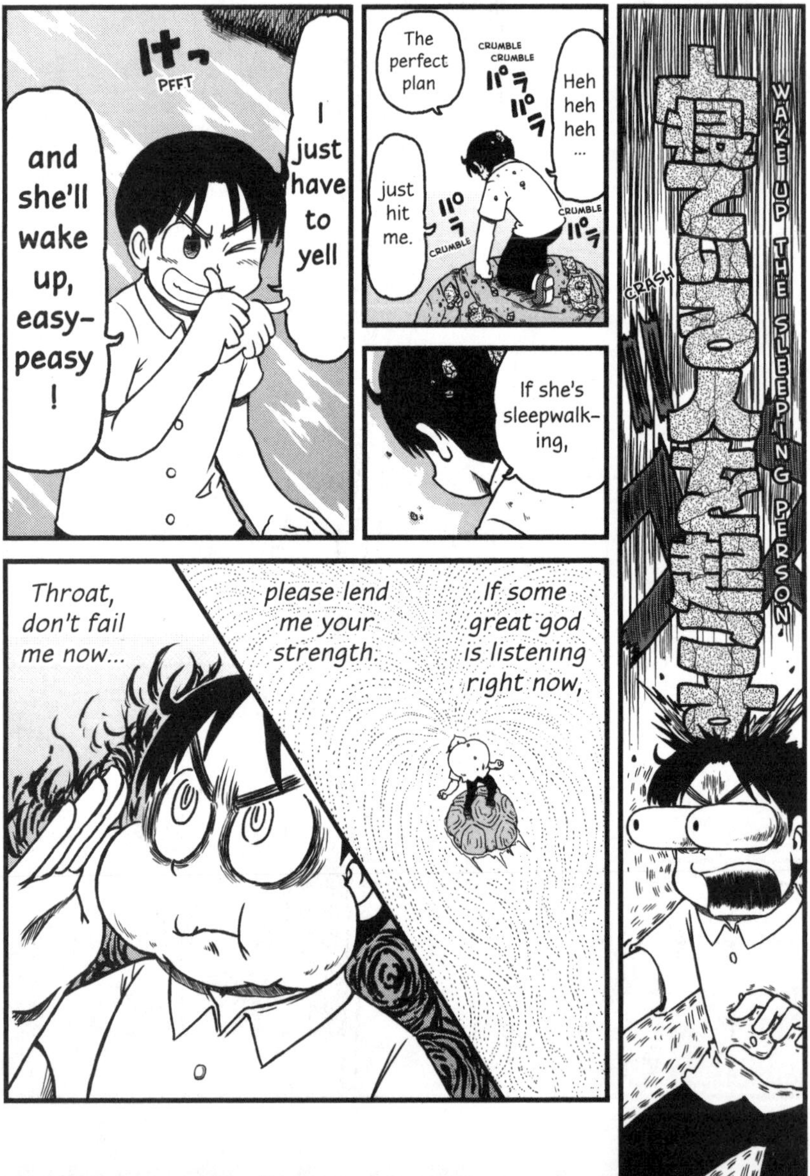
CRUMBLE CRUMBLE
パラ パラ
Heh heh heh...
The perfect plan
CRUMBLE
パラ
CRUMBLE
パラ
just hit me.
If she's sleepwalking,
I just have to yell
けっ
PFFT
and she'll wake up, easy-peasy!
If some great god is listening right now,
please lend me your strength.
Throat, don't fail me now...
寝ている人を起こす
WAKE UP THE SLEEPING PERSON
CRASH

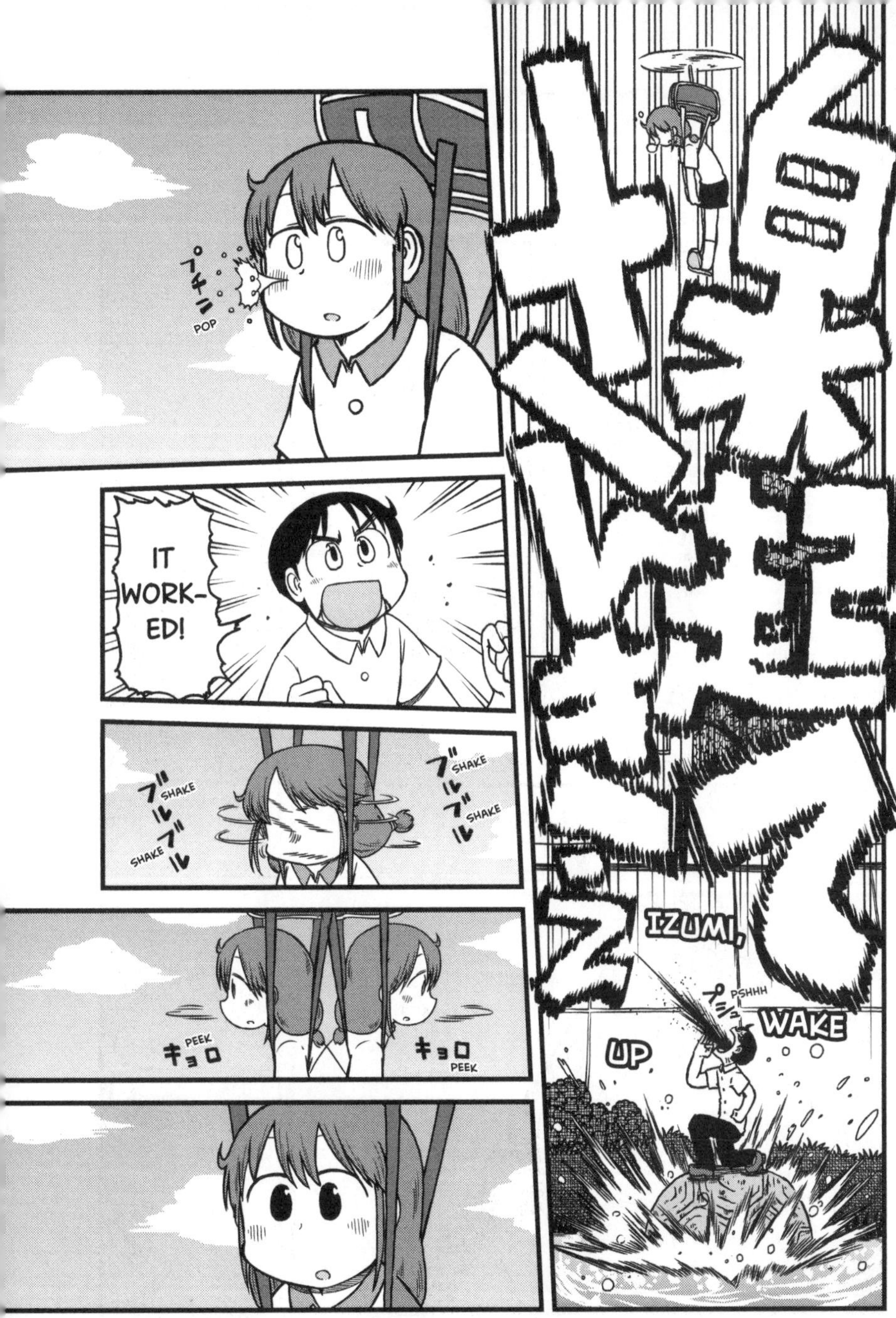
IZUMI, WAKE UP
プシュ
PSHHH
プチン
POP
IT WORK-ED!
ブルブル
SHAKE
SHAKE
ブルブル
SHAKE
SHAKE
キョロ
PEEK
キョロ
PEEK

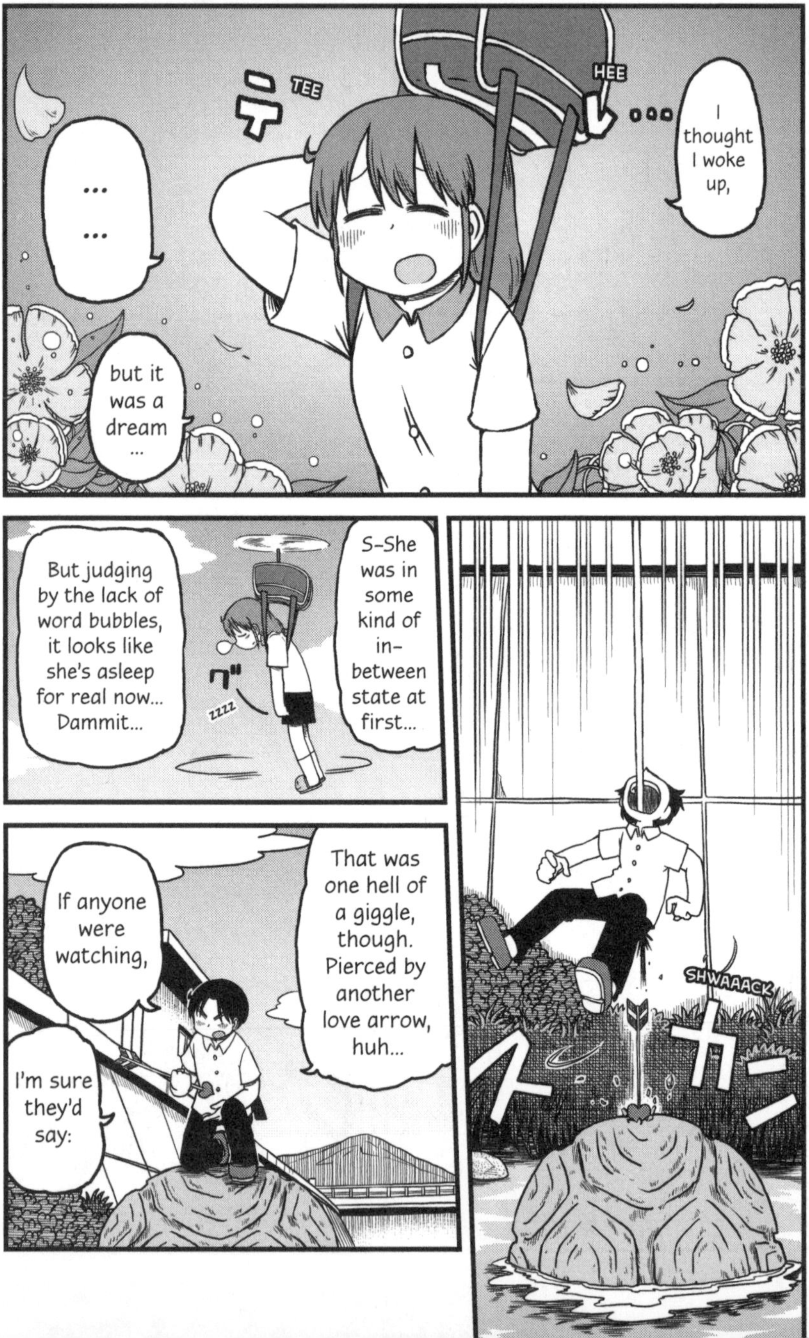
I thought I woke up,
HEE
TEE
... ...
but it was a dream ...
SHWAAACK
S-She was in some kind of in-between state at first...
But judging by the lack of word bubbles, it looks like she's asleep for real now... Dammit...
zzzz
That was one hell of a giggle, though. Pierced by another love arrow, huh...
If anyone were watching,
I'm sure they'd say:

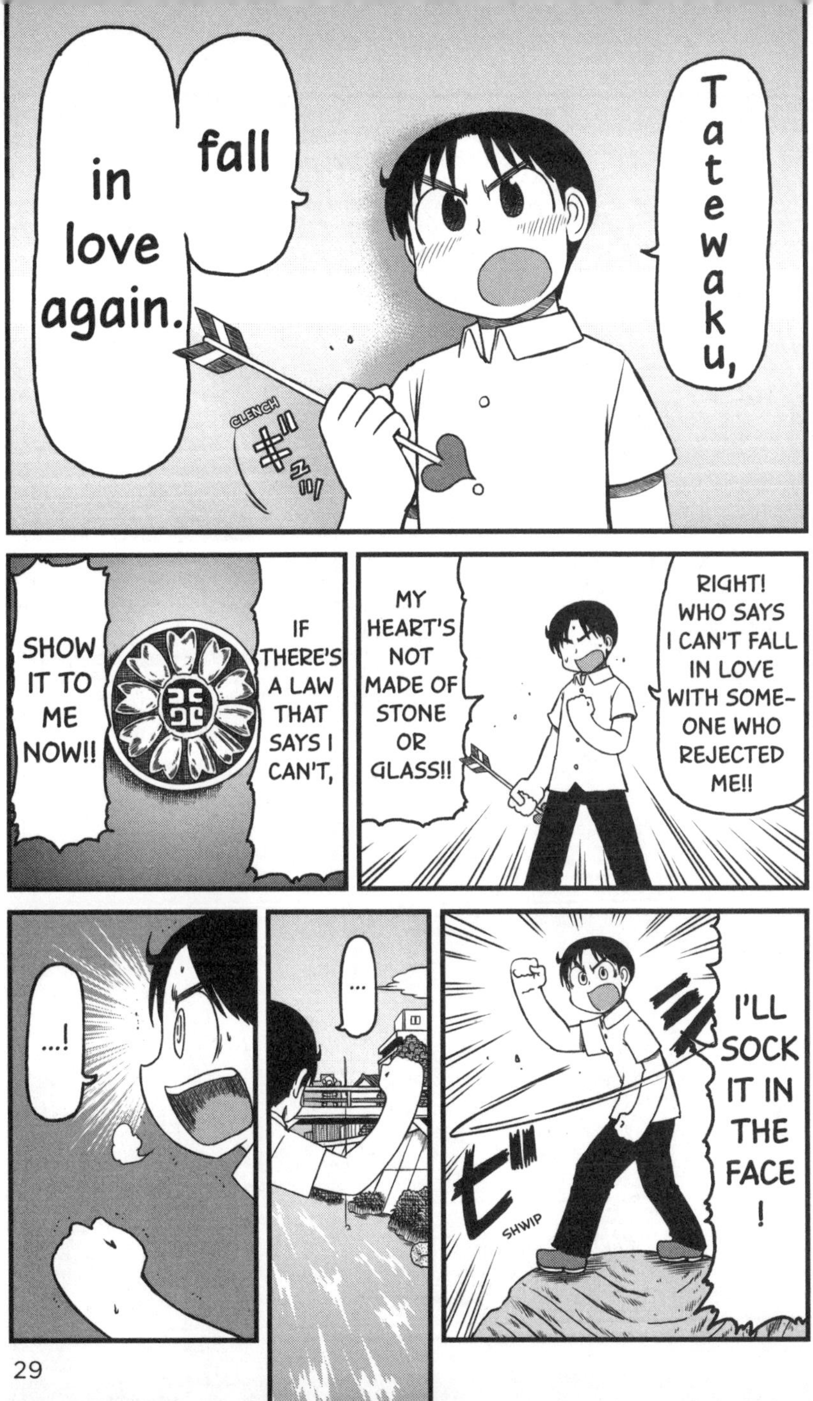
Tatewaku,
fall in love again.
CLENCH
RIGHT! WHO SAYS I CAN'T FALL IN LOVE WITH SOME-ONE WHO REJECTED ME!!
MY HEART'S NOT MADE OF STONE OR GLASS!!
IF THERE'S A LAW THAT SAYS I CAN'T,
SHOW IT TO ME NOW!!
I'LL SOCK IT IN THE FACE!
SHWIP
...
...!

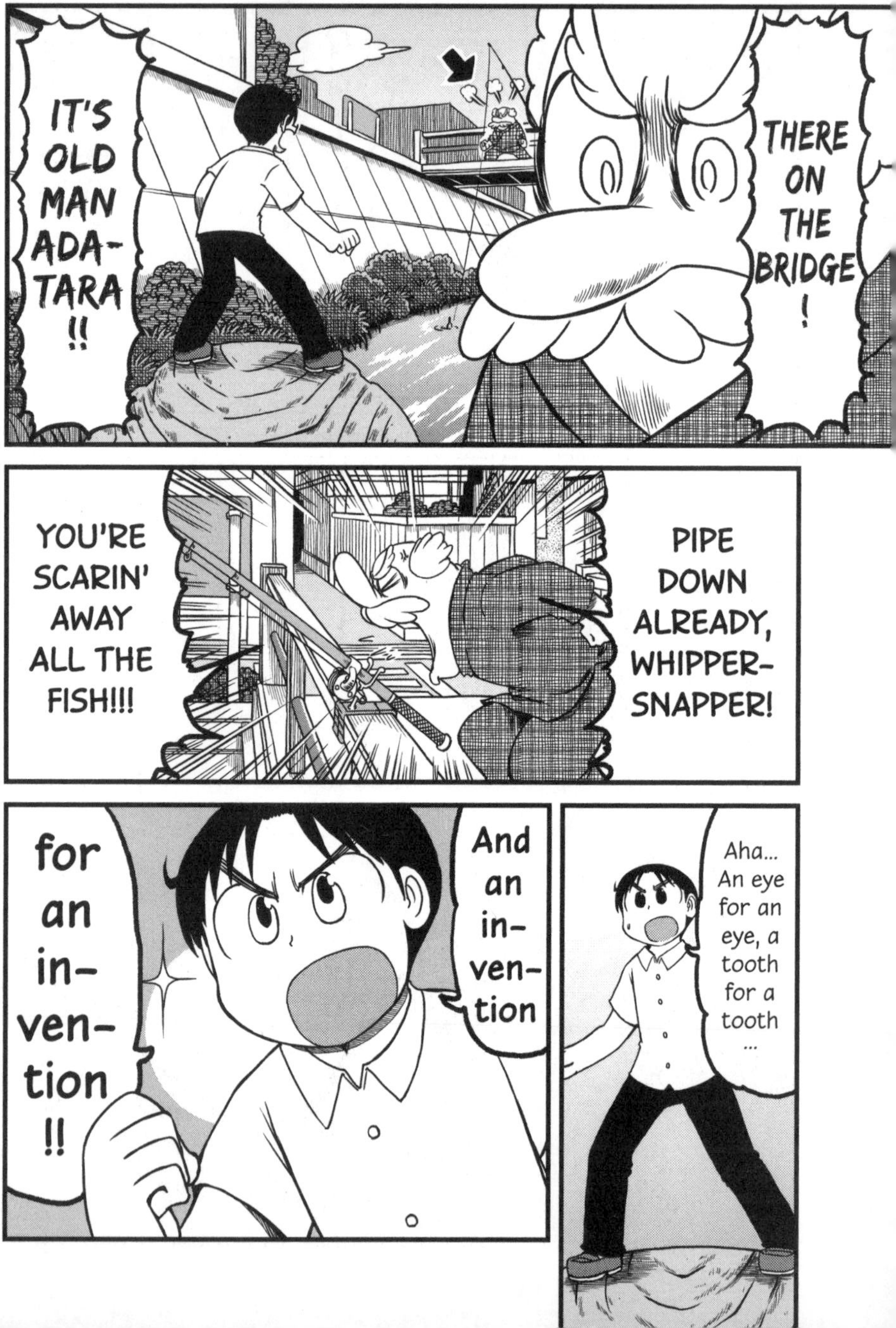
THERE ON THE BRIDGE!
IT'S OLD MAN ADATARA!!
PIPE DOWN ALREADY, WHIPPERSNAPPER!
YOU'RE SCARIN' AWAY ALL THE FISH!!!
Aha... An eye for an eye, a tooth for a tooth...
And an invention
for an invention!!

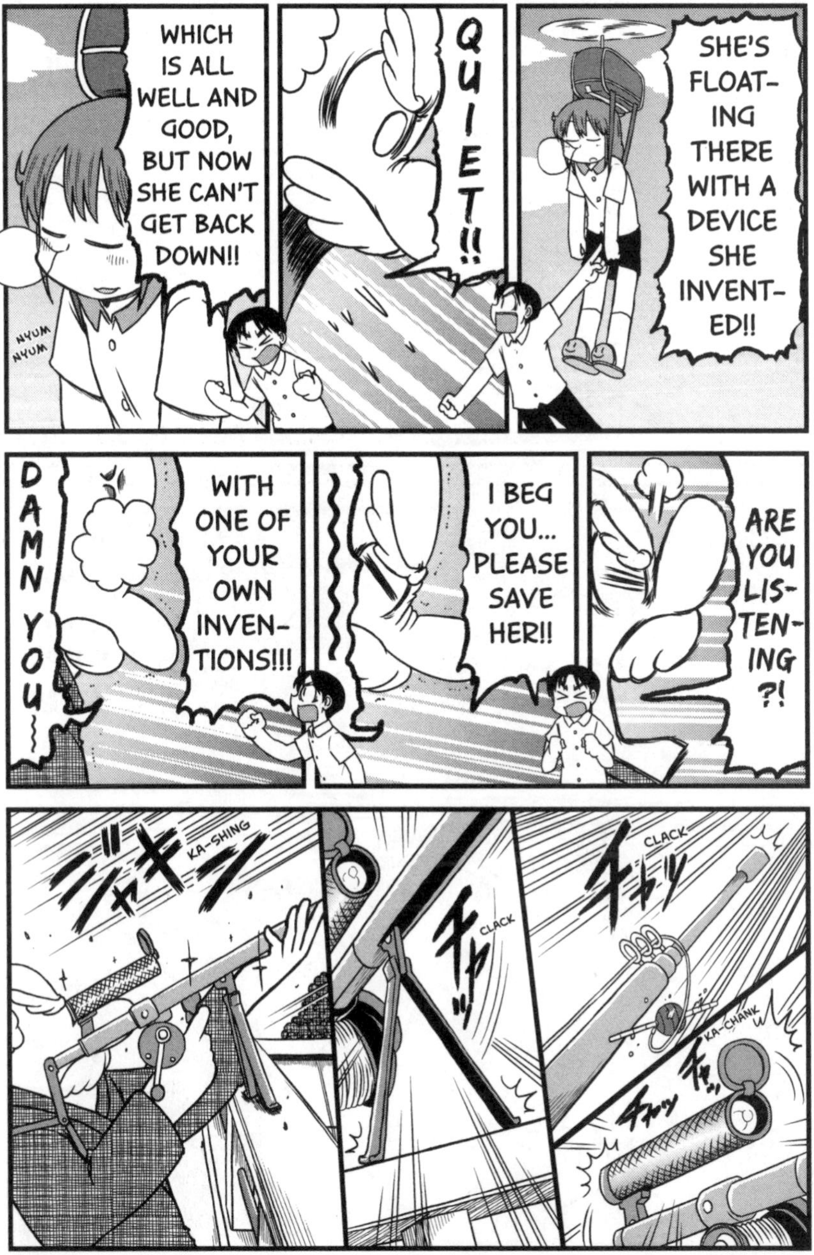
SHE'S FLOATING THERE WITH A DEVICE SHE INVENTED!!
QUIET!!
WHICH IS ALL WELL AND GOOD, BUT NOW SHE CAN'T GET BACK DOWN!!
NYUM NYUM
ARE YOU LISTENING?!
I BEG YOU... PLEASE SAVE HER!!
WITH ONE OF YOUR OWN INVENTIONS!!!
DAMN YOU~
CLACK
KA-CHANK
CLACK
KA-SHING

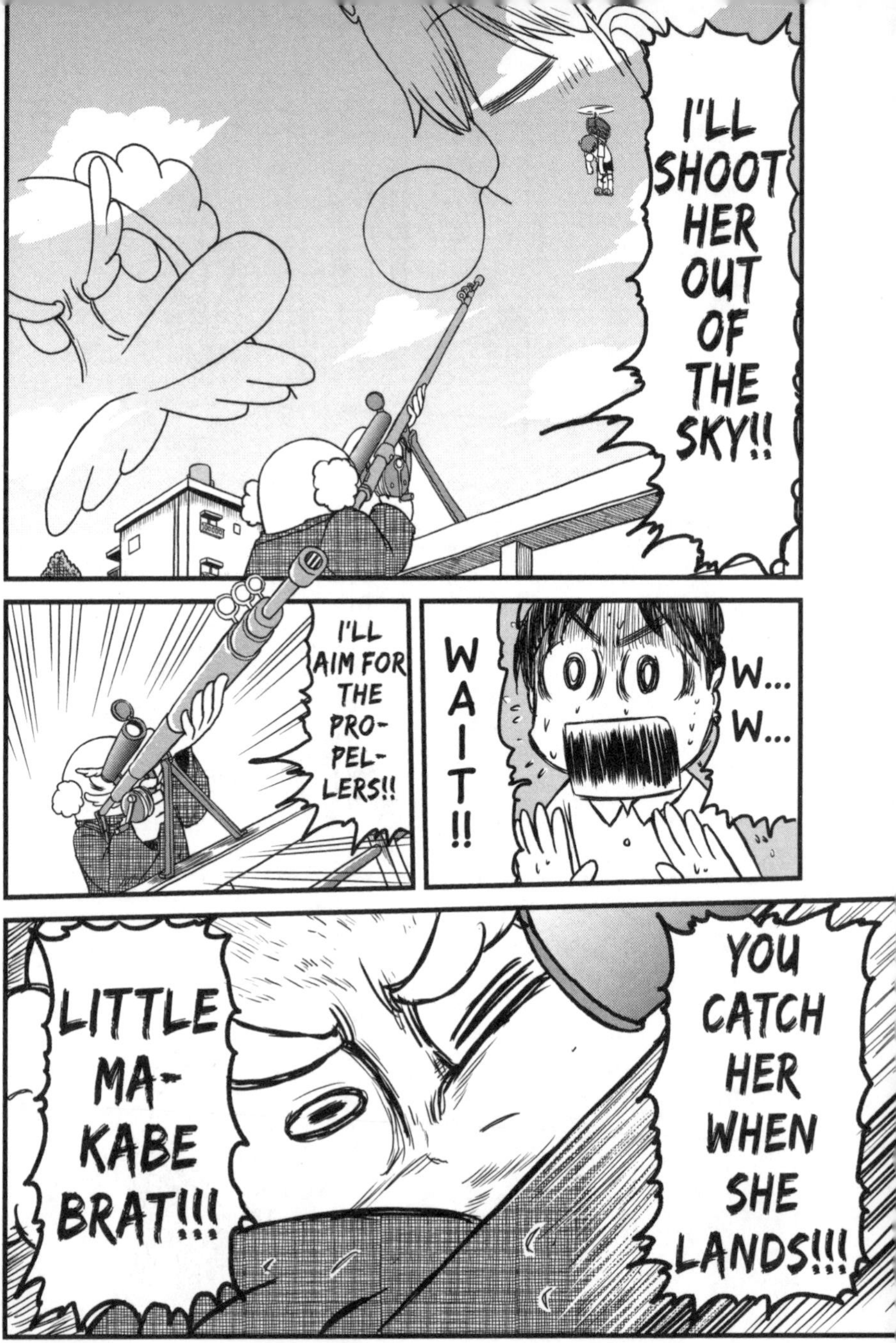
I'LL SHOOT HER OUT OF THE SKY!!
W... W...
WAIT!!
I'LL AIM FOR THE PRO-PEL-LERS!!
YOU CATCH HER WHEN SHE LANDS!!!
LITTLE MA-KABE BRAT!!!

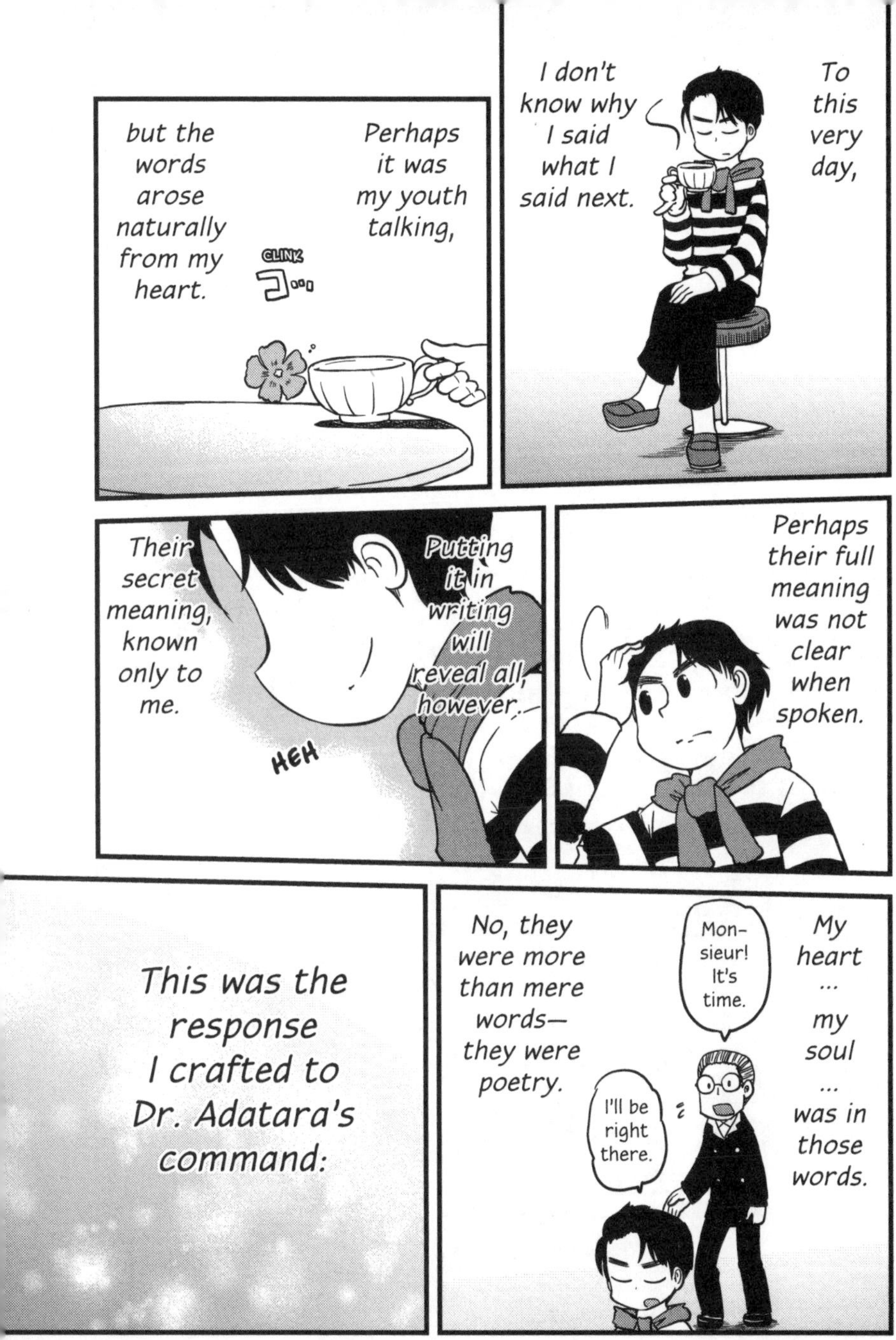
To this very day,
I don't know why I said what I said next.
Perhaps it was my youth talking,
but the words arose naturally from my heart.
CLINK
コ
Perhaps their full meaning was not clear when spoken.
Putting it in writing will reveal all, however.
Their secret meaning, known only to me.
HEH
My heart ... my soul ... was in those words.
Monsieur! It's time.
No, they were more than mere words—they were poetry.
I'll be right there.
This was the response I crafted to Dr. Adatara's command:

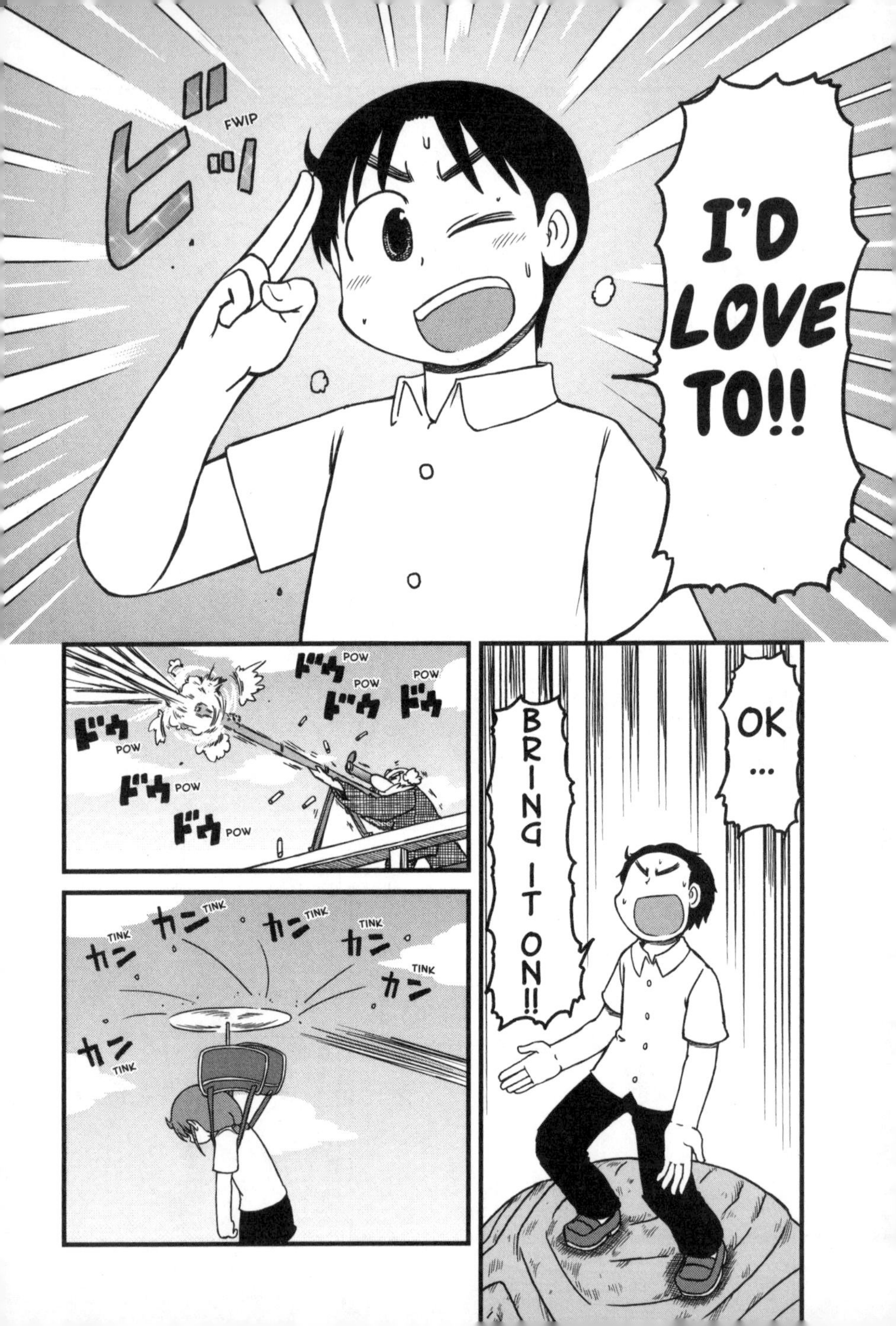
ビッ
FWIP
I'D LOVE TO!!
OK ...
BRING IT ON!!
ドウ POW
ドウ POW
ドウ POW
ドウ POW
ドウ POW
ドウ POW
カン TINK
カン TINK
カン TINK
カン TINK
カン TINK
カン TINK

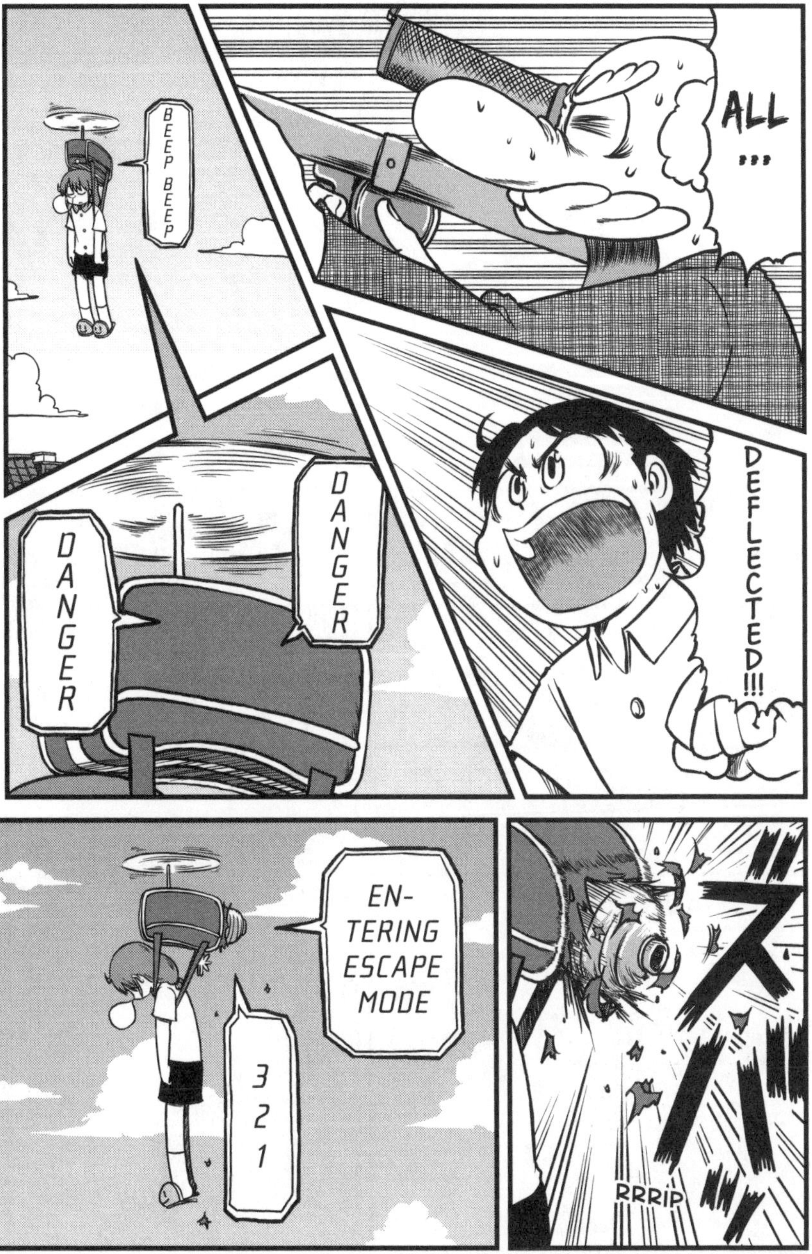
ALL ...
BEEP BEEP
DEFLECTED!!!
DANGER
DANGER
ズバ
RRRIP
EN-TERING ESCAPE MODE
3 2 1

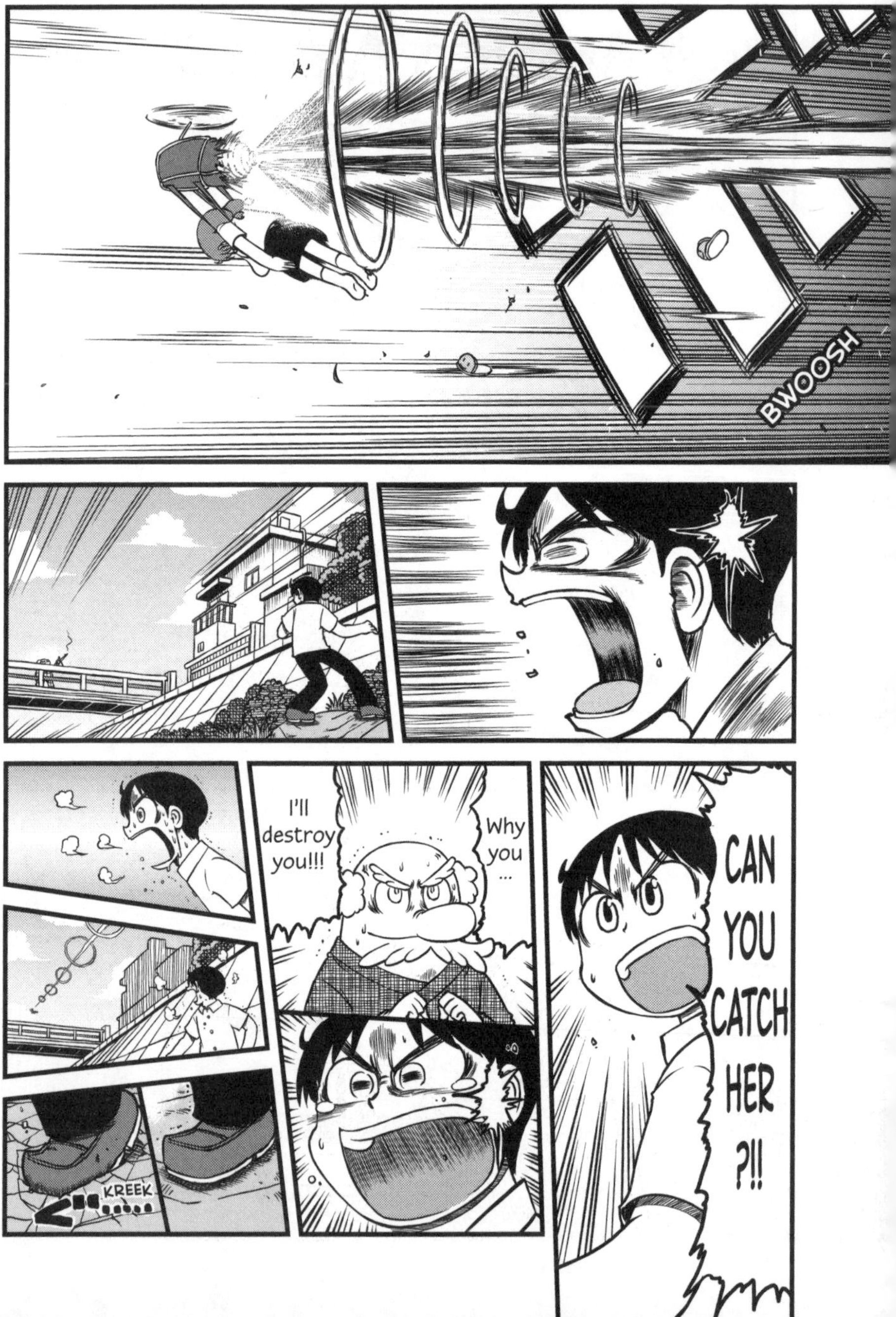
BWOOSH
CAN YOU CATCH HER ?!!
Why you ...
I'll destroy you!!!
KREEK

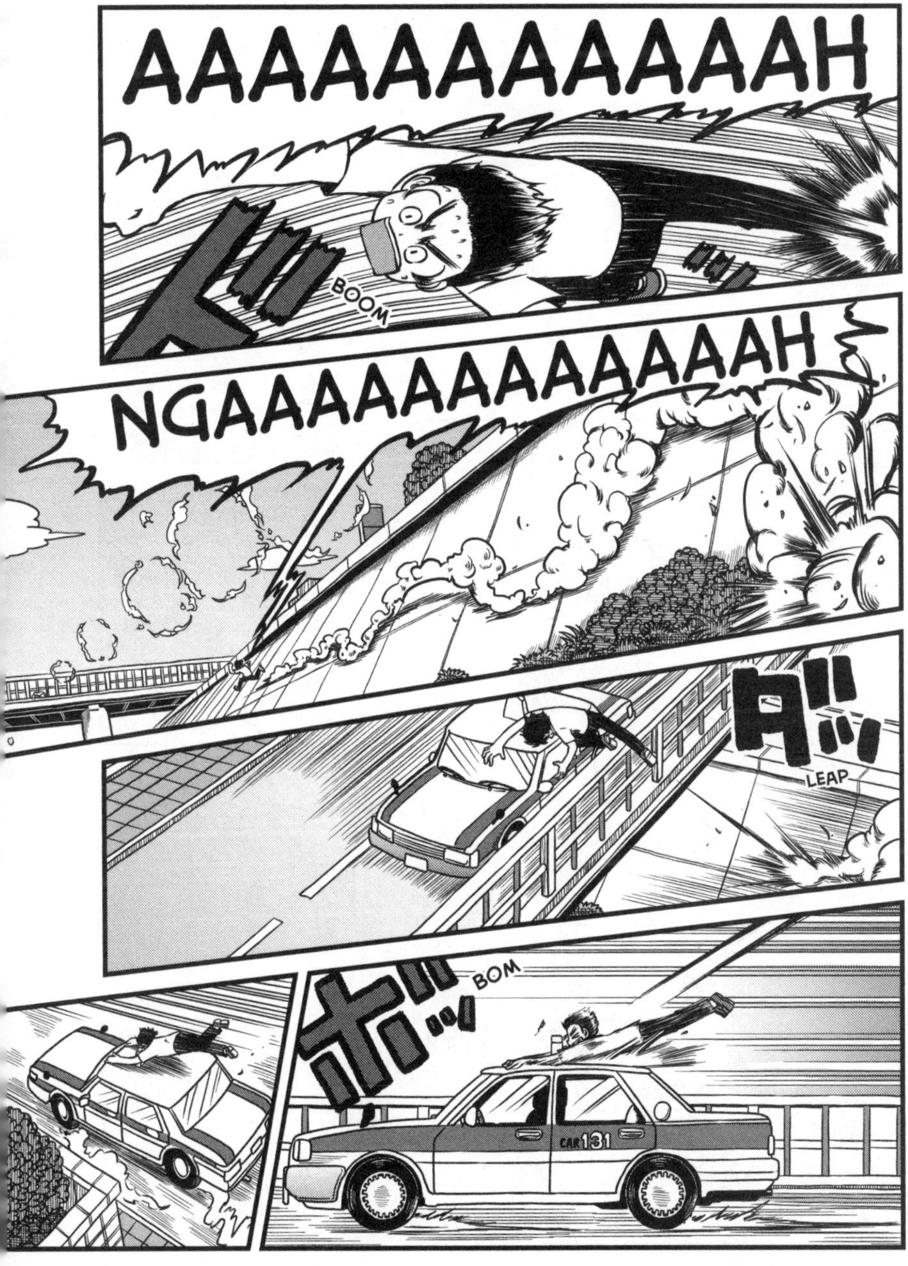
AAAAAAAAAAAH
BOOM
NGAAAAAAAAAAAH
LEAP
BOM
CAR 131

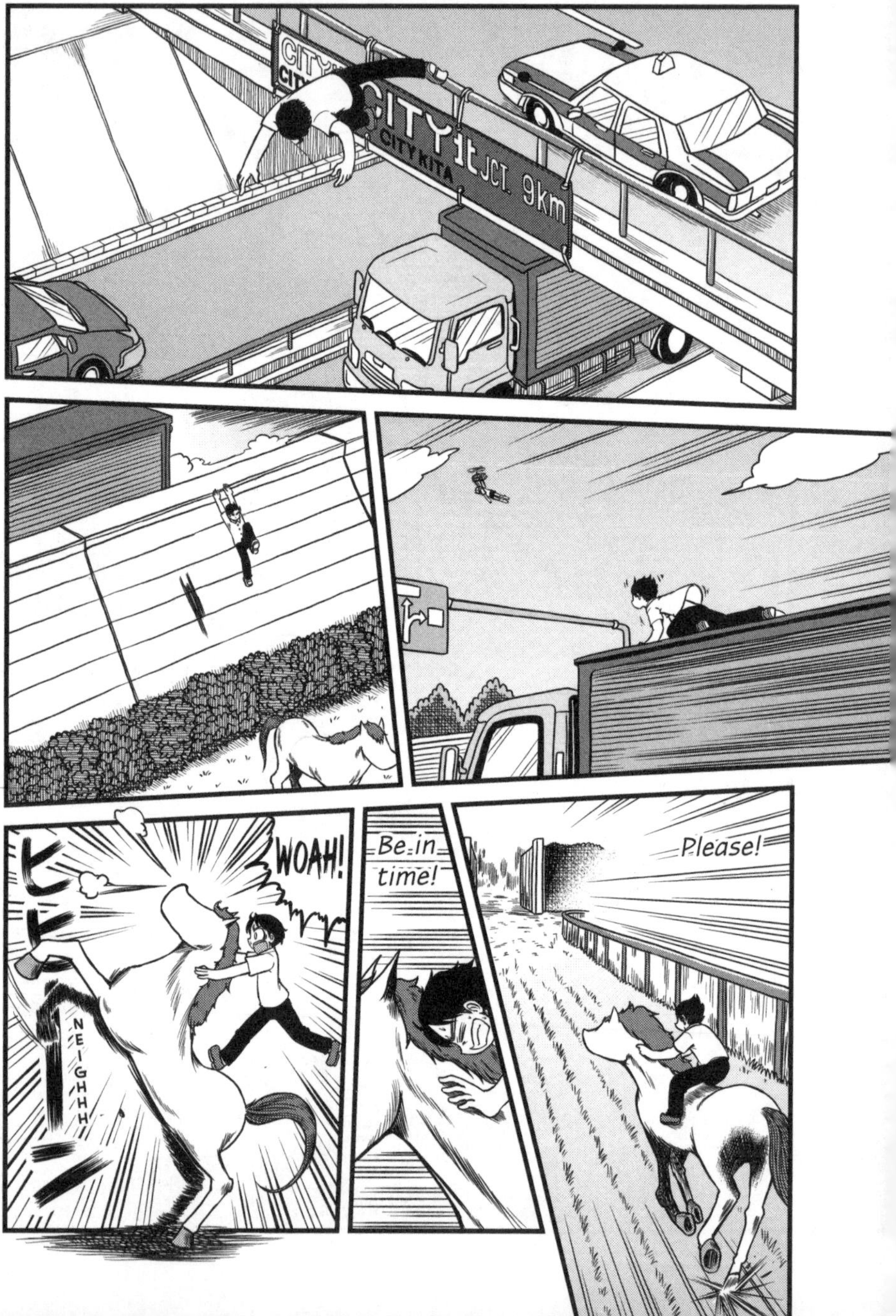
CITY北
CITY KITA
JCT. 9km
Please!
Be in time!
WOAH!
NEIGHHH

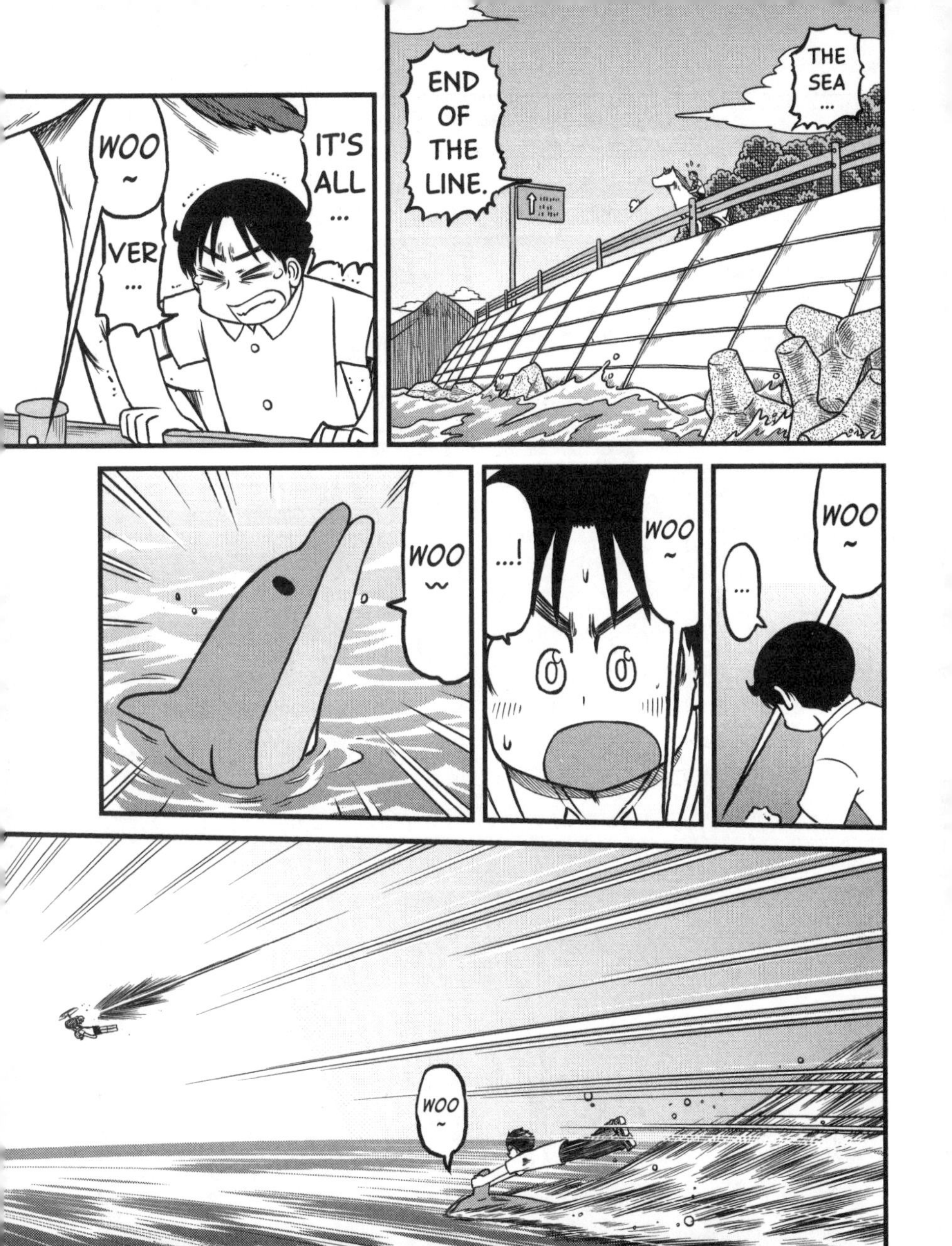
THE SEA ...
END OF THE LINE.
IT'S ALL ...
WOO ~ VER ...
WOO ~
...
WOO ~
...!
WOO ~~
WOO ~

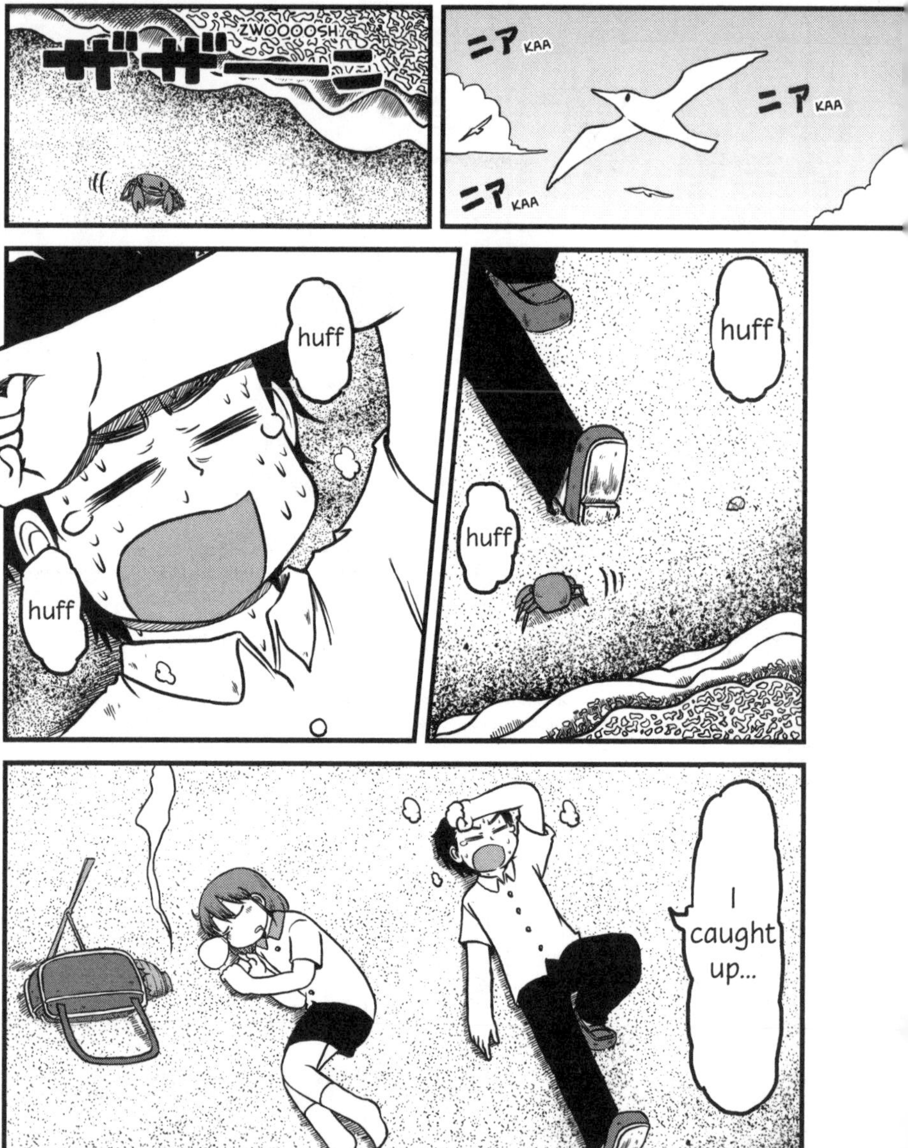
ニア KAA
ニア KAA
ニア KAA
ザザーン
ZWOOOOSH
huff
huff
huff
huff
I caught up...

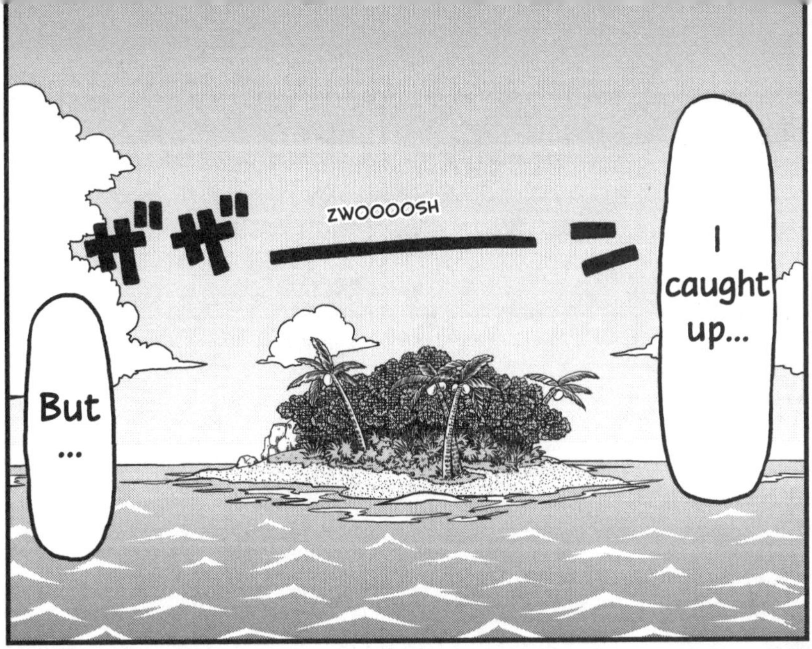
I caught up...
ZWOOOOSH
ザザーーン
But ...

Chapter 140 Riko Izumi Goes Sleepwalking 4

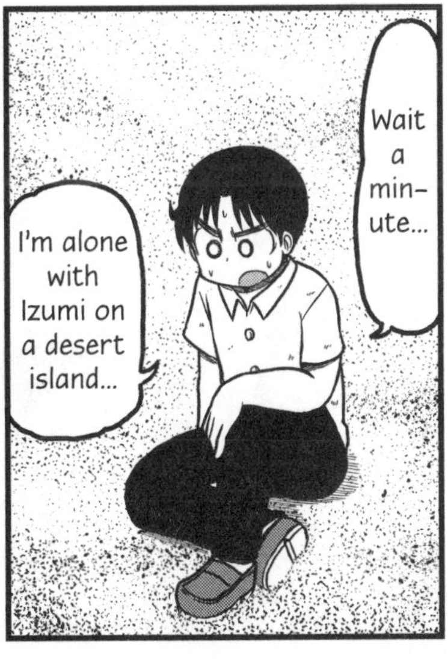
Wait a min-ute...
I'm alone with Izumi on a desert island...

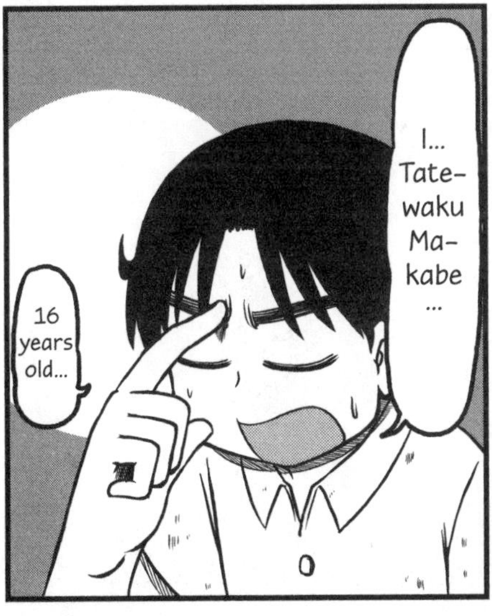
I... Tate-waku Ma-kabe ...
16 years old...

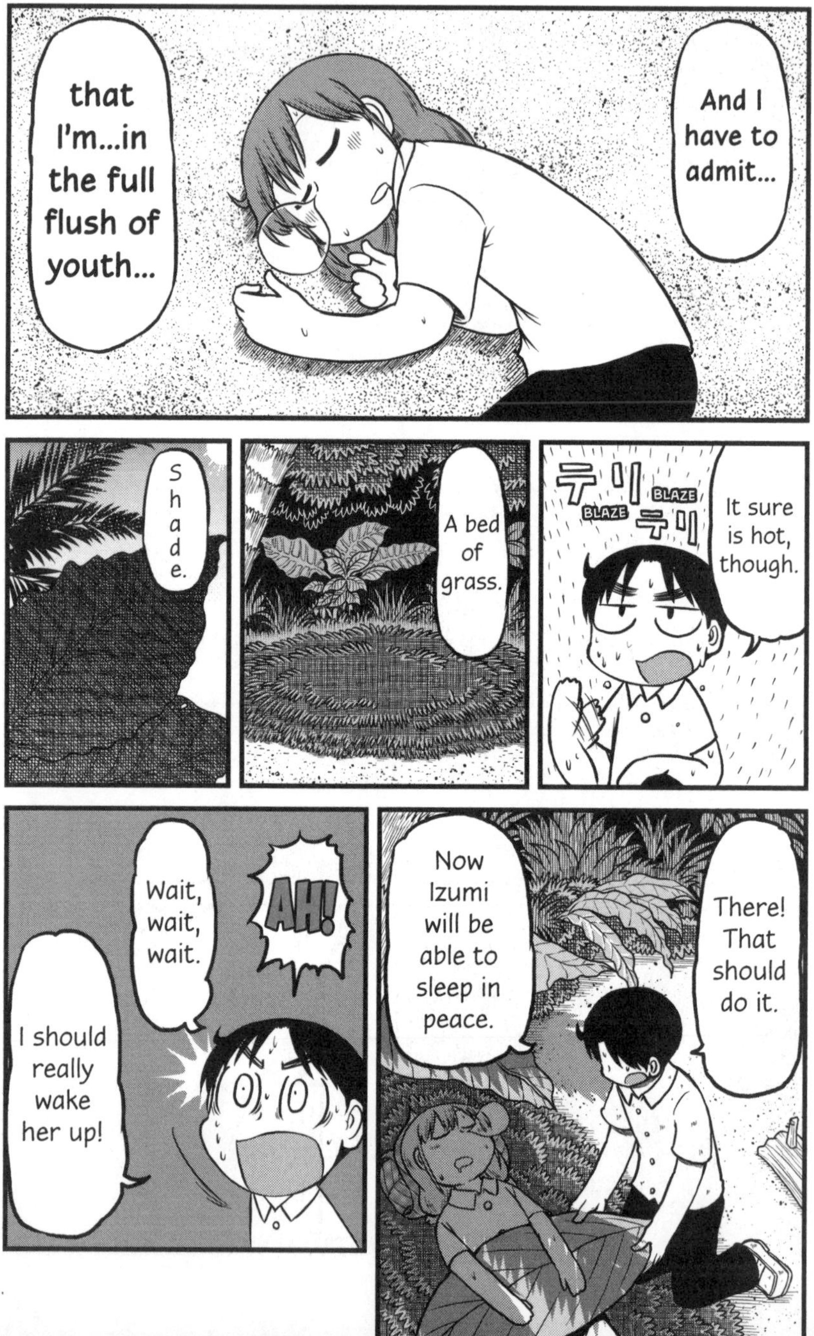
And I have to admit...
that I'm...in the full flush of youth...
BLAZE
BLAZE
It sure is hot, though.
A bed of grass.
Shade.
There! That should do it.
Now Izumi will be able to sleep in peace.
AH!
Wait, wait, wait.
I should really wake her up!

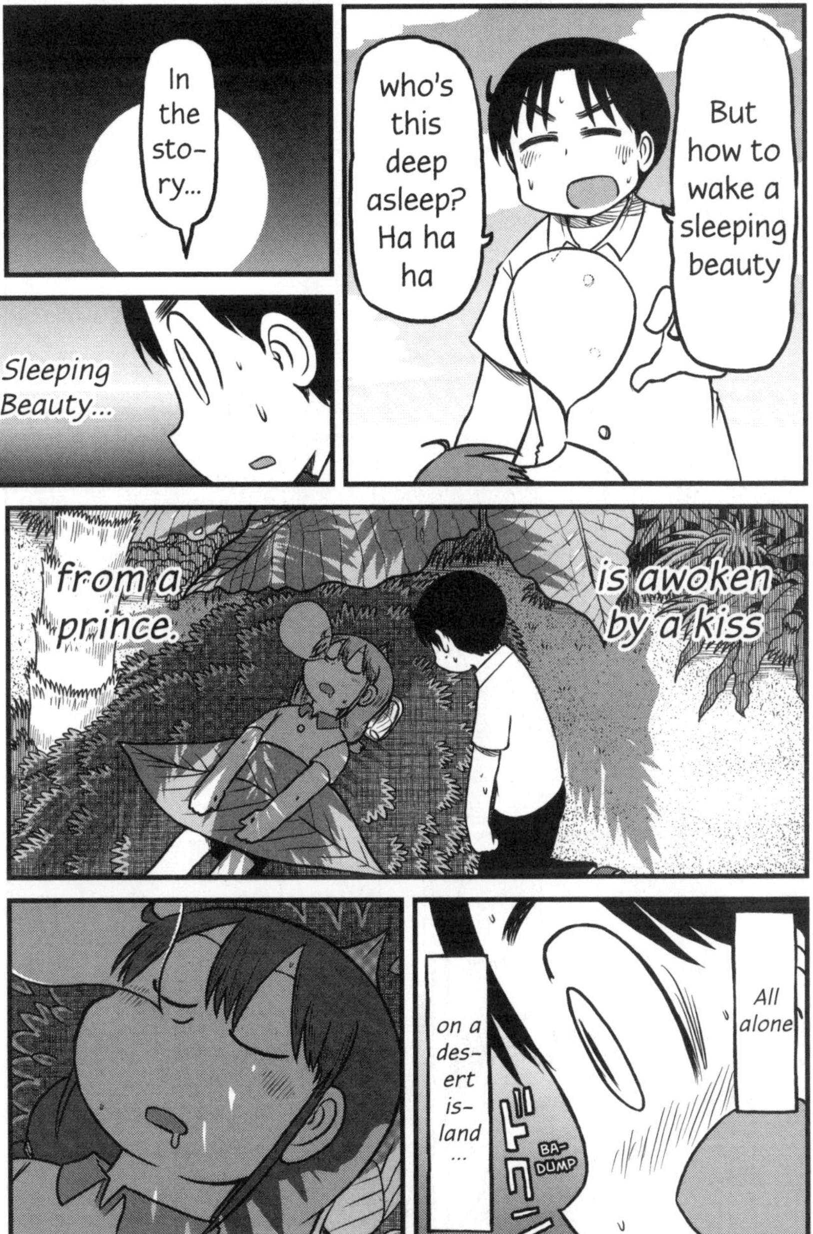
But how to wake a sleeping beauty
who's this deep asleep? Ha ha ha
In the sto-ry...
Sleeping Beauty...
is awoken by a kiss
from a prince.
All alone
on a des-ert is-land ...
BA-DUMP

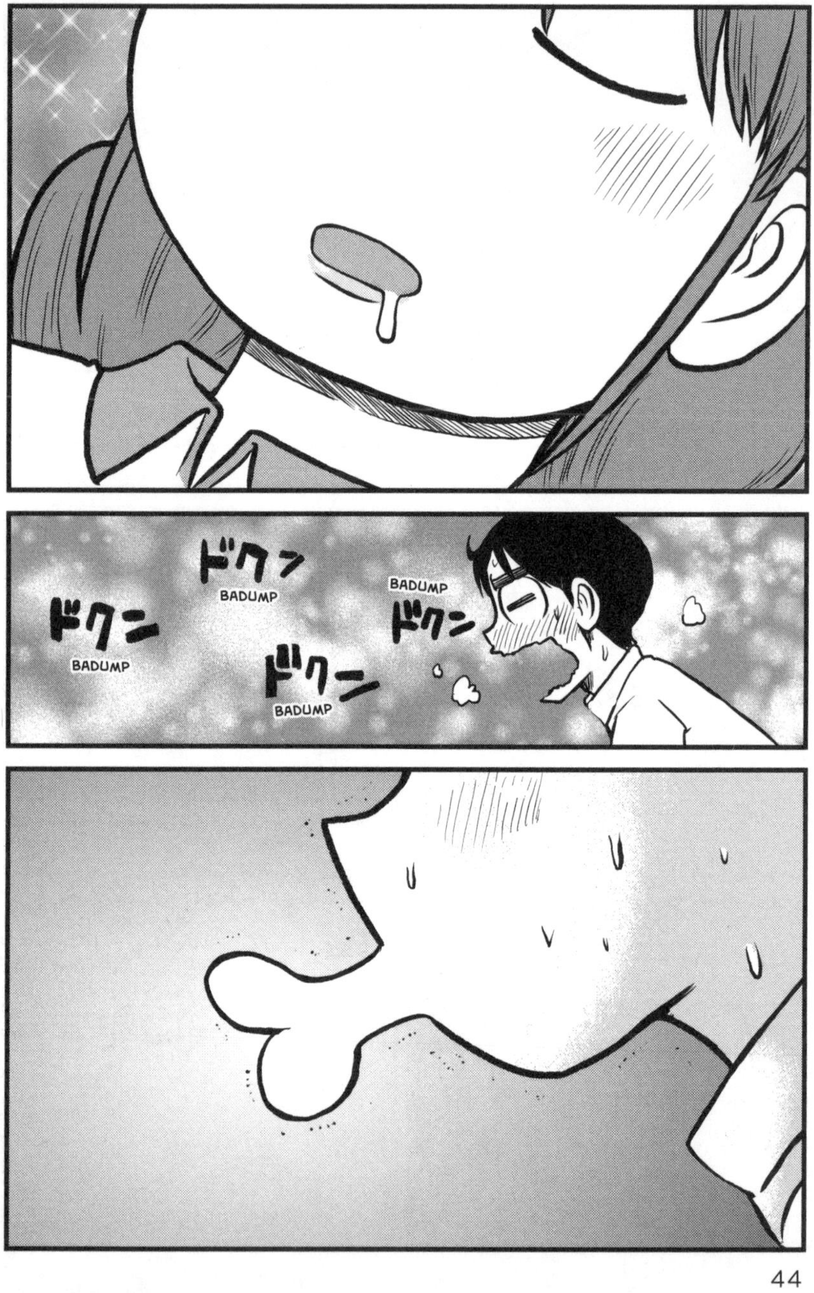

BADUMP
ドクン
ドクン
BADUMP
ドクン
BADUMP
ドクン
BADUMP

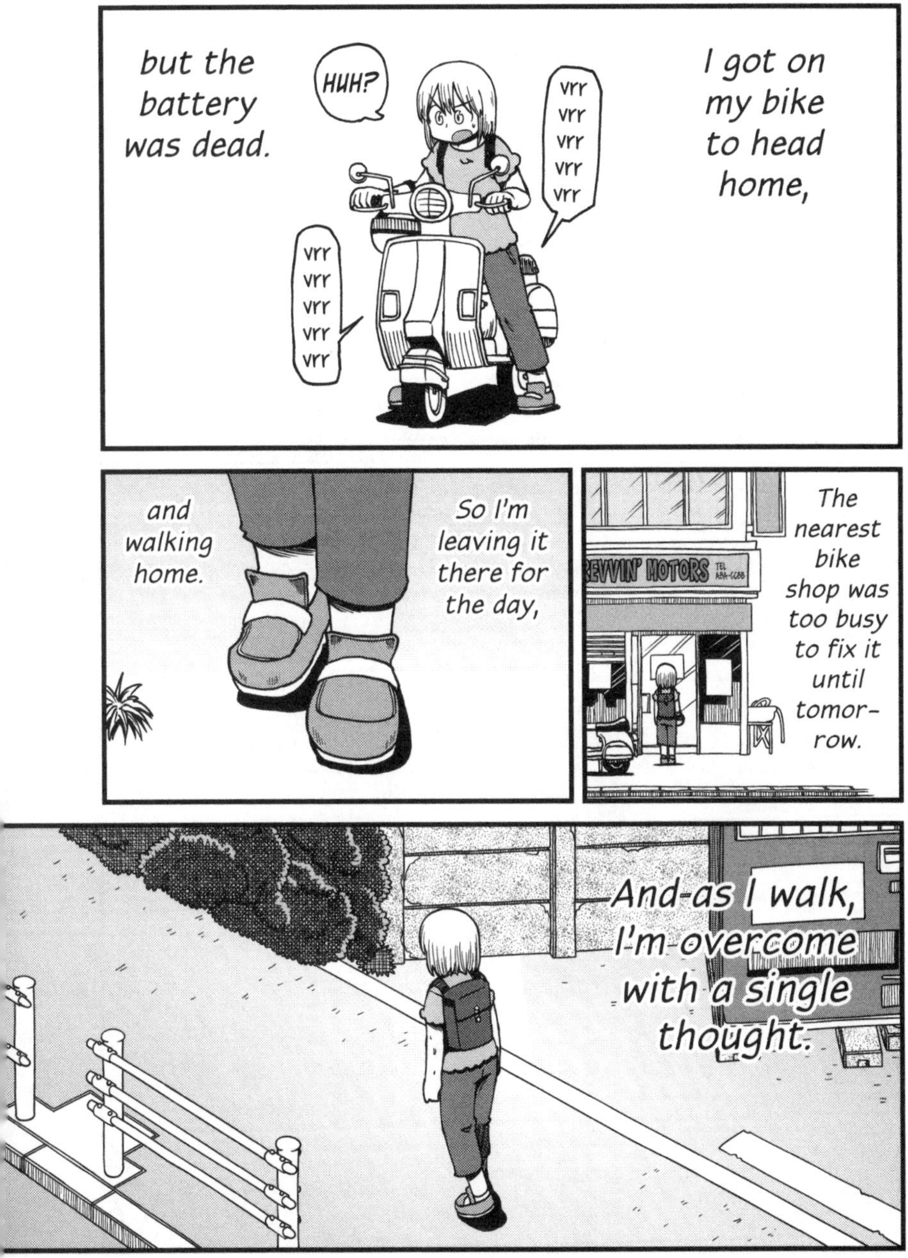
I got on my bike to head home,
vrr vrr vrr vrr vrr
HUH?
but the battery was dead.
vrr vrr vrr vrr vrr
The nearest bike shop was too busy to fix it until tomor-row.
EVVIN' MOTORS
So I'm leaving it there for the day,
and walking home.
And as I walk, I'm overcome with a single thought.

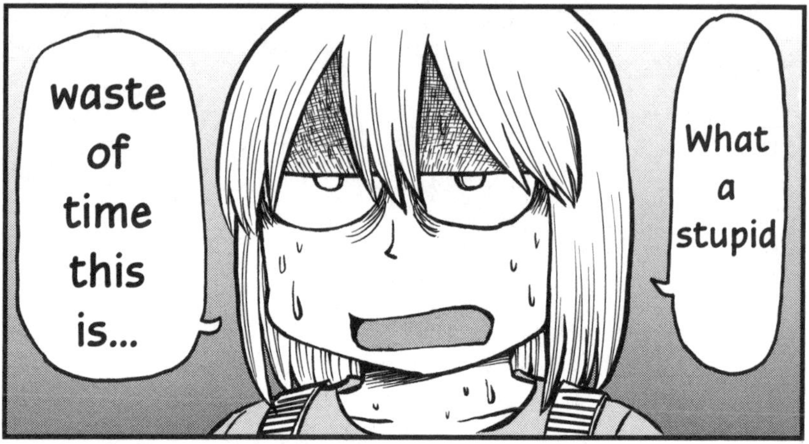
What a stupid
waste of time this is...

Chapter 141 The CITY Minus Tatewaku and Riko Izumi

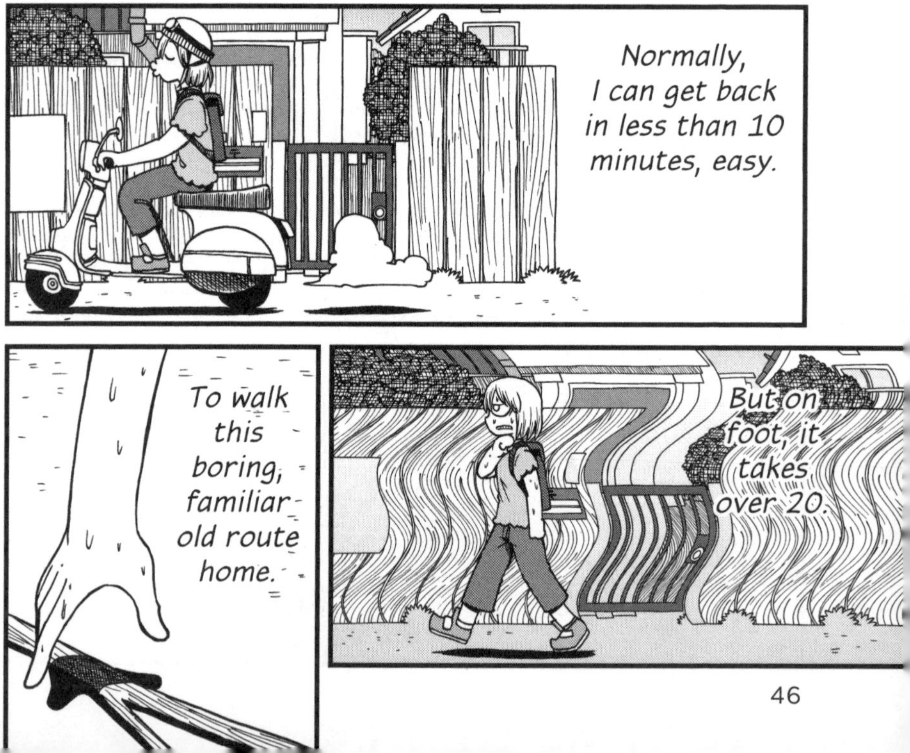
Normally, I can get back in less than 10 minutes, easy.
But on foot, it takes over 20.
To walk this boring, familiar old route home.

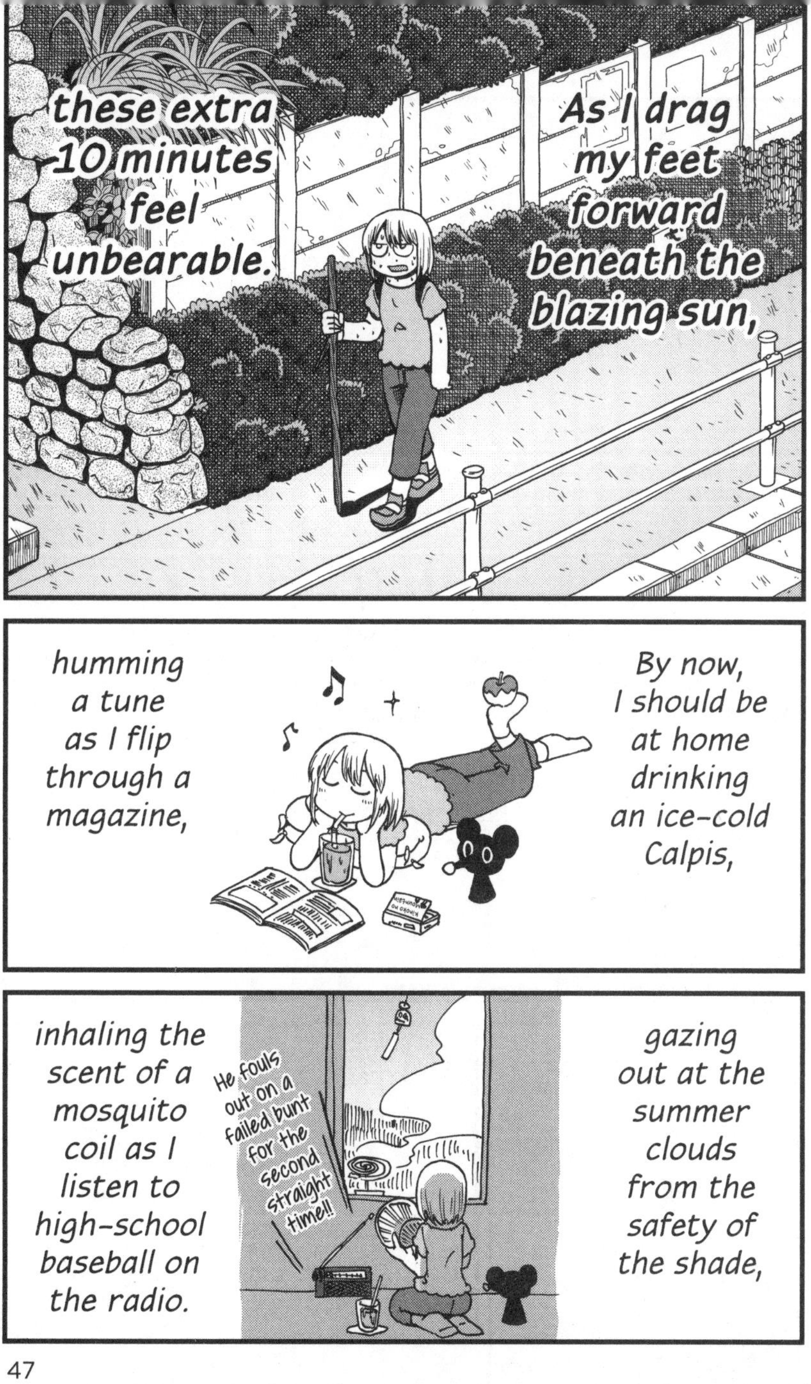
As I drag my feet forward beneath the blazing sun,
these extra 10 minutes feel unbearable.
By now, I should be at home drinking an ice-cold Calpis,
humming a tune as I flip through a magazine,
gazing out at the summer clouds from the safety of the shade,
He fouls out on a failed bunt for the second straight time!!
inhaling the scent of a mosquito coil as I listen to high-school baseball on the radio.

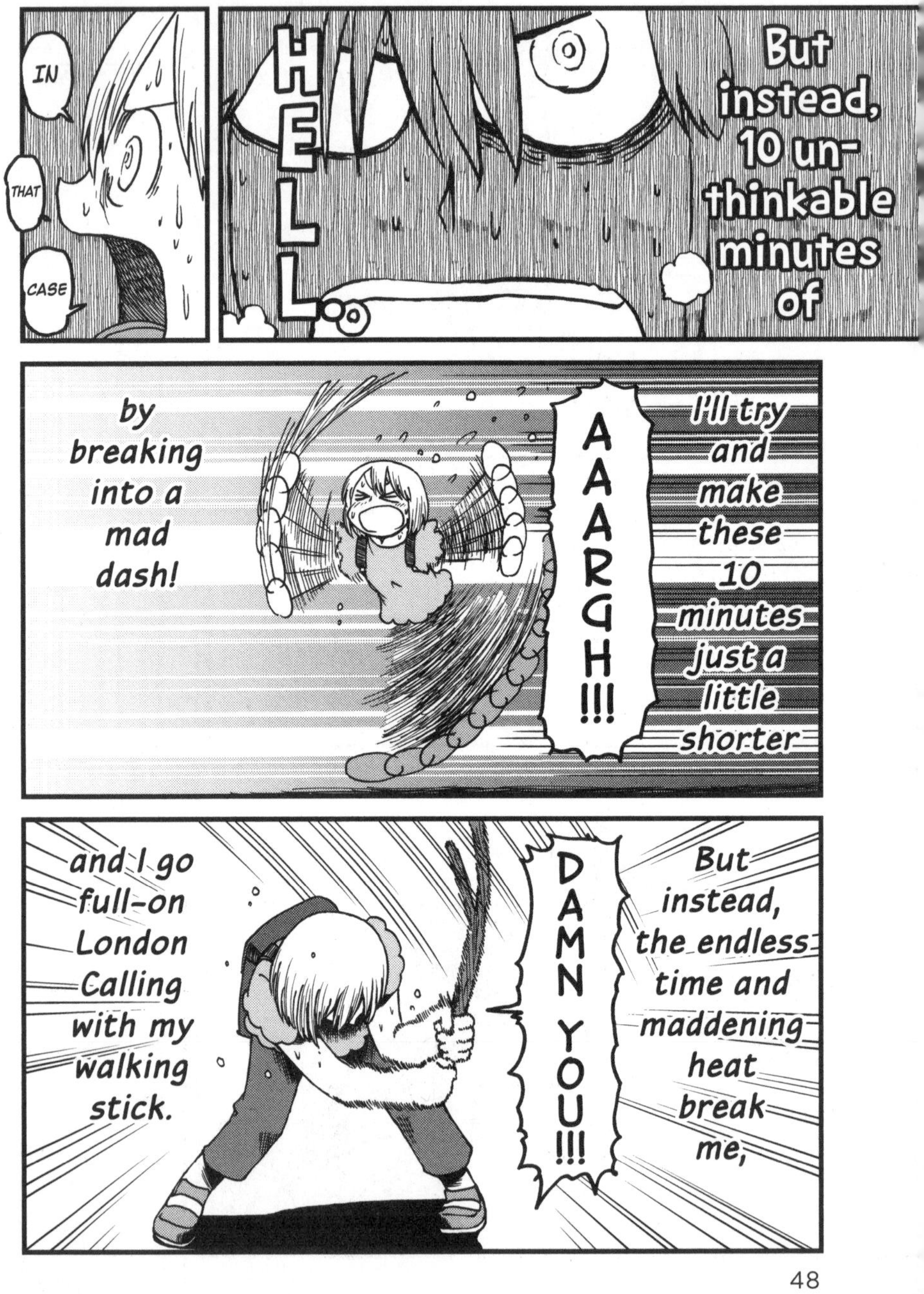

But instead, 10 un-thinkable minutes of
HELL...
IN
THAT
CASE
I'll try and make these 10 minutes just a little shorter
AAARGH!!!
by breaking into a mad dash!
But instead, the endless time and maddening heat break me,
DAMN YOU!!!
and I go full-on London Calling with my walking stick.

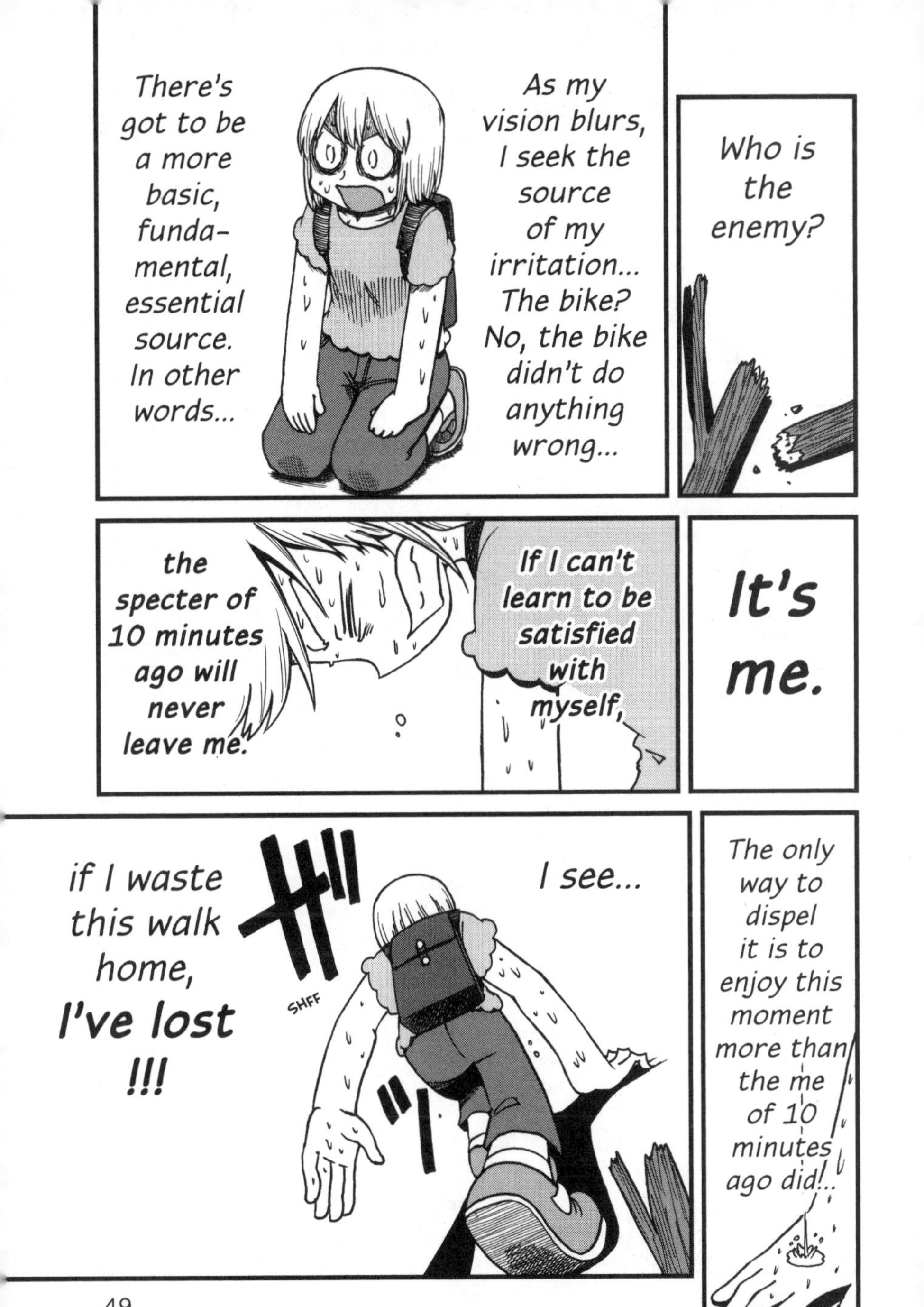

Who is the enemy?
As my vision blurs, I seek the source of my irritation... The bike? No, the bike didn't do anything wrong...
There's got to be a more basic, funda-mental, essential source. In other words...
It's me.
If I can't learn to be satisfied with myself,
the specter of 10 minutes ago will never leave me.
The only way to dispel it is to enjoy this moment more than the me of 10 minutes ago did!..
I see...
SHFF
if I waste this walk home, I've lost !!!

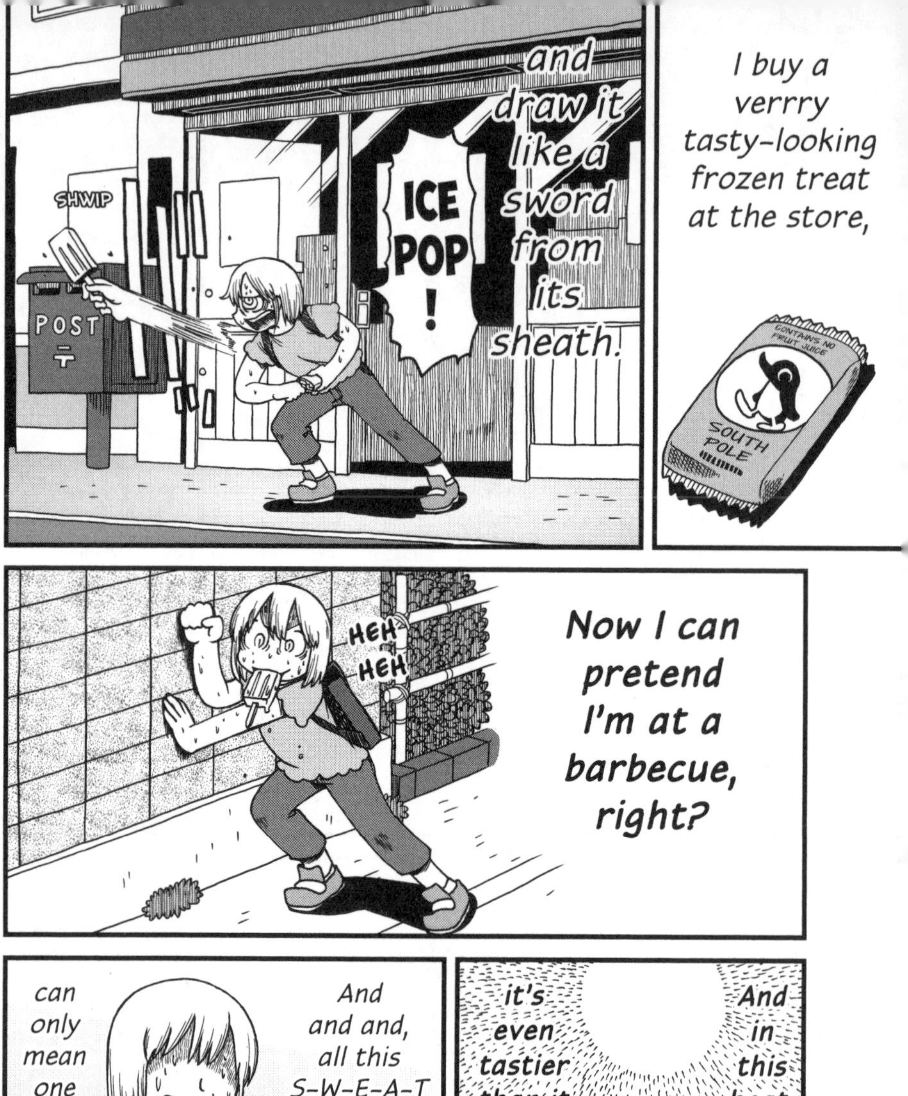
I buy a verrry tasty-looking frozen treat at the store,
CONTAINS NO FRUIT JUICE
SOUTH POLE
and draw it like a sword from its sheath.
ICE POP!
SHWIP
POST
Now I can pretend I'm at a barbecue, right?
HEH HEH
And in this heat,
it's even tastier than it would be at home.
And and and, all this S-W-E-A-T
can only mean one thing:
PLIP

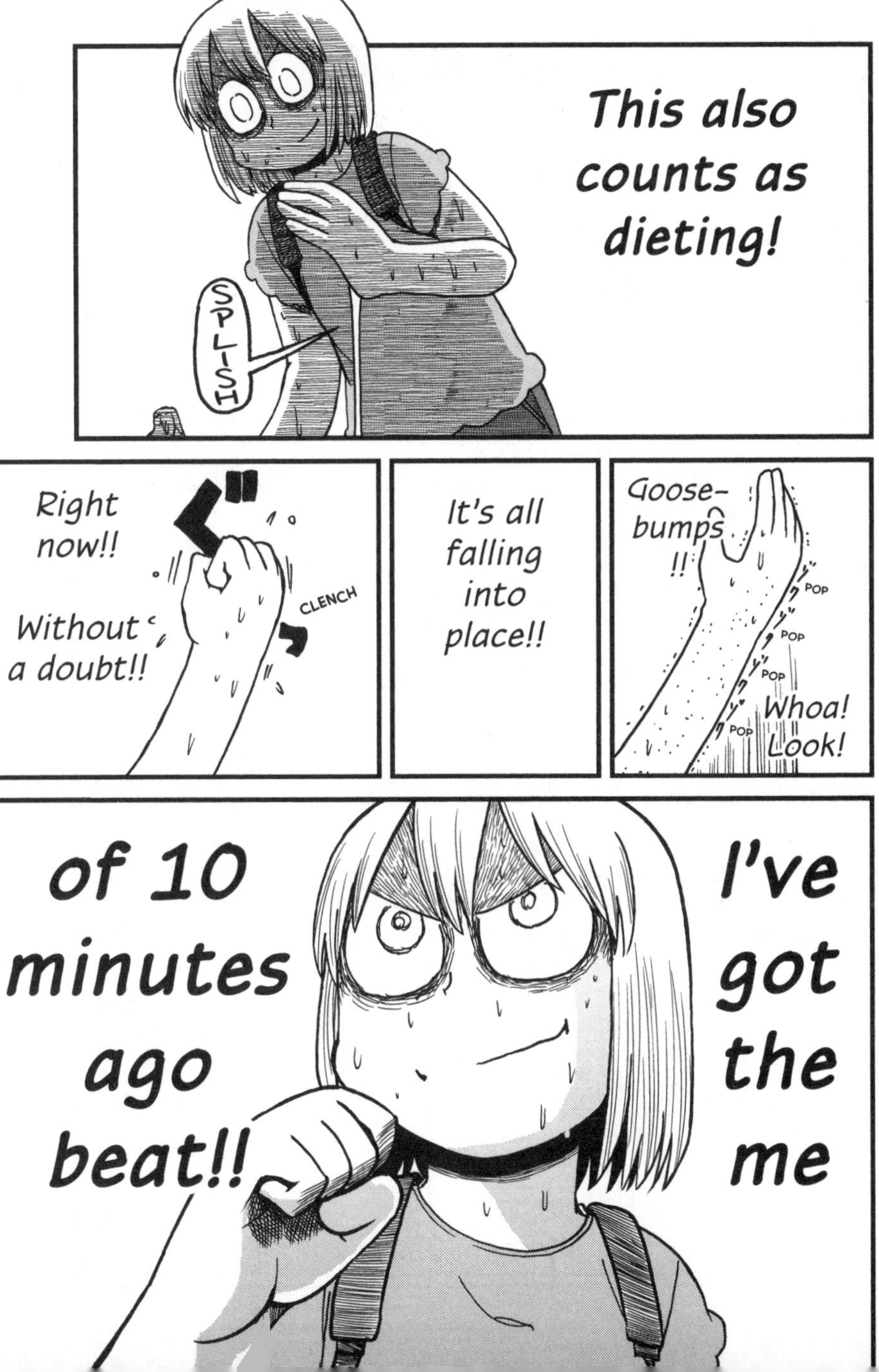
This also counts as dieting!
SPLISH
Goose-bumps!!
POP
POP
POP
POP
Whoa! Look!
It's all falling into place!!
Right now!!
CLENCH
Without a doubt!!
I've got the me
of 10 minutes ago beat!!

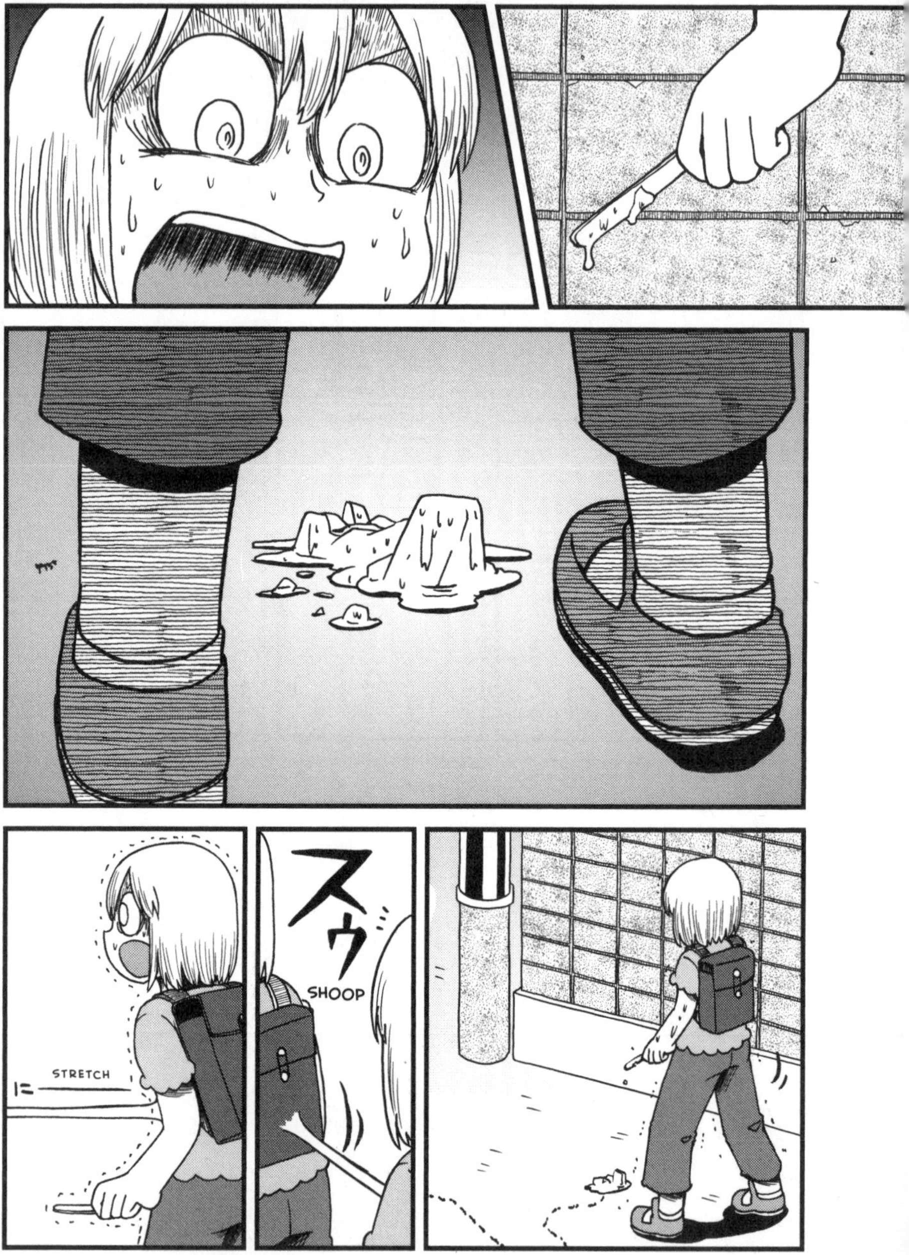
スウ
SHOOP
に
STRETCH

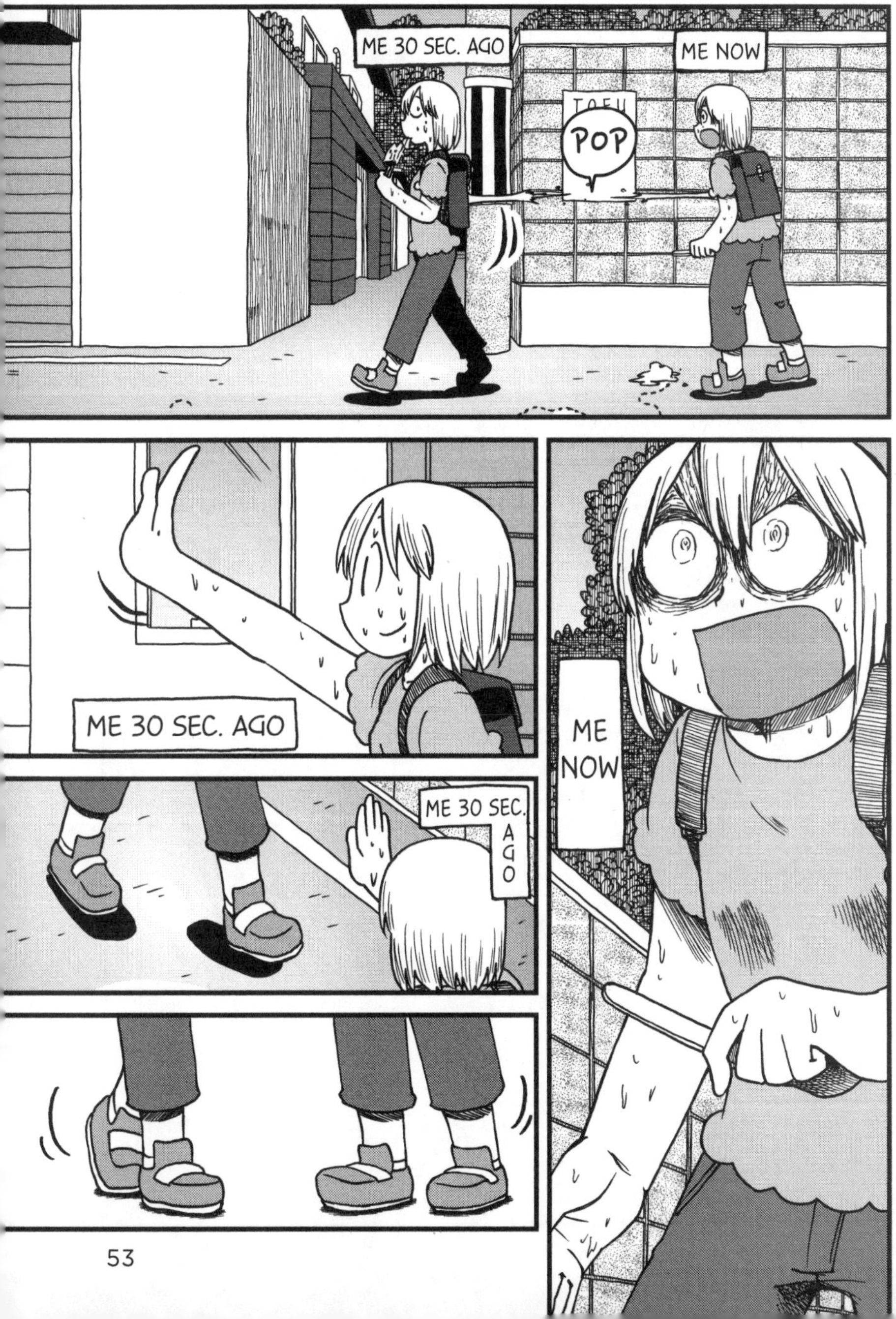

ME NOW
POP
ME 30 SEC. AGO
ME NOW
ME 30 SEC. AGO
ME 30 SEC. AGO

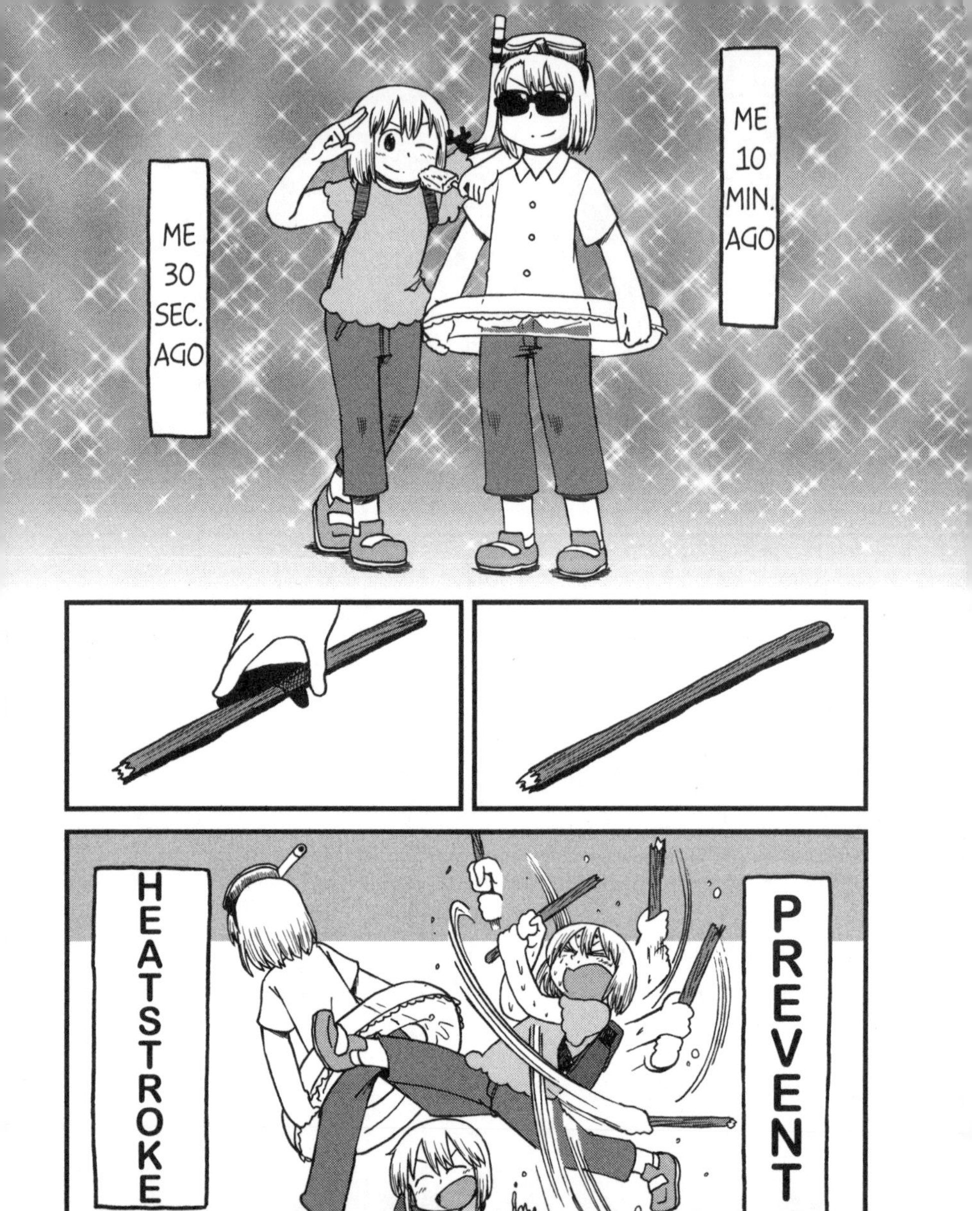
ME 10 MIN. AGO
ME 30 SEC. AGO
PREVENT
HEATSTROKE

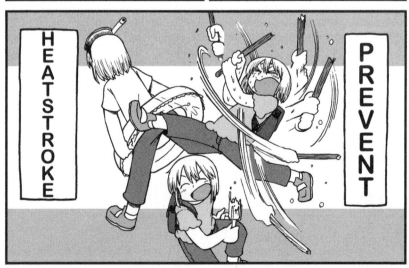

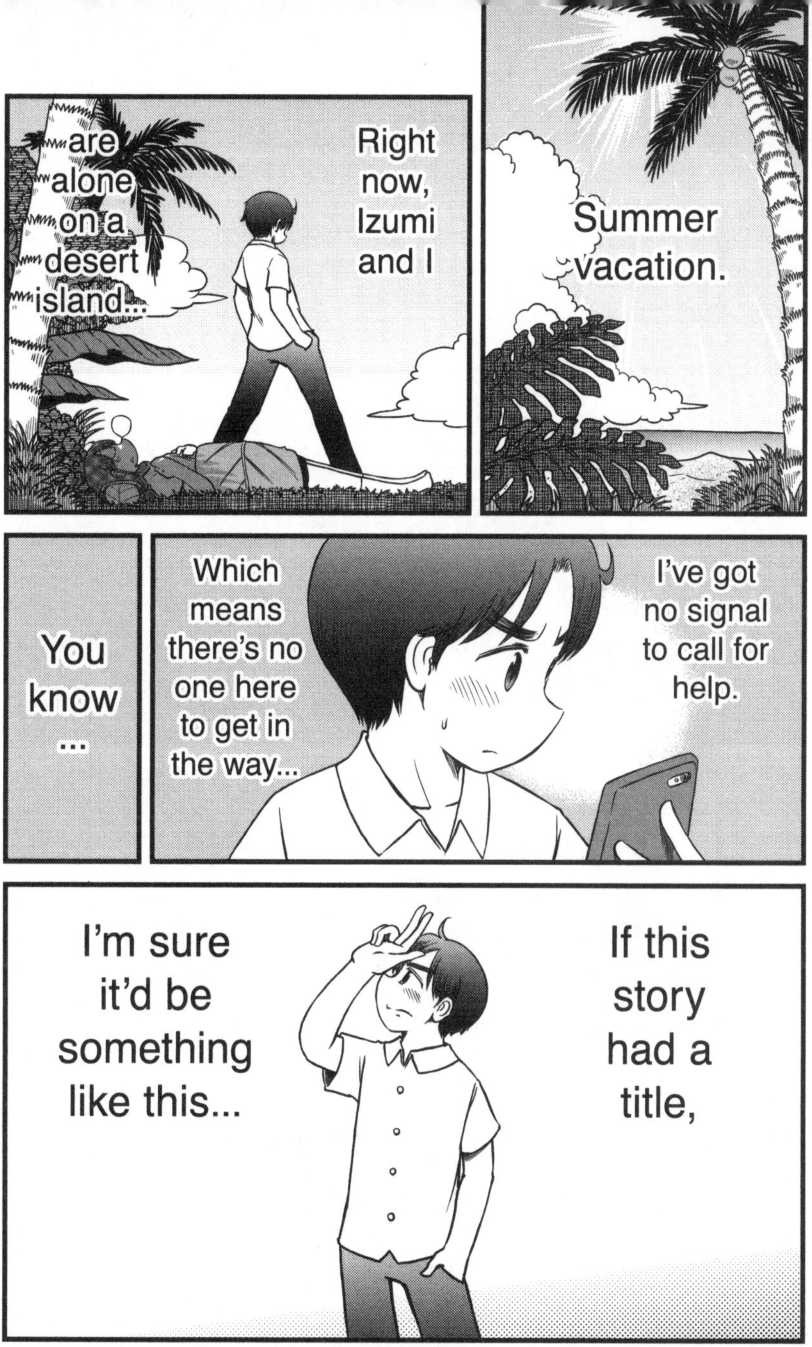
Summer vacation.
Right now, Izumi and I
are alone on a desert island...
I've got no signal to call for help.
Which means there's no one here to get in the way...
You know ...
If this story had a title,
I'm sure it'd be something like this...

SUMMERTIME

BLUES

TatewaQ Makabe

#1 HOW FAR AROUND THE BASES
WILL THIS SUMMER EXPERIENCE TAKE HIM?!

LOST ON A PAROPICAL ISLAND
OF SEDUCTION

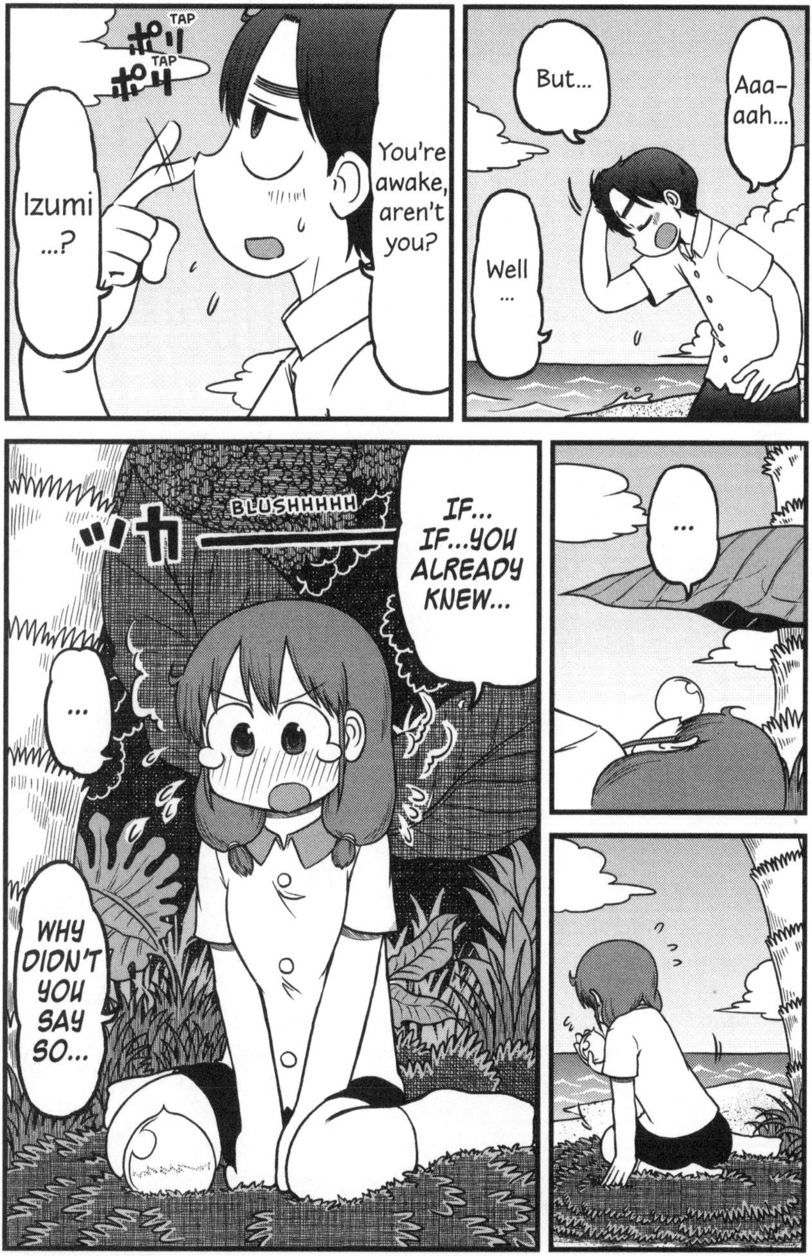
Aaa-aah...
But...
Well...
You're awake, aren't you?
ポリ
TAP
ポリ
TAP
Izumi...?
...
IF... IF...YOU ALREADY KNEW...
BLUSHHHHH
ッカー
...
WHY DIDN'T YOU SAY SO...

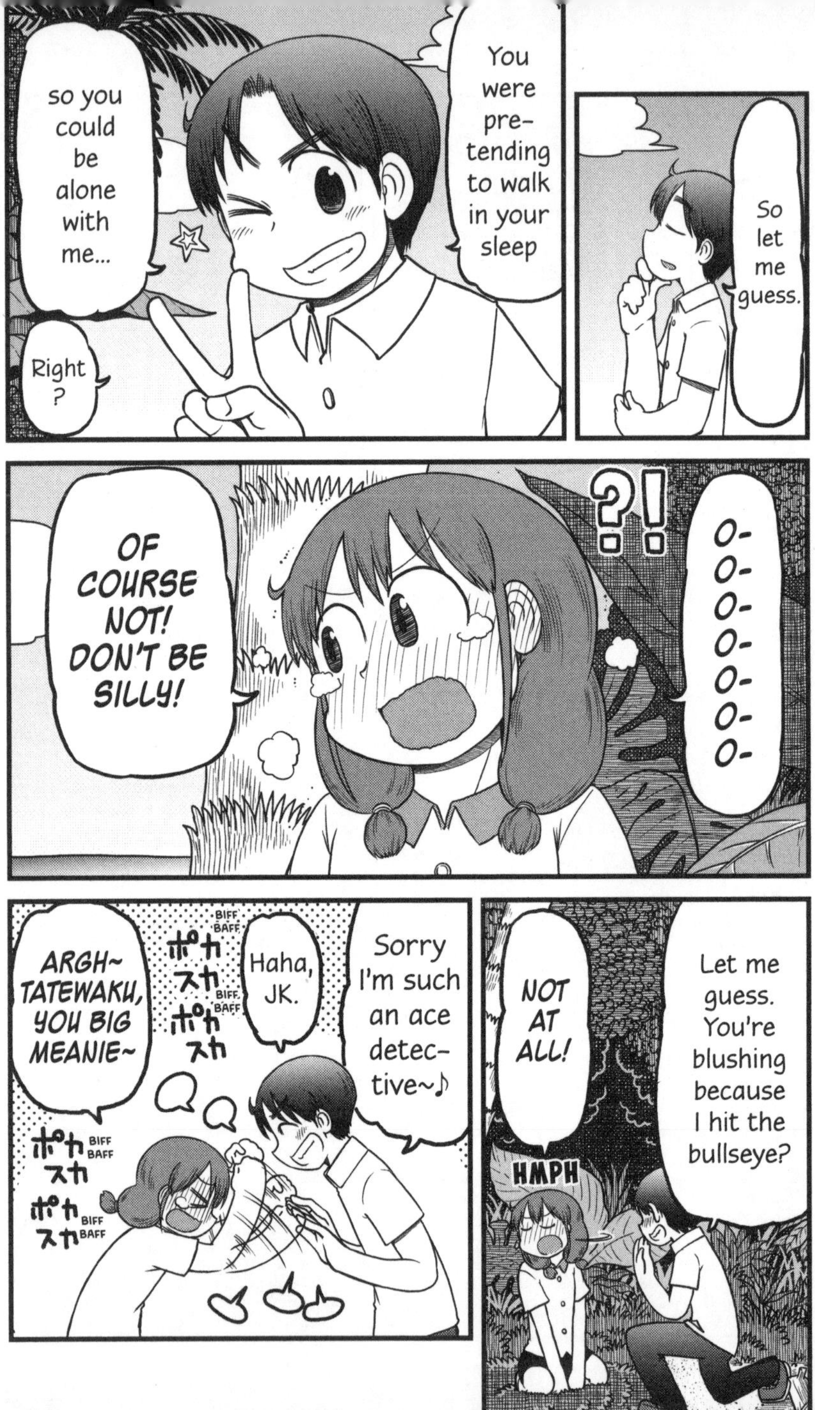
So let me guess.
You were pre-tending to walk in your sleep
so you could be alone with me...
Right?
?!
O-O-O-O-O-O-O-
OF COURSE NOT! DON'T BE SILLY!
Let me guess. You're blushing because I hit the bullseye?
NOT AT ALL!
HMPH
Sorry I'm such an ace detec-tive~♪
Haha, JK.
ポカスカ BIFF BAFF
ポカスカ BIFF BAFF
ARGH~ TATEWAKU, YOU BIG MEANIE~
ポカスカ BIFF BAFF
ポカスカ BIFF BAFF

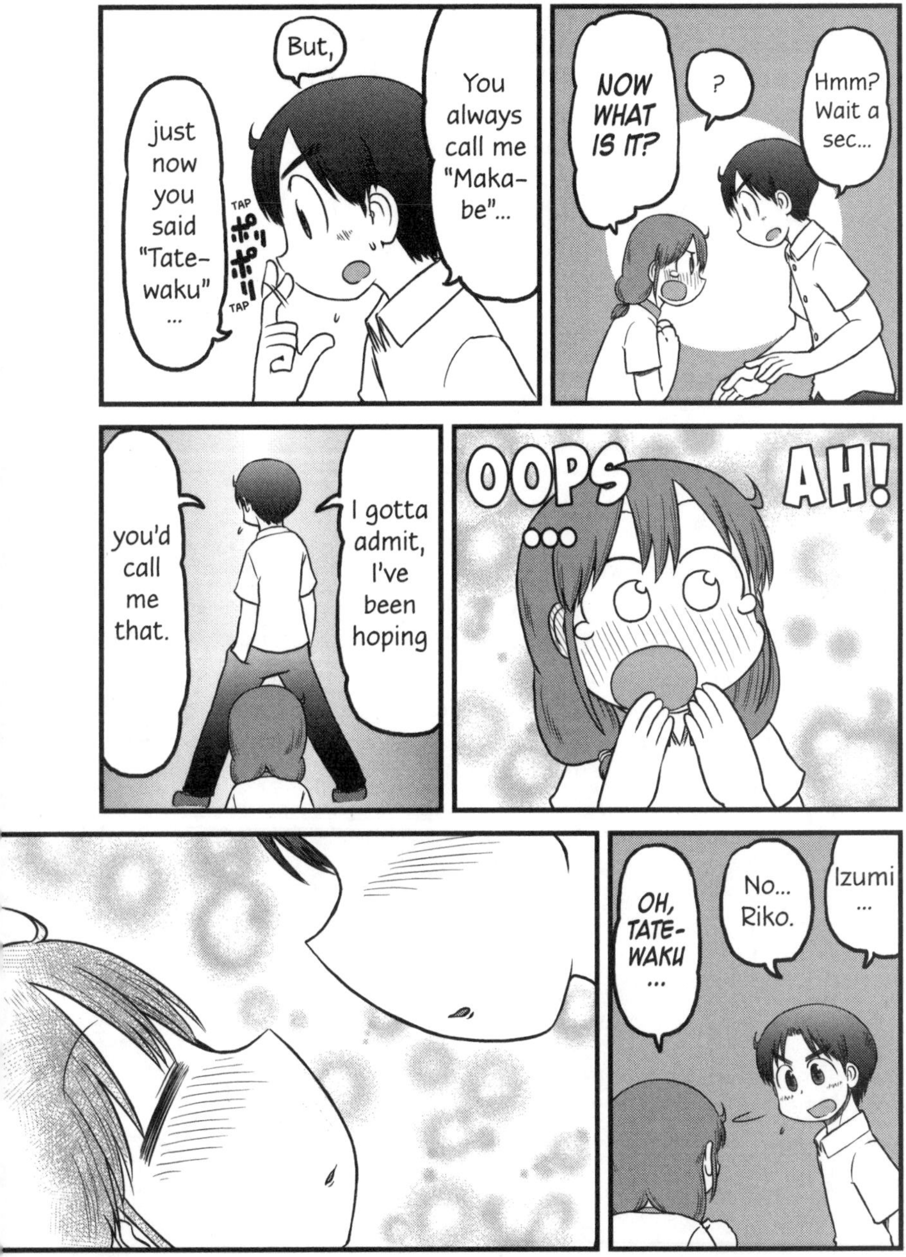
Hmm? Wait a sec...
?
NOW WHAT IS IT?
You always call me "Maka-be"...
But,
just now you said "Tate-waku" ...
TAP ポリ ポリ TAP
AH!
OOPS ...
I gotta admit, I've been hoping
you'd call me that.
Izumi ...
No... Riko.
OH, TATE-WAKU ...

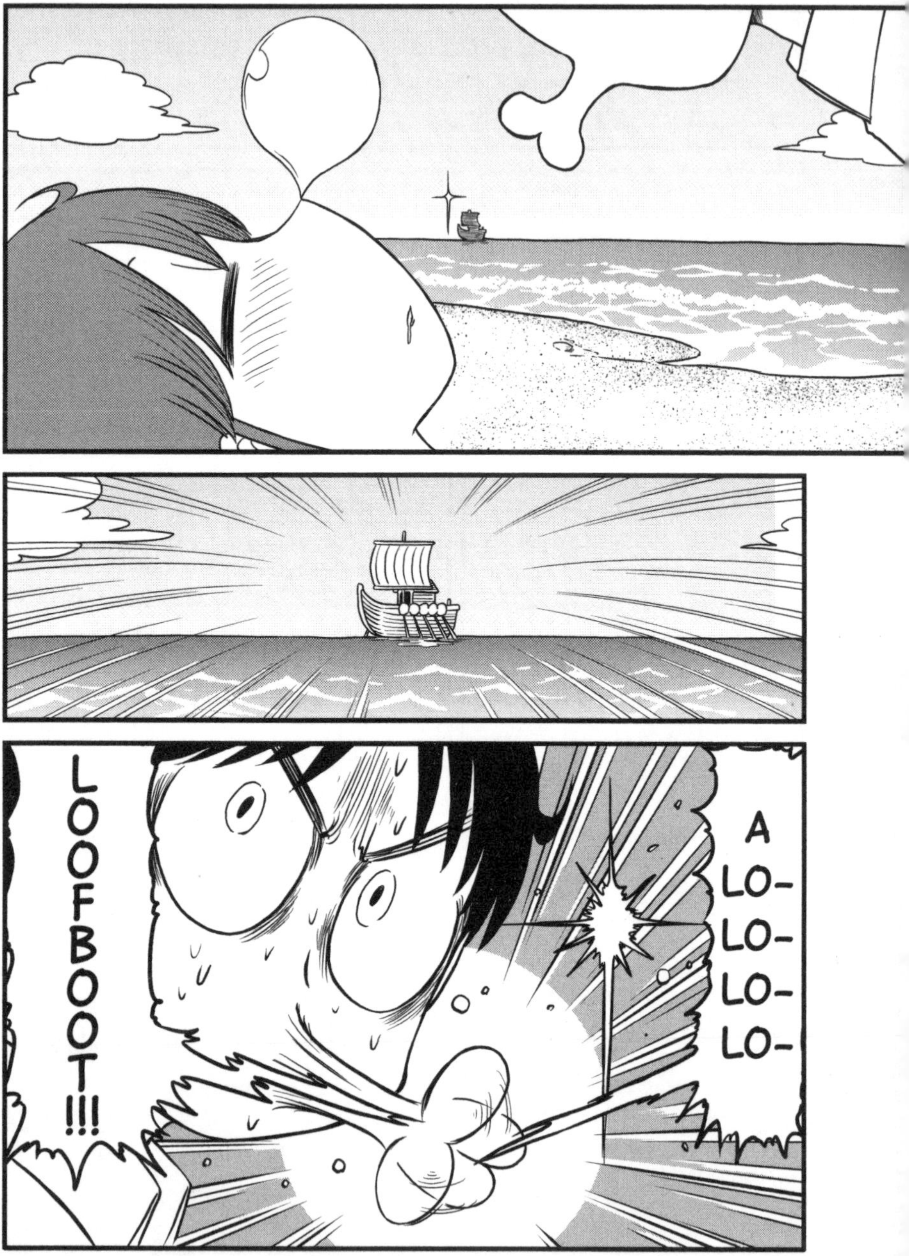
A LO-LO-LO-LO-LO-
LOOFBOOT!!!

Chapter 142 ◇ Riko Izumi Goes Sleepwalking 5

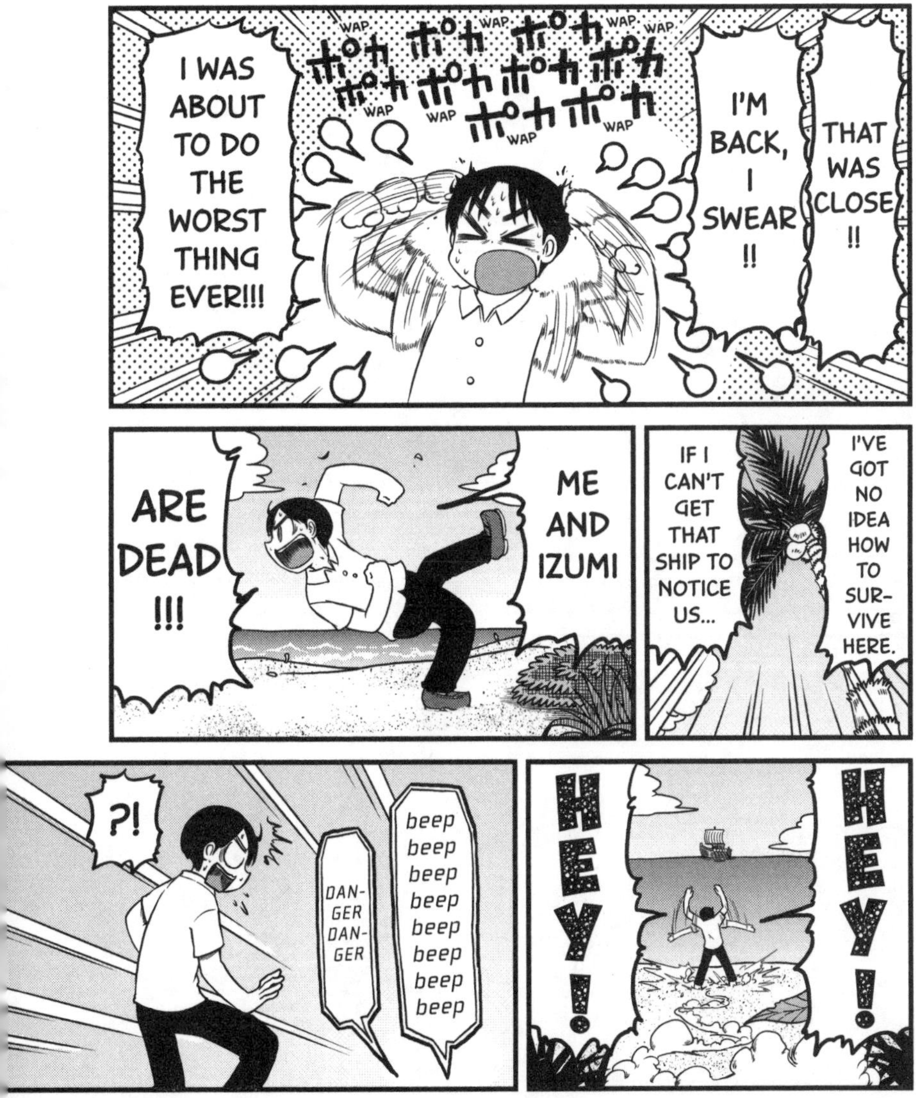
THAT WAS CLOSE!!
I'M BACK, I SWEAR!!
WAP WAP WAP WAP WAP WAP WAP WAP
I WAS ABOUT TO DO THE WORST THING EVER!!!
I'VE GOT NO IDEA HOW TO SURVIVE HERE.
IF I CAN'T GET THAT SHIP TO NOTICE US...
ME AND IZUMI
ARE DEAD!!!
HEY!
HEY!
beep beep beep beep beep beep beep beep
DANGER DANGER
?!

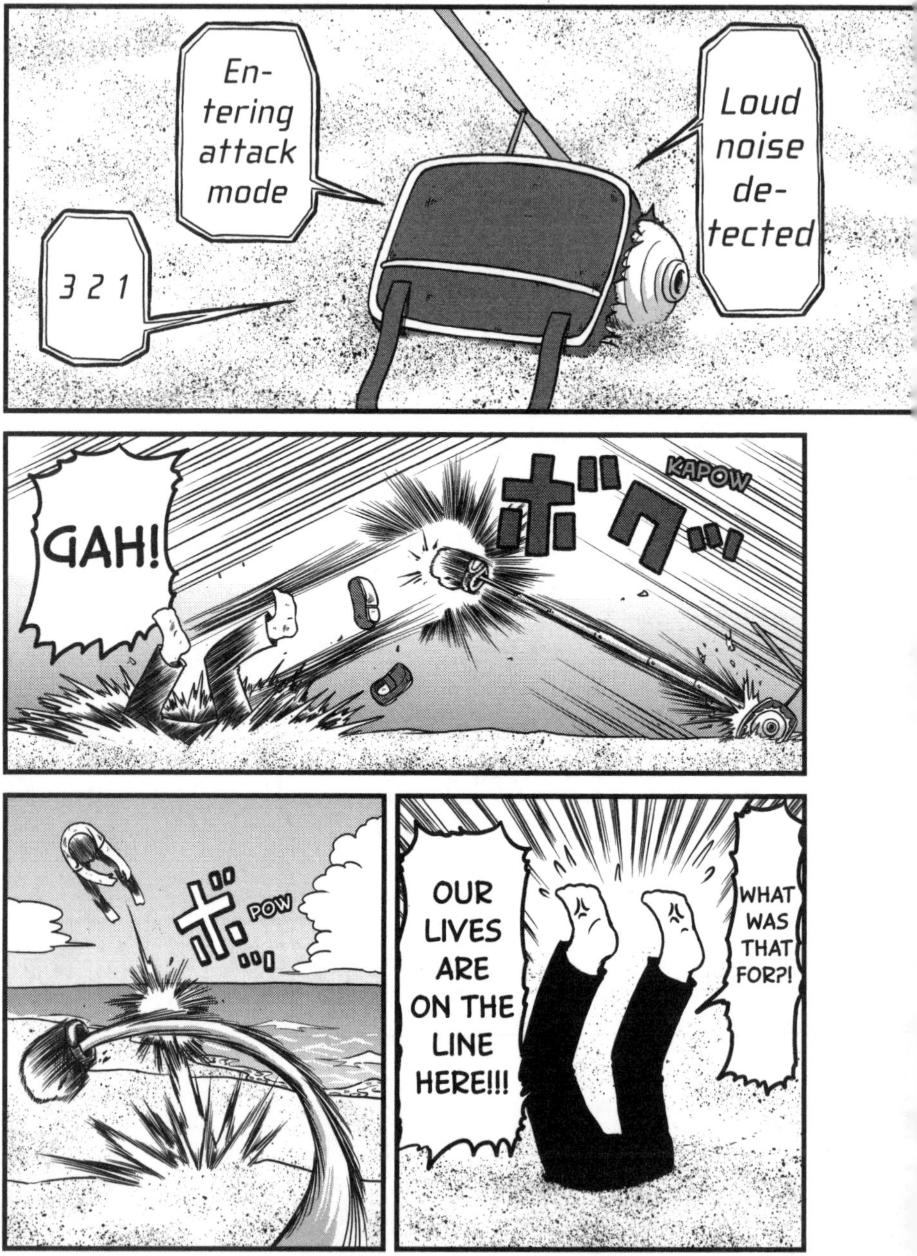
Loud noise de- tected
En- tering attack mode
3 2 1
ボグッ
KAPOW
GAH!
WHAT WAS THAT FOR?!
OUR LIVES ARE ON THE LINE HERE!!!
ボッ
POW

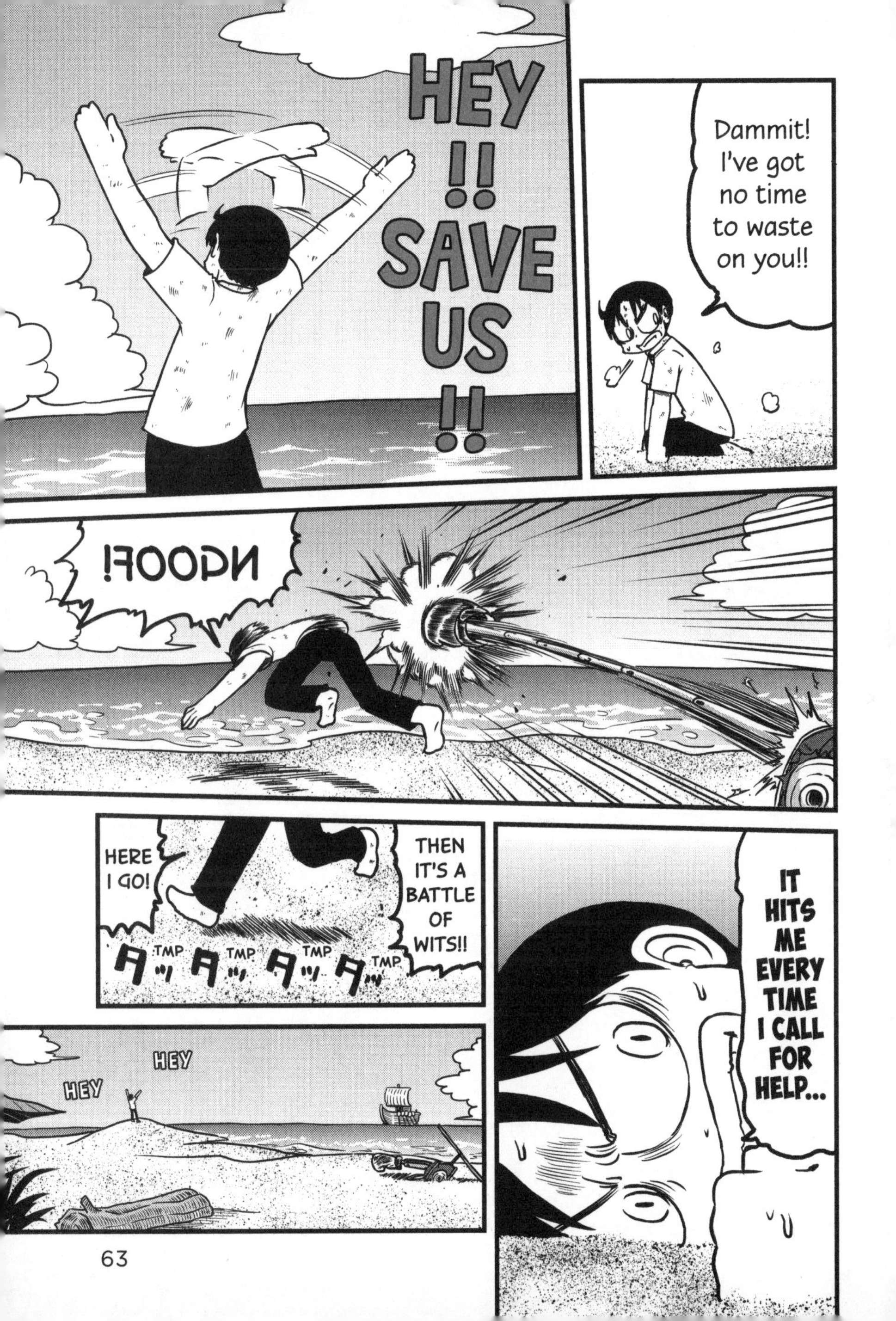

Dammit! I've got no time to waste on you!!
HEY!! SAVE US!!
NGOOF!
IT HITS ME EVERY TIME I CALL FOR HELP...
THEN IT'S A BATTLE OF WITS!!
HERE I GO!
TMP TMP TMP TMP
HEY
HEY

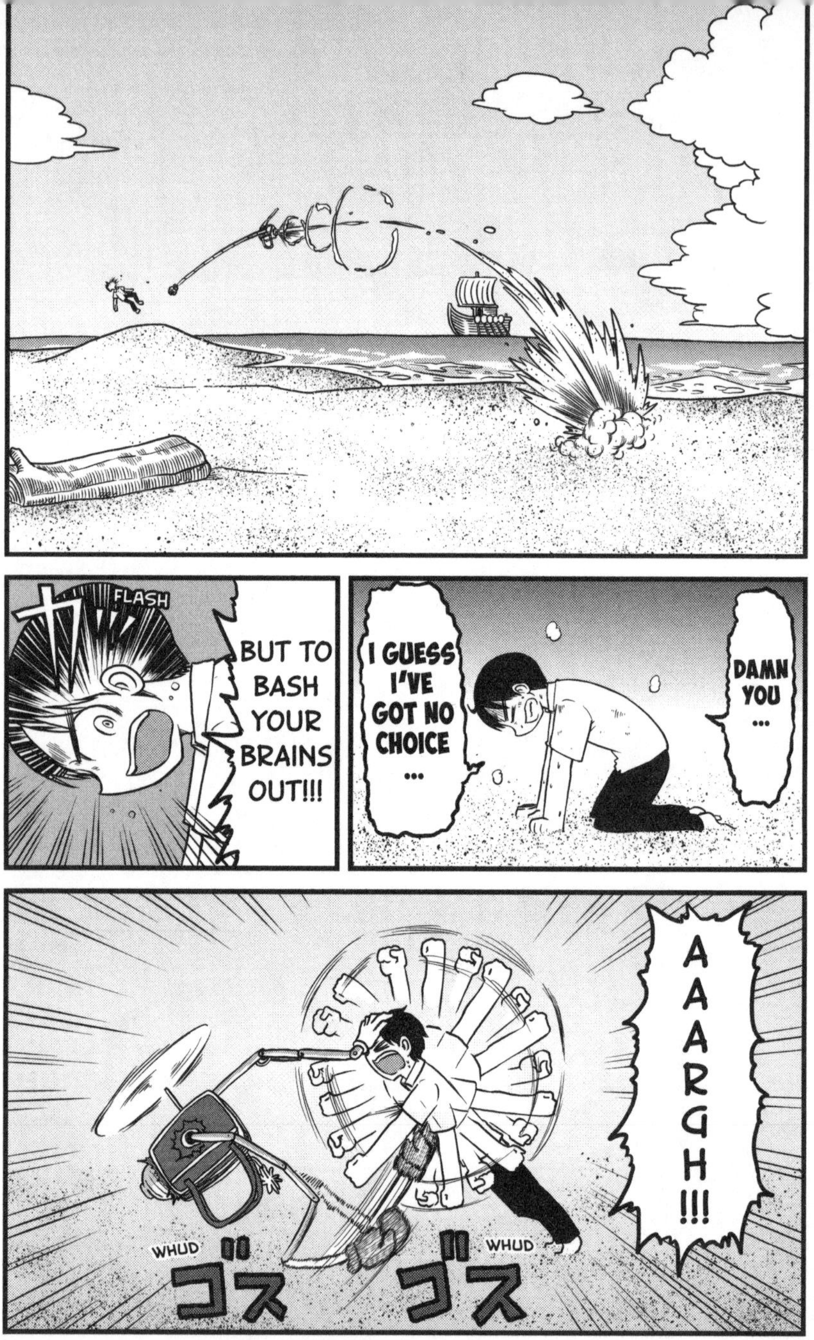
DAMN YOU ...
I GUESS I'VE GOT NO CHOICE ...
FLASH
BUT TO BASH YOUR BRAINS OUT!!!
AAAARGH!!!
WHUD
ゴス
WHUD
ゴス

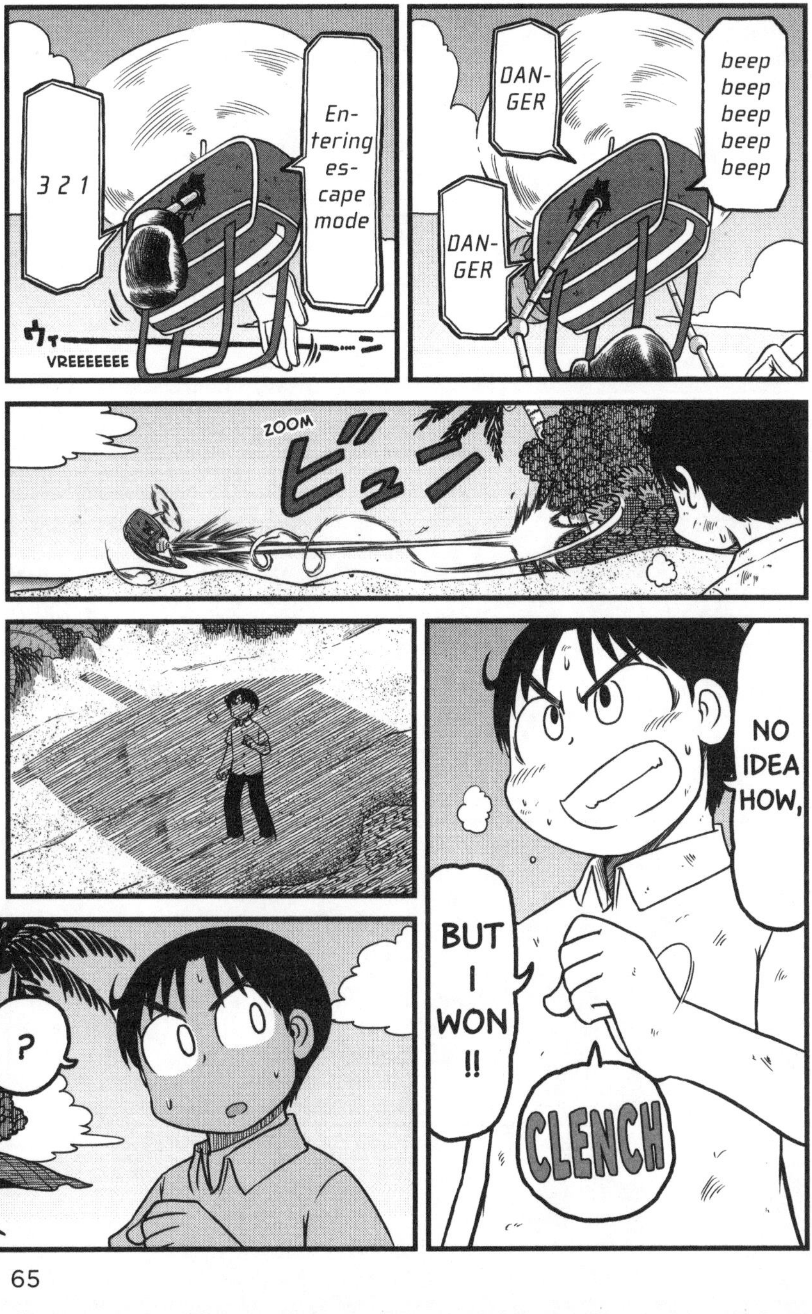
beep beep beep beep beep
DAN-GER
DAN-GER
En-tering es-cape mode
3 2 1
VREEEEEEE
ZOOM
ビュン
NO IDEA HOW,
BUT I WON!!
CLENCH
?

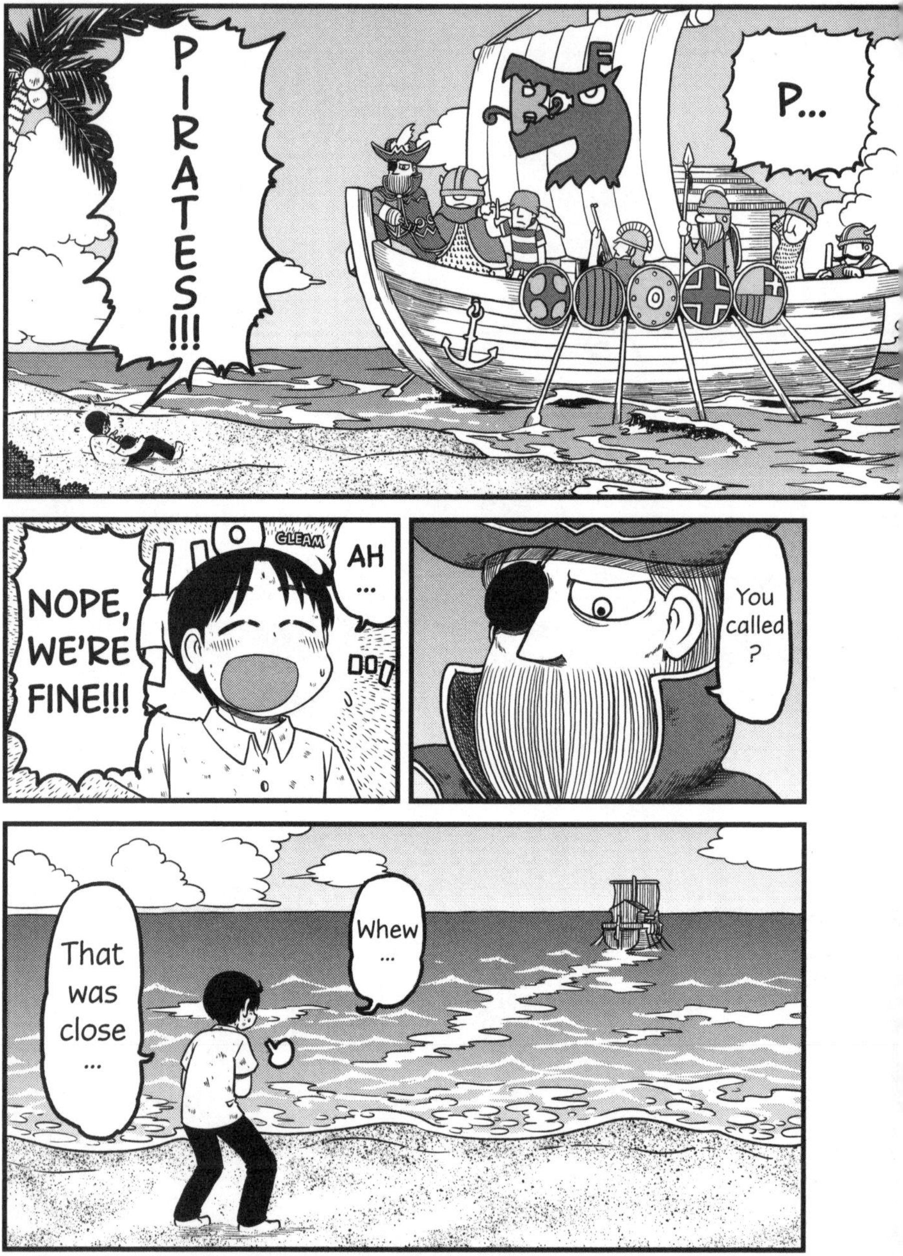
P...
PIRATES!!!
You called?
AH ...
GLEAM
NOPE, WE'RE FINE!!!
Whew ...
That was close ...

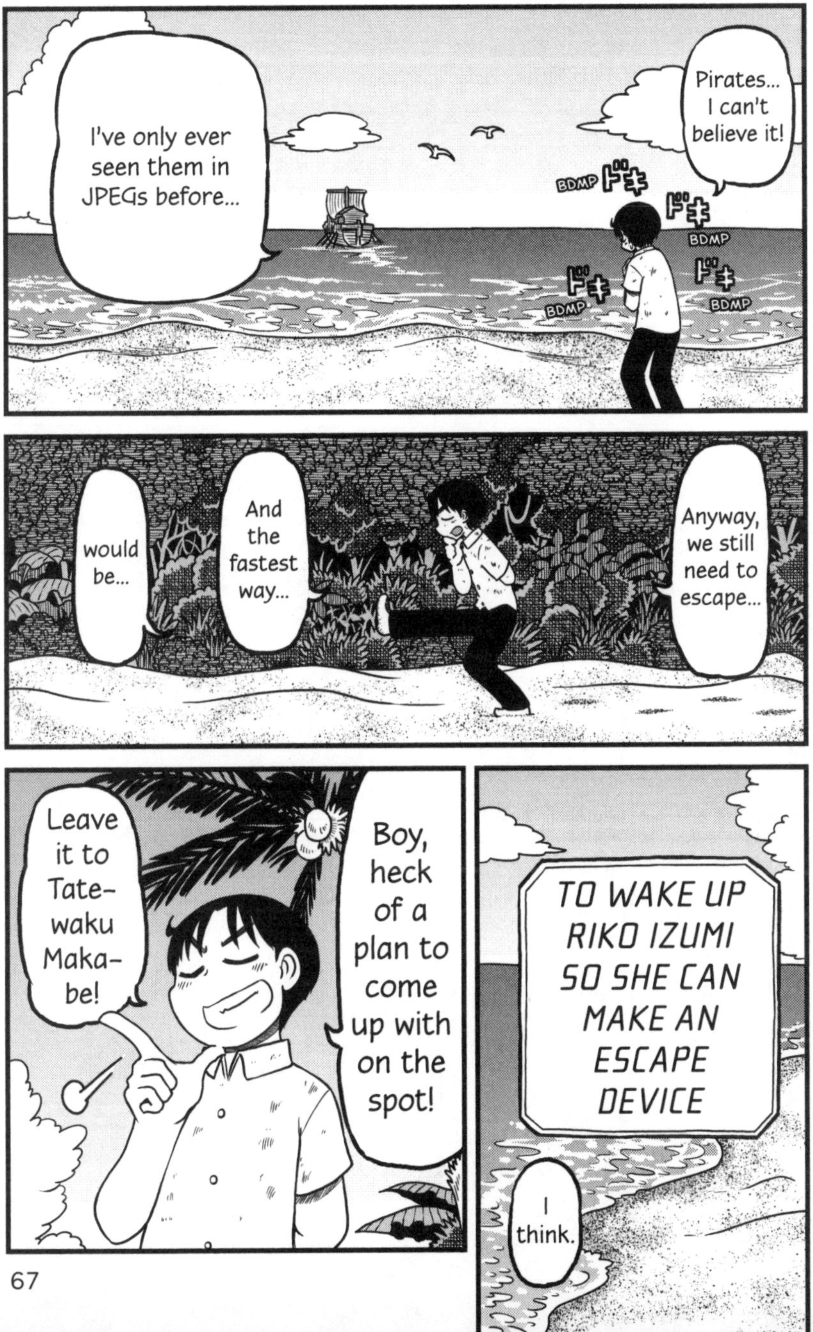
Pirates... I can't believe it!
BDMP ドキ
ドキ BDMP
ドキ BDMP
ドキ BDMP
I've only ever seen them in JPEGs before...
Anyway, we still need to escape...
And the fastest way...
would be...
TO WAKE UP RIKO IZUMI SO SHE CAN MAKE AN ESCAPE DEVICE
I think.
Boy, heck of a plan to come up with on the spot!
Leave it to Tate-waku Maka-be!

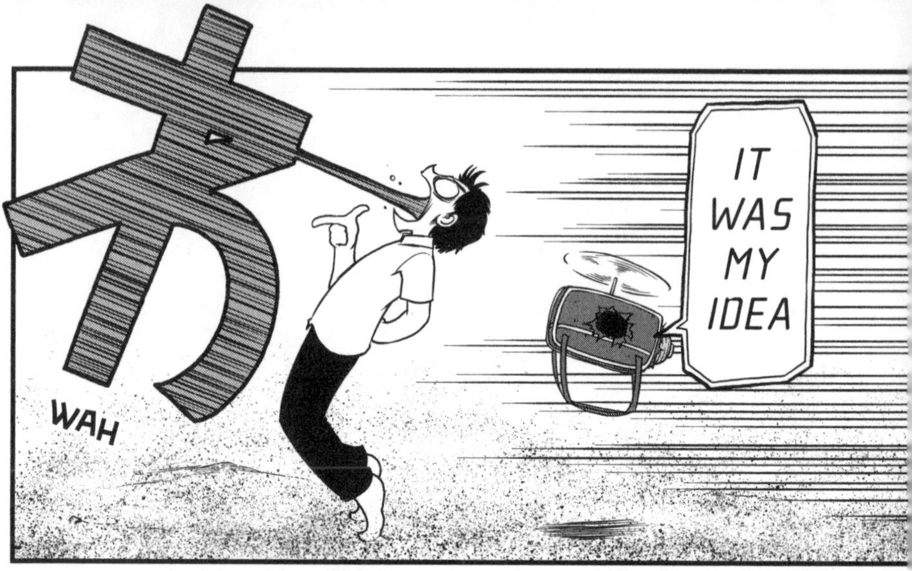
IT WAS MY IDEA
WAH

Chapter 143 Riko Izumi Goes Sleepwalking 6

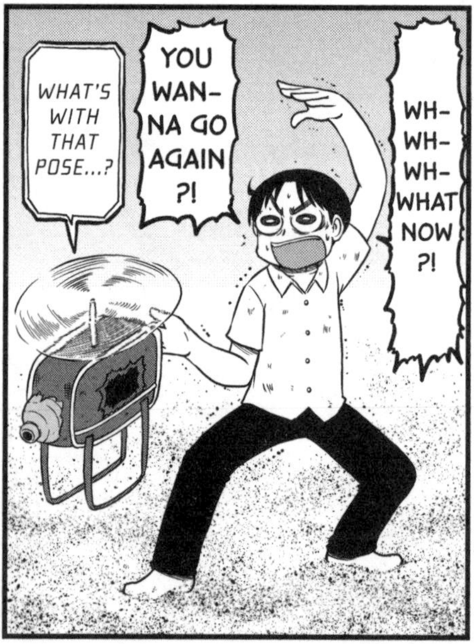
WH-WH-WH-WHAT NOW?!
YOU WAN-NA GO AGAIN?!
WHAT'S WITH THAT POSE...?

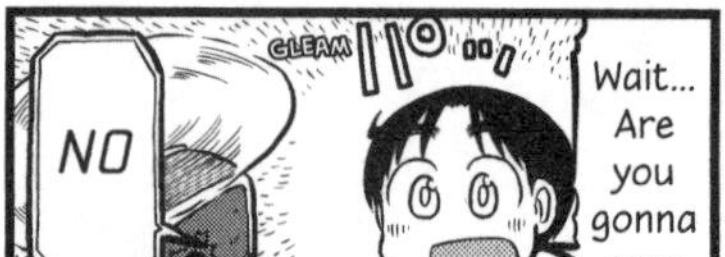
GLEAM
Wait... Are you gonna save us?!
NO

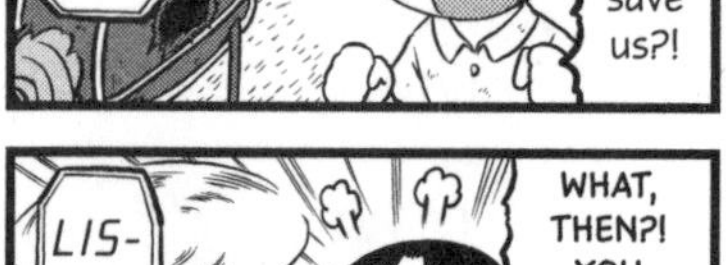
WHAT, THEN?! YOU PLANNING TO LEAVE ME HERE ALONE?!
LIS-TEN TO ME

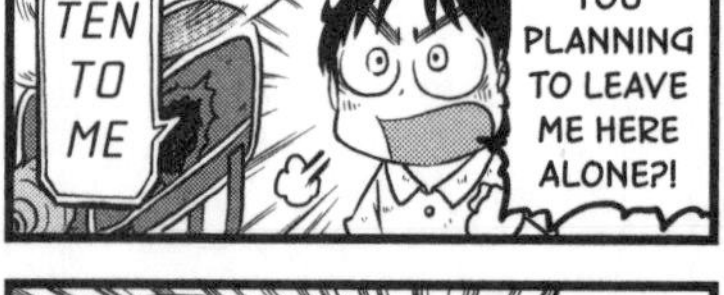
THIS MEANS WAR!!!
LOOK

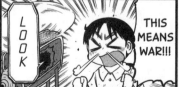

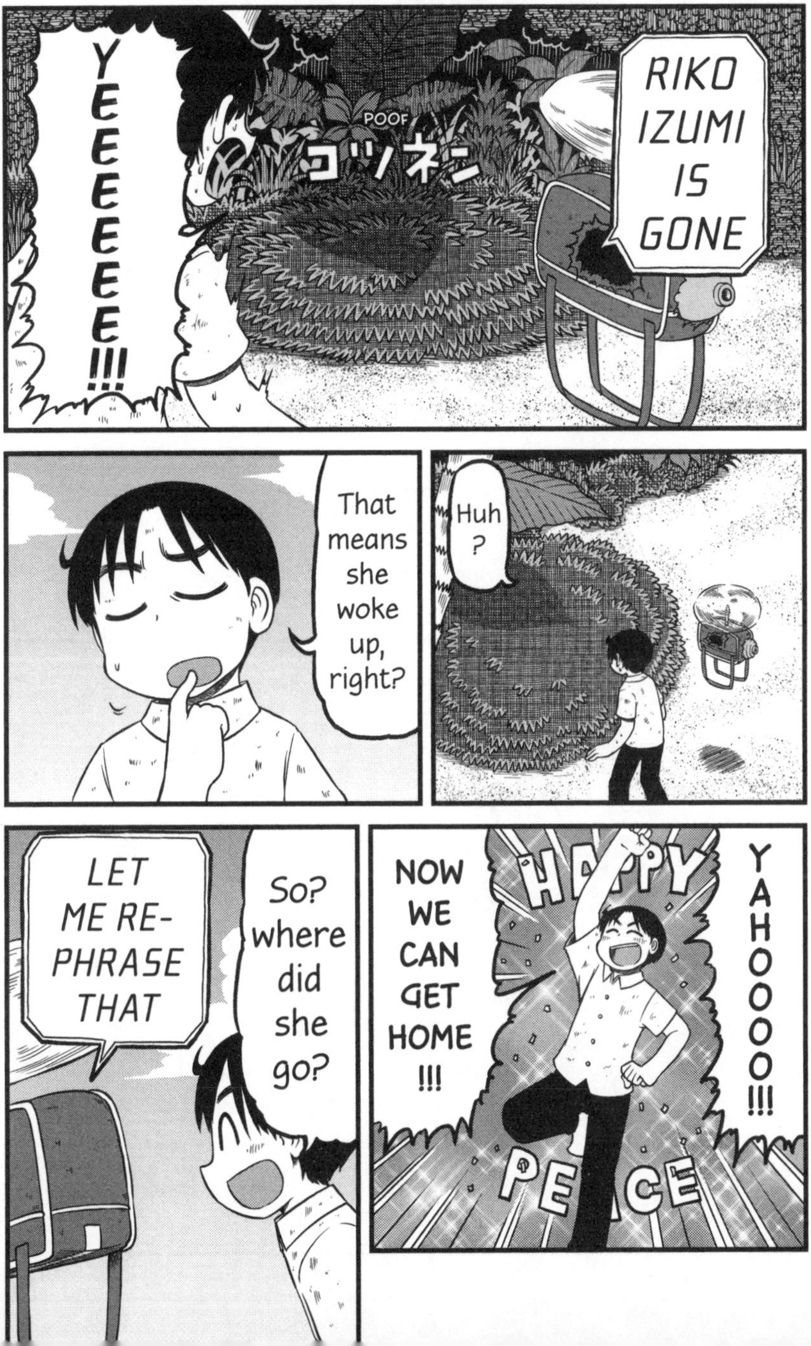
RIKO IZUMI IS GONE
POOF
コツネン
YEEEEEEEE!!!
Huh?
That means she woke up, right?
YAHOOOOO!!!
HAPPY
NOW WE CAN GET HOME!!!
PEACE
So? where did she go?
LET ME RE-PHRASE THAT

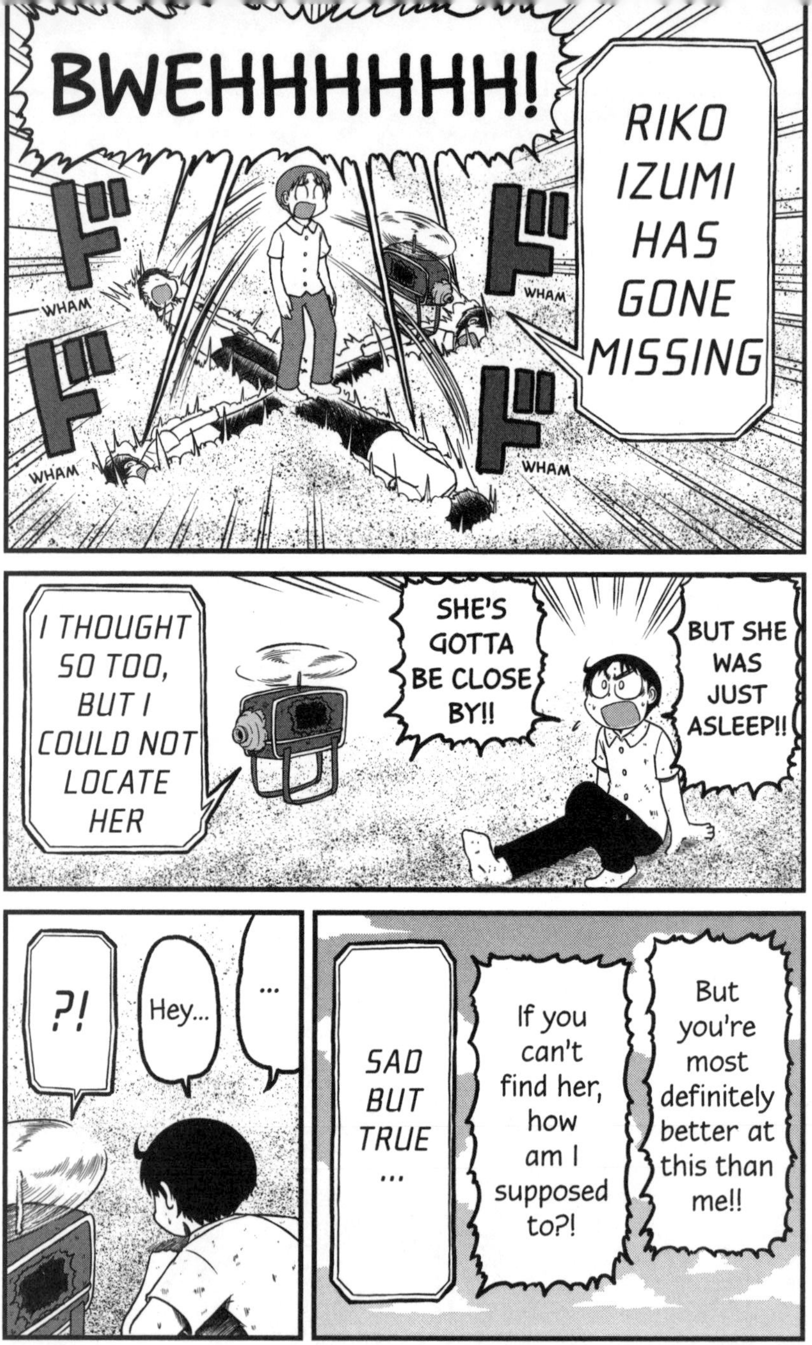
RIKO IZUMI HAS GONE MISSING
BWEHHHHHH!
ド
WHAM
ド
WHAM
ド
WHAM
ド
WHAM
BUT SHE WAS JUST ASLEEP!!
SHE'S GOTTA BE CLOSE BY!!
I THOUGHT SO TOO, BUT I COULD NOT LOCATE HER
But you're most definitely better at this than me!!
If you can't find her, how am I supposed to?!
SAD BUT TRUE ...
...
Hey...
?!

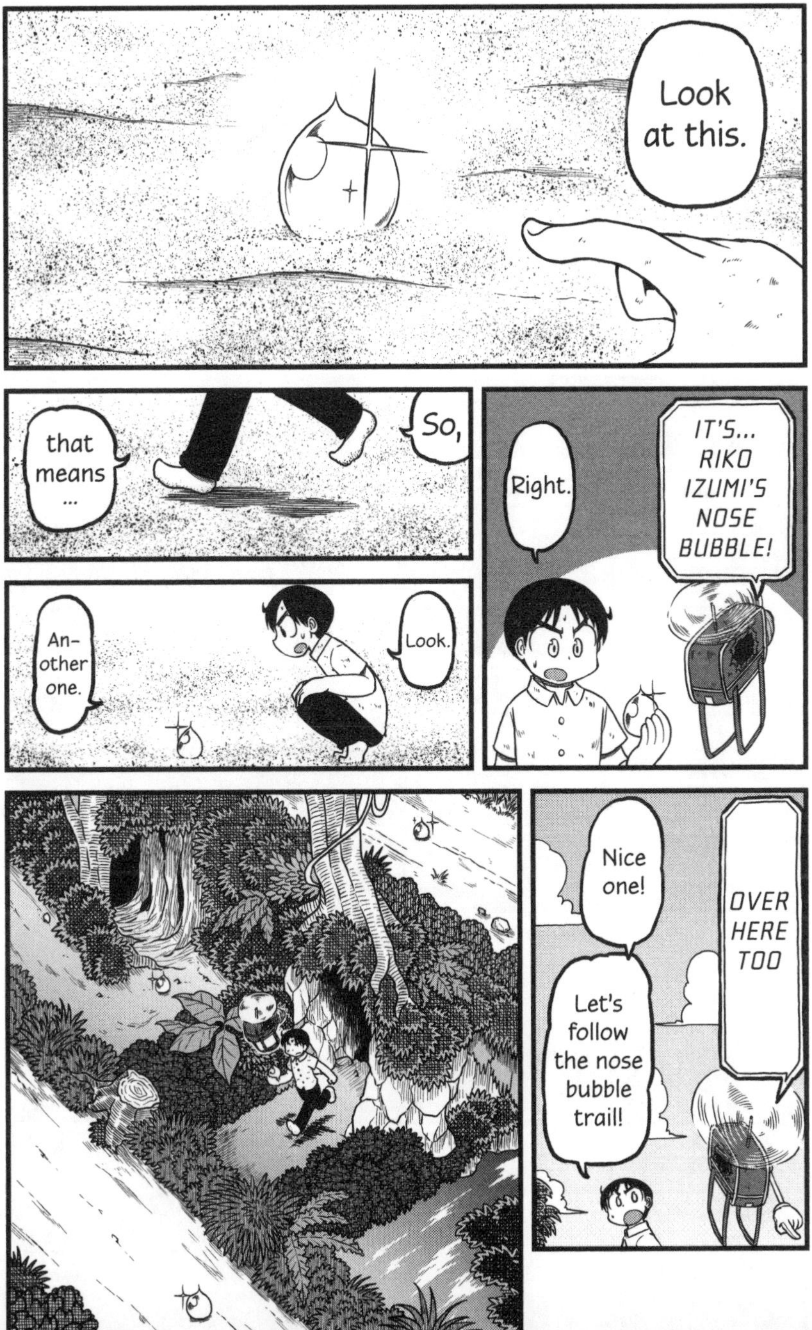
Look at this.
IT'S... RIKO IZUMI'S NOSE BUBBLE!
Right.
So,
that means ...
Look.
An-other one.
OVER HERE TOO
Nice one!
Let's follow the nose bubble trail!

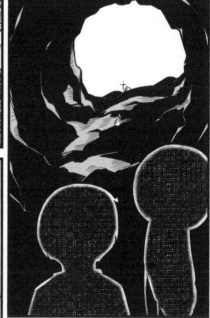

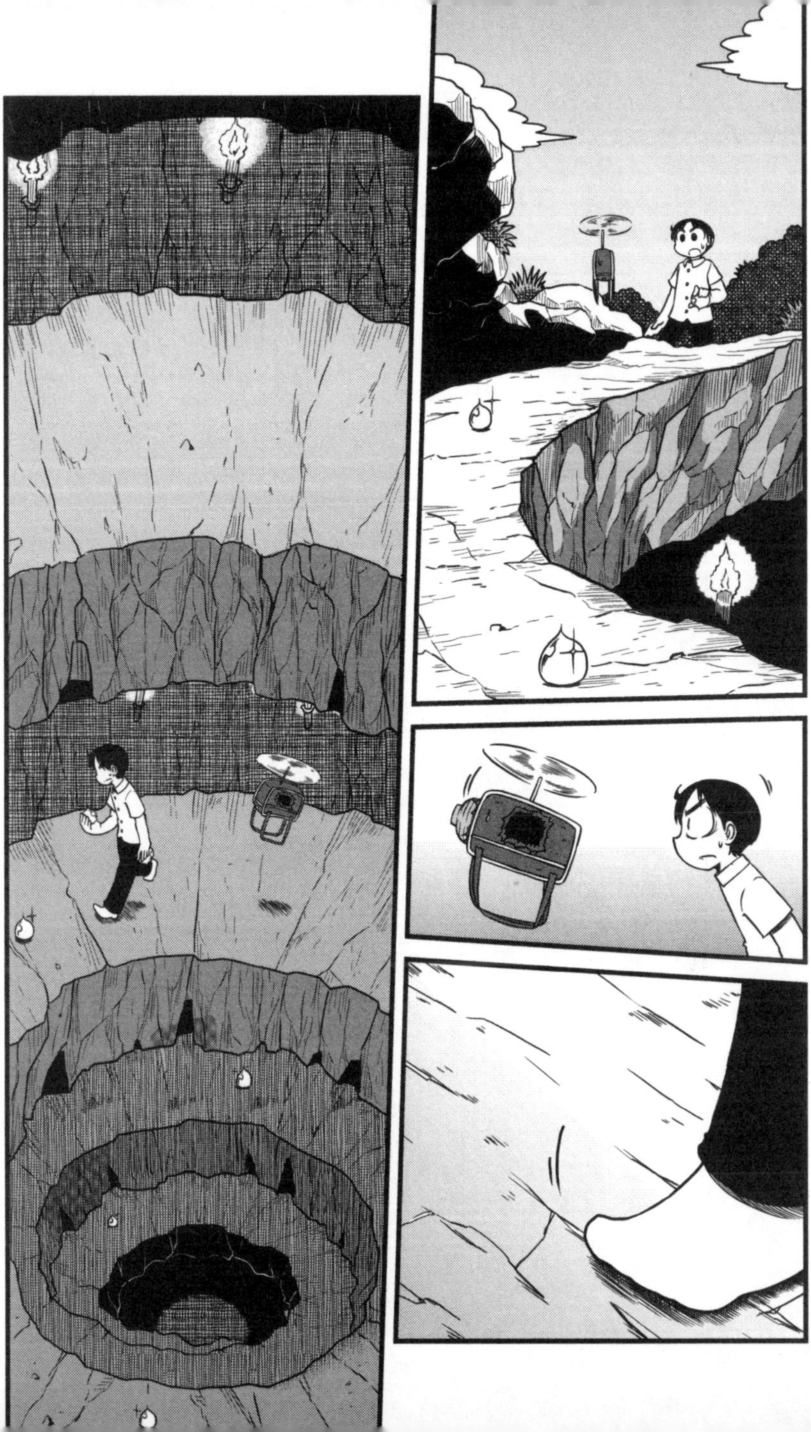

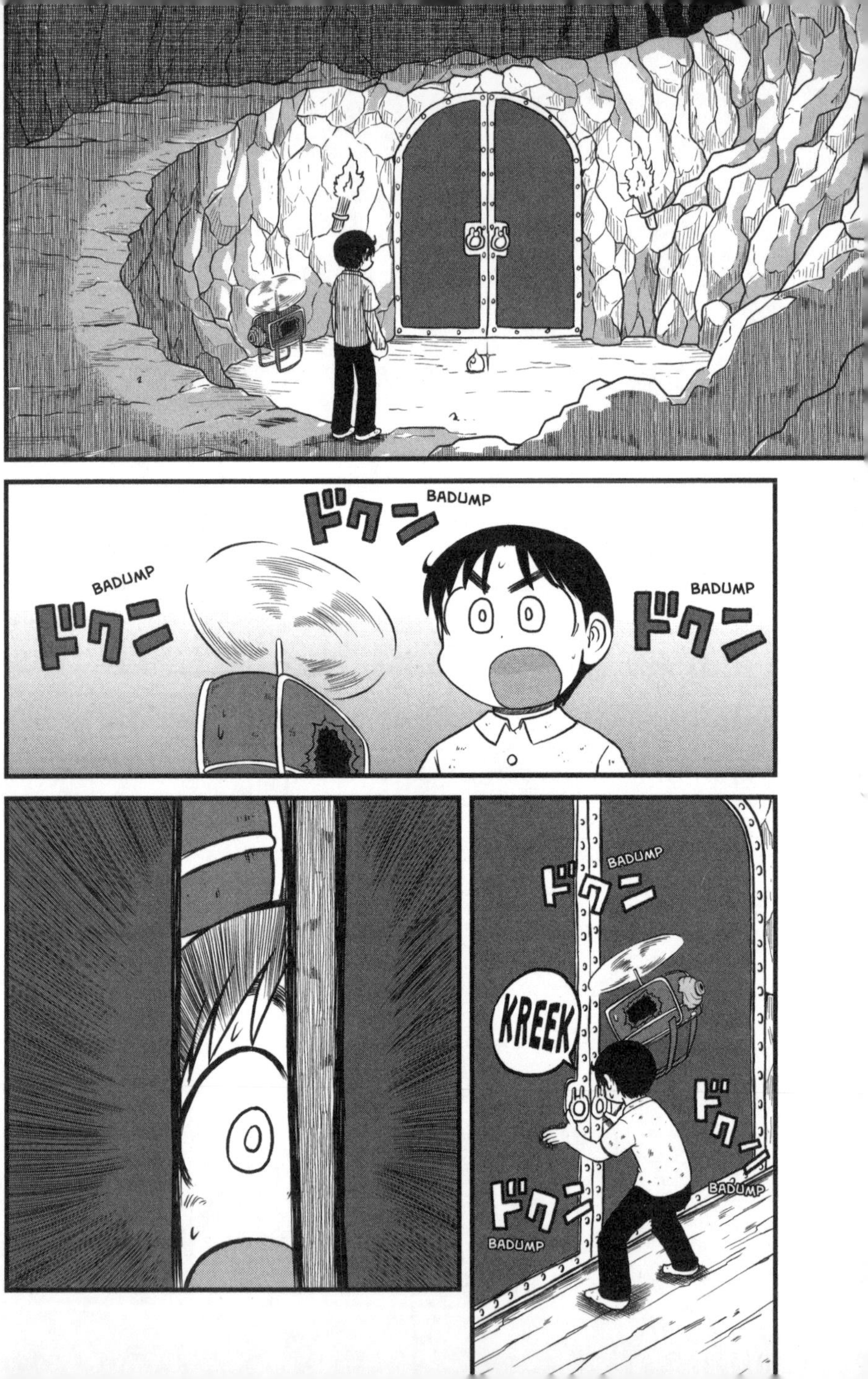
BADUMP
ドクン
BADUMP
ドクン
BADUMP
ドクン
BADUMP
ドクン
KREEK
ドクン
BADUMP
ドクン
BADUMP

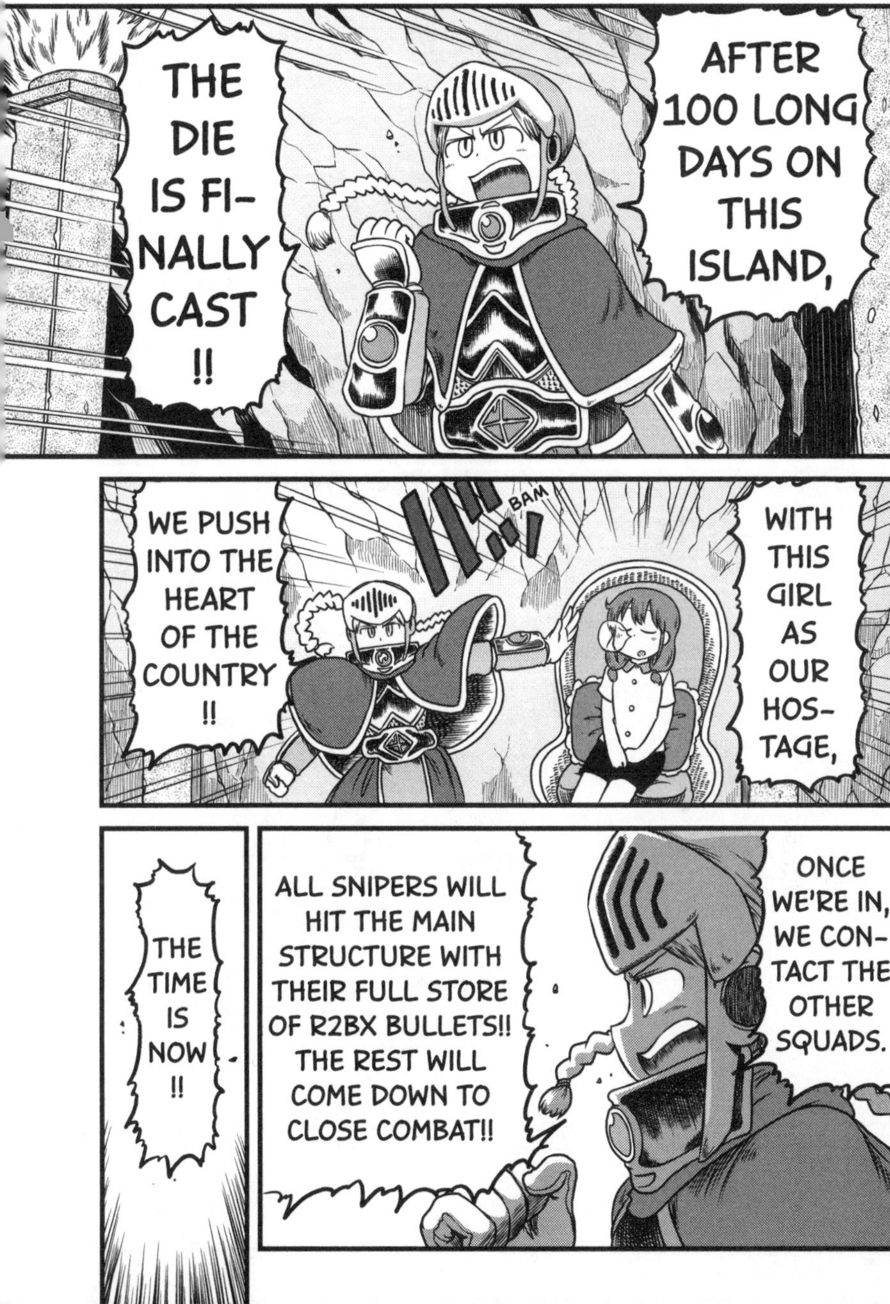
AFTER 100 LONG DAYS ON THIS ISLAND,
THE DIE IS FI-NALLY CAST!!
WITH THIS GIRL AS OUR HOS-TAGE,
BAM
WE PUSH INTO THE HEART OF THE COUNTRY!!
ONCE WE'RE IN, WE CON-TACT THE OTHER SQUADS.
ALL SNIPERS WILL HIT THE MAIN STRUCTURE WITH THEIR FULL STORE OF R2BX BULLETS!! THE REST WILL COME DOWN TO CLOSE COMBAT!!
THE TIME IS NOW!!

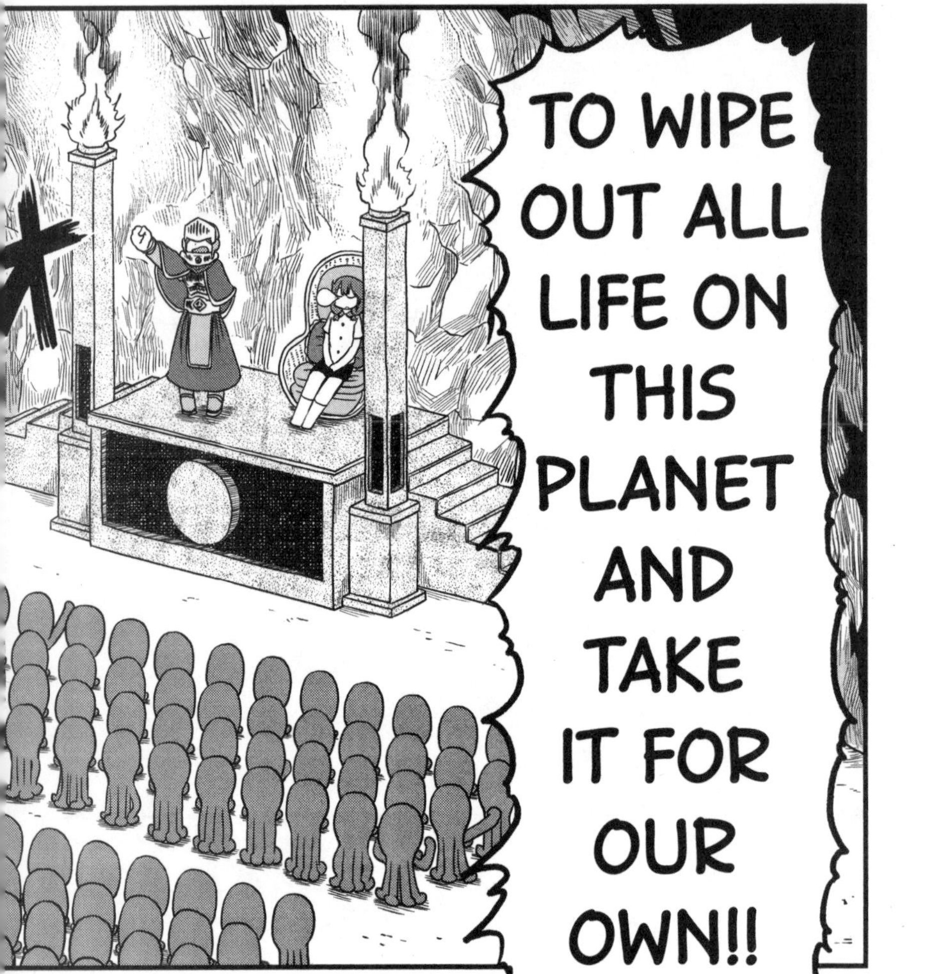
TO WIPE OUT ALL LIFE ON THIS PLANET AND TAKE IT FOR OUR OWN!!

Chapter 144 Riko Izumi Goes Sleepwalking 7

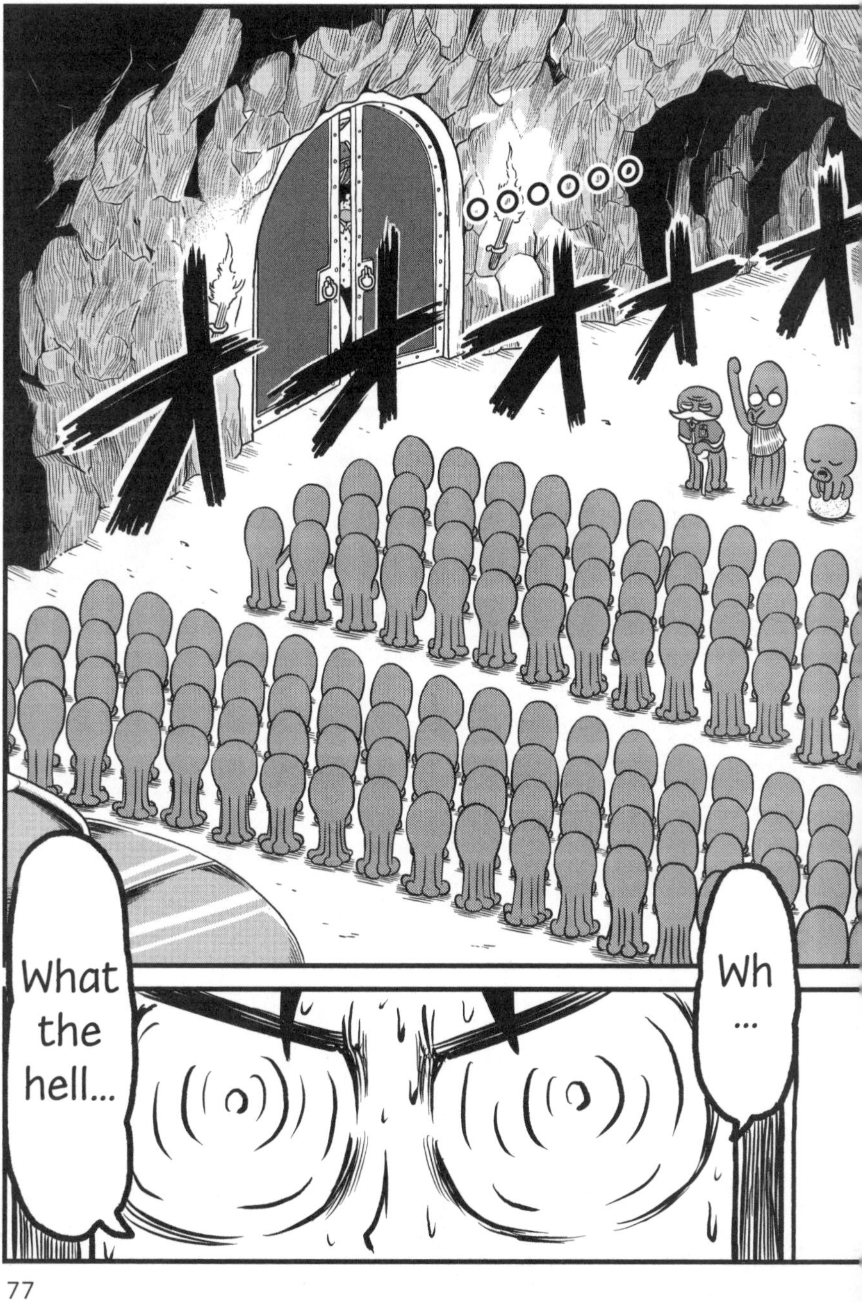
Wh...
What the hell...

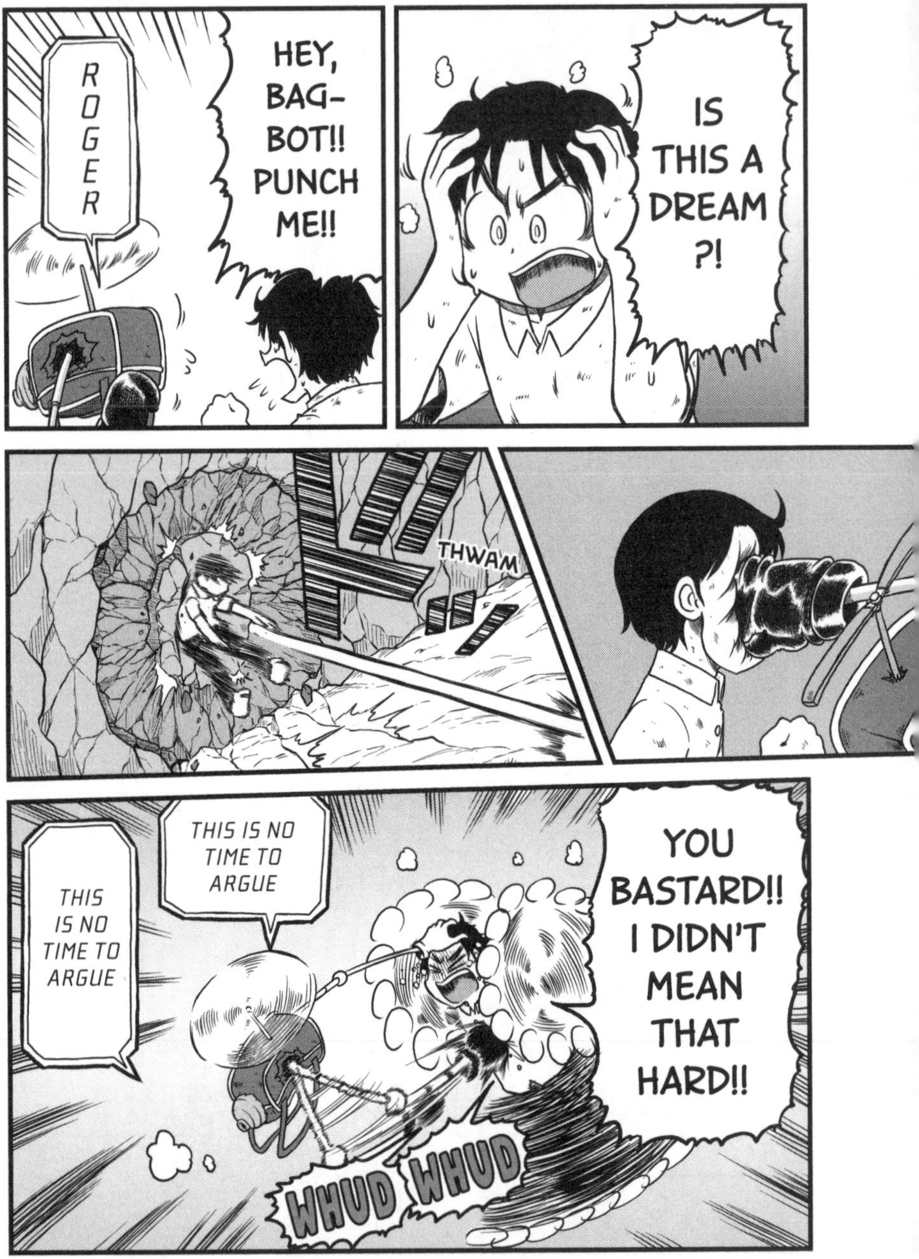
IS THIS A DREAM ?!
HEY, BAG-BOT!! PUNCH ME!!
ROGER
THWAM
YOU BASTARD!! I DIDN'T MEAN THAT HARD!!
THIS IS NO TIME TO ARGUE
THIS IS NO TIME TO ARGUE
WHUD WHUD

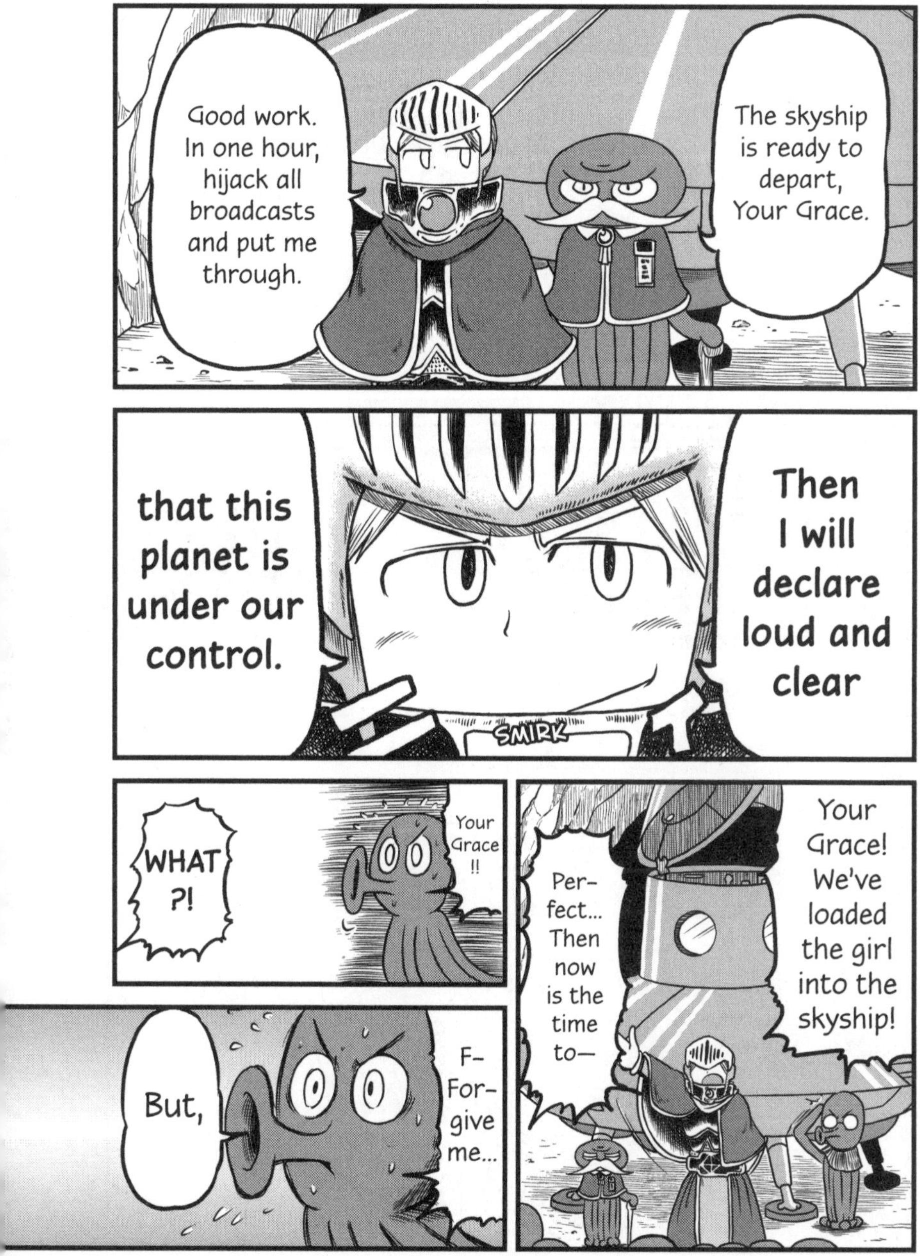
The skyship is ready to depart, Your Grace.
Good work. In one hour, hijack all broadcasts and put me through.
Then I will declare loud and clear
that this planet is under our control.
SMIRK
Your Grace! We've loaded the girl into the skyship!
Per-fect... Then now is the time to—
Your Grace !!
WHAT ?!
F-For-give me...
But,

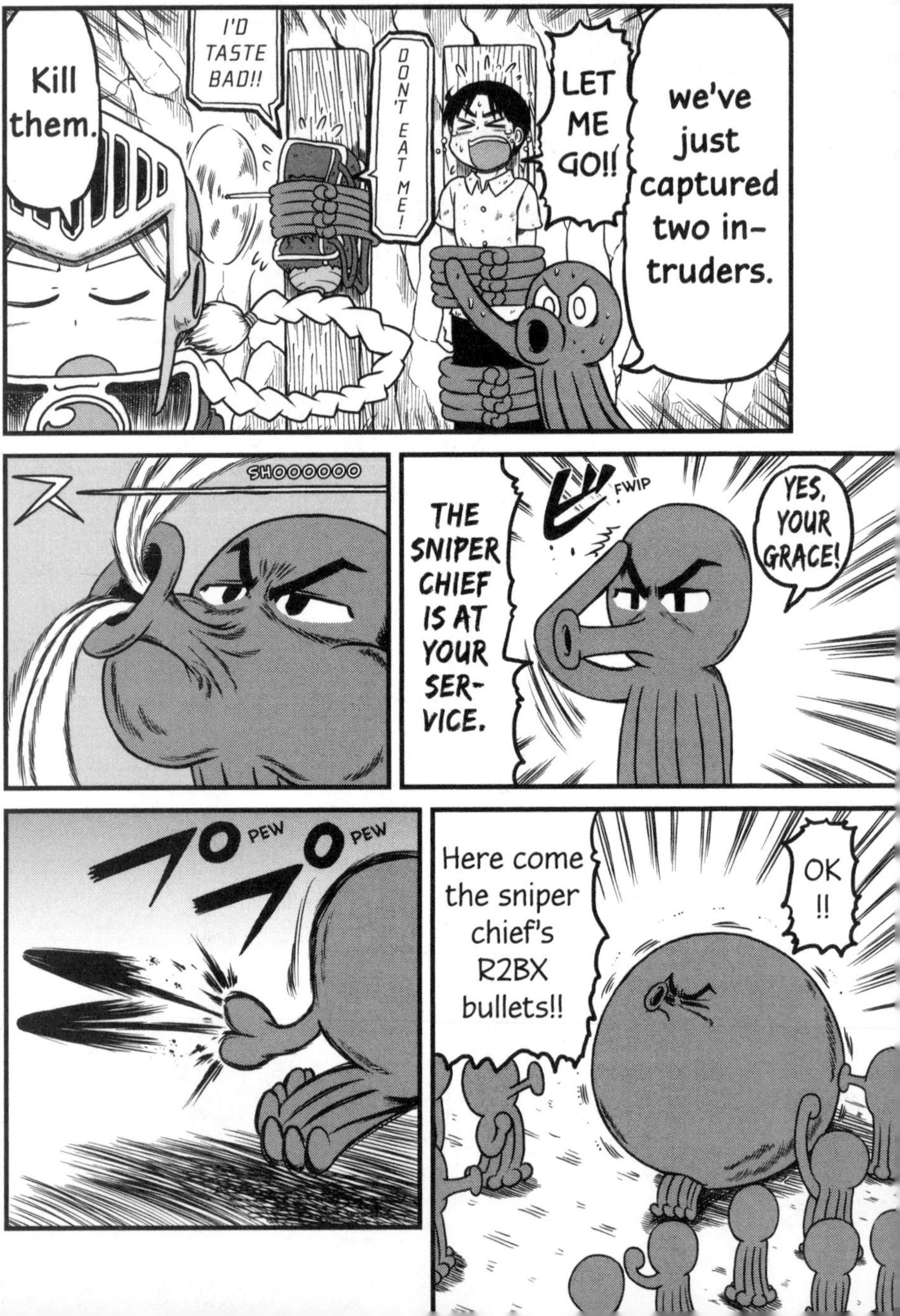
we've just captured two in-truders.
LET ME GO!!
DON'T EAT ME!
I'D TASTE BAD!!
Kill them.
YES, YOUR GRACE!
FWIP
THE SNIPER CHIEF IS AT YOUR SER-VICE.
SHOOOOOO
OK !!
Here come the sniper chief's R2BX bullets!!
PEW
PEW

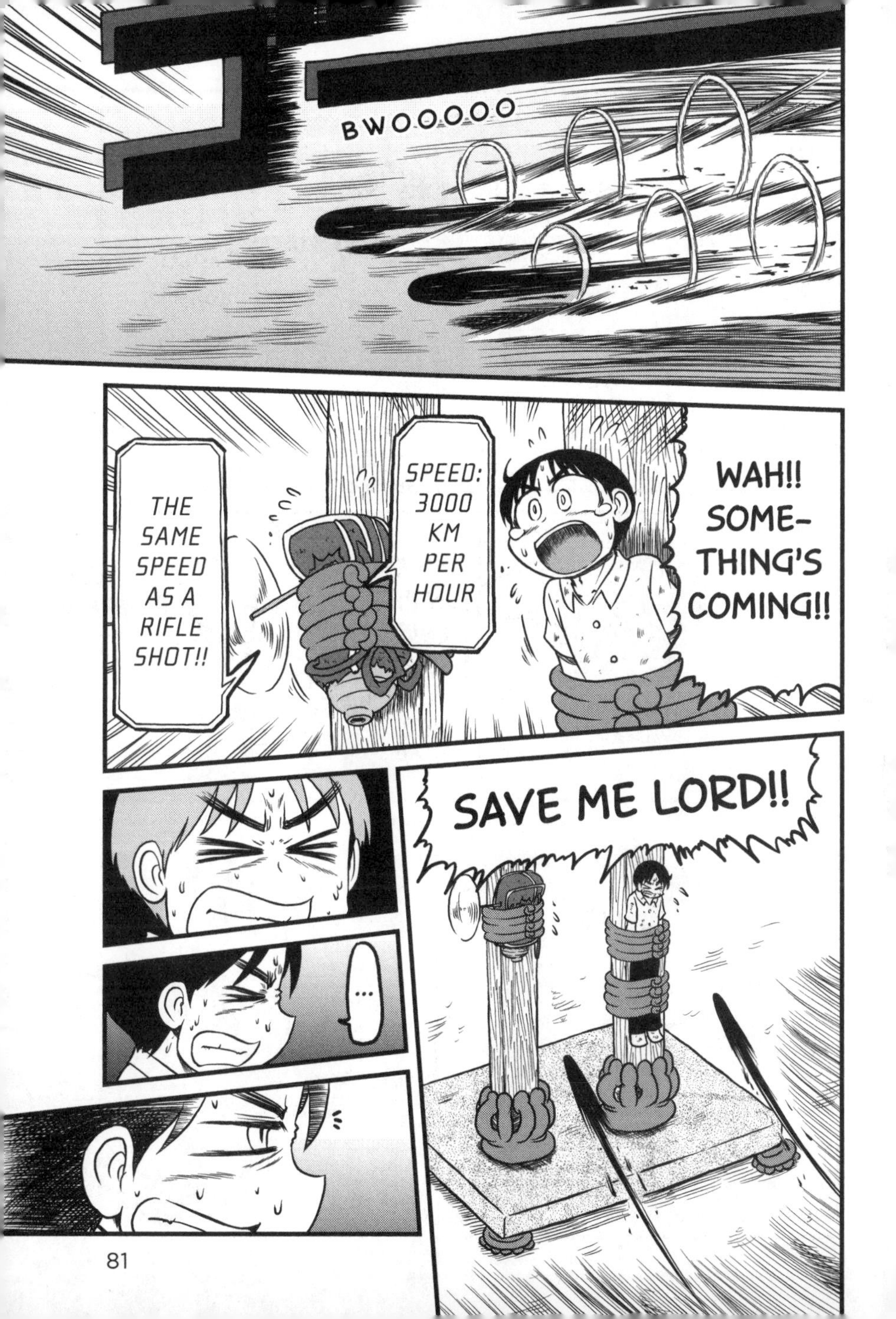
BWOOOOOO
WAH!! SOME-THING'S COMING!!
SPEED: 3000 KM PER HOUR
THE SAME SPEED AS A RIFLE SHOT!!
SAVE ME LORD!!
...

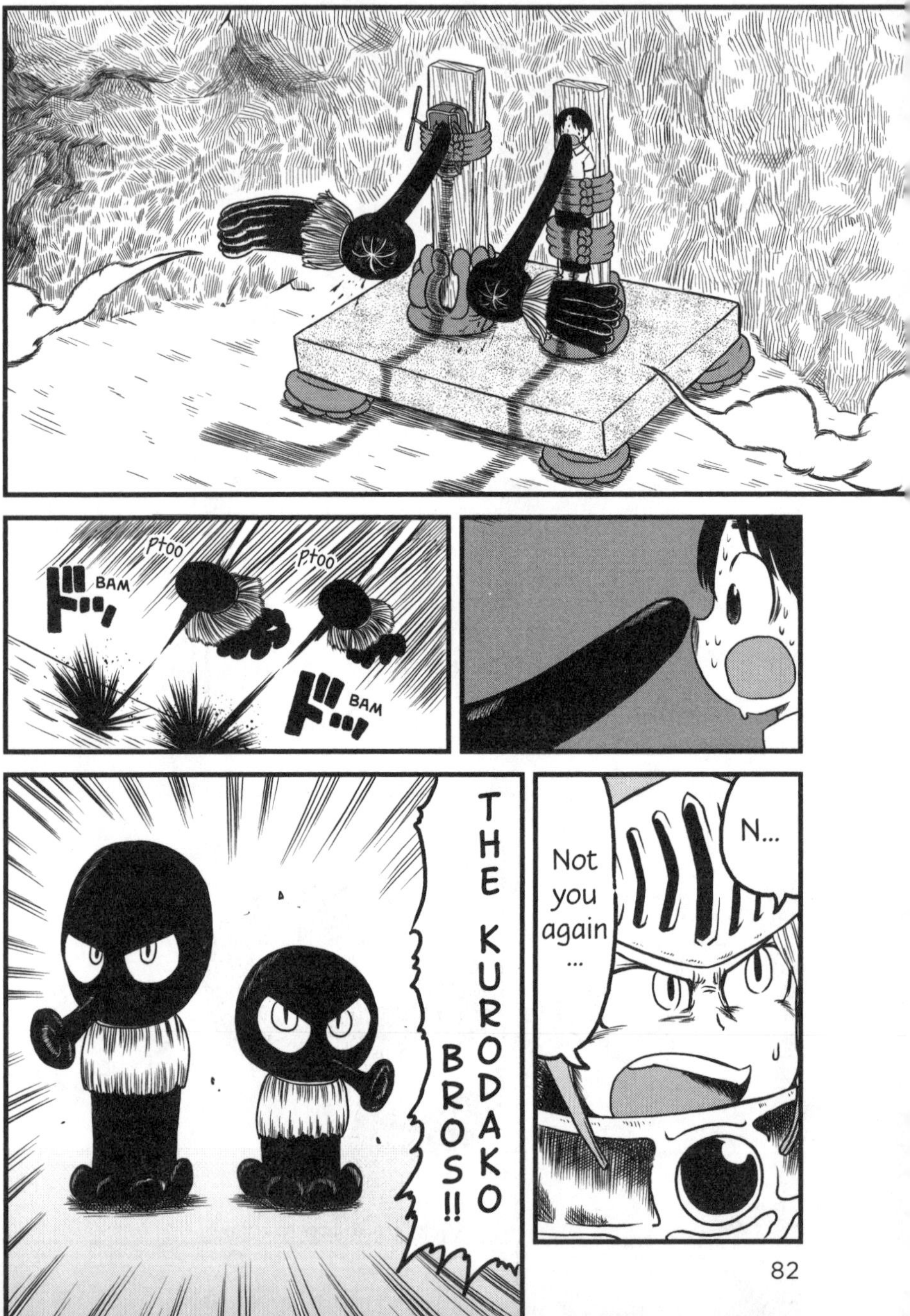
Ptoo
Ptoo
ドッ
BAM
ドッ
BAM
N...
Not you again ...
THE KURODAKO BROS!!

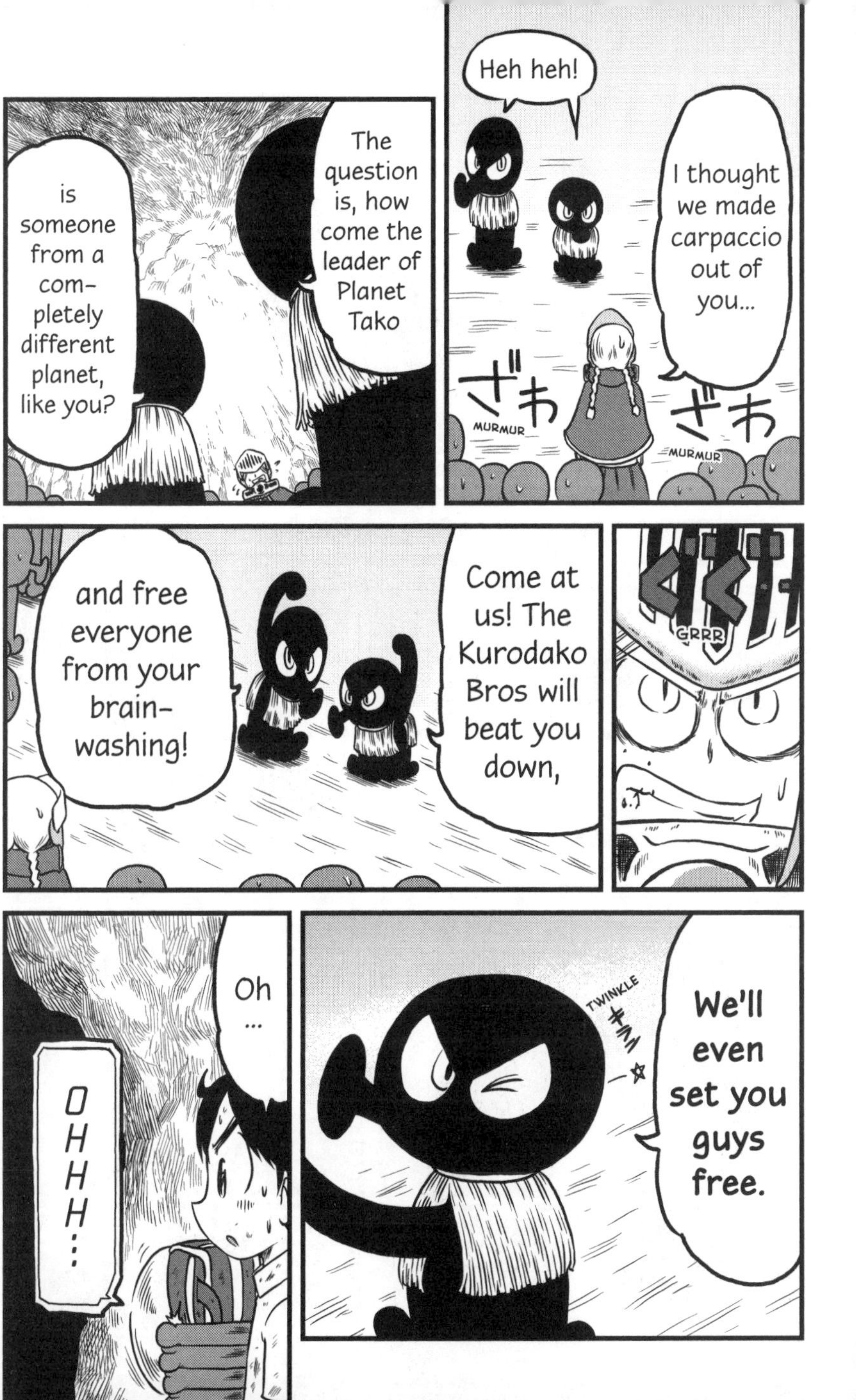

Heh heh!
I thought we made carpaccio out of you...
ざわ
MURMUR
ざわ
MURMUR
The question is, how come the leader of Planet Tako
is someone from a com-pletely different planet, like you?
GRRR
Come at us! The Kurodako Bros will beat you down,
and free everyone from your brain-washing!
We'll even set you guys free.
TWINKLE
Oh ...
OHHH...

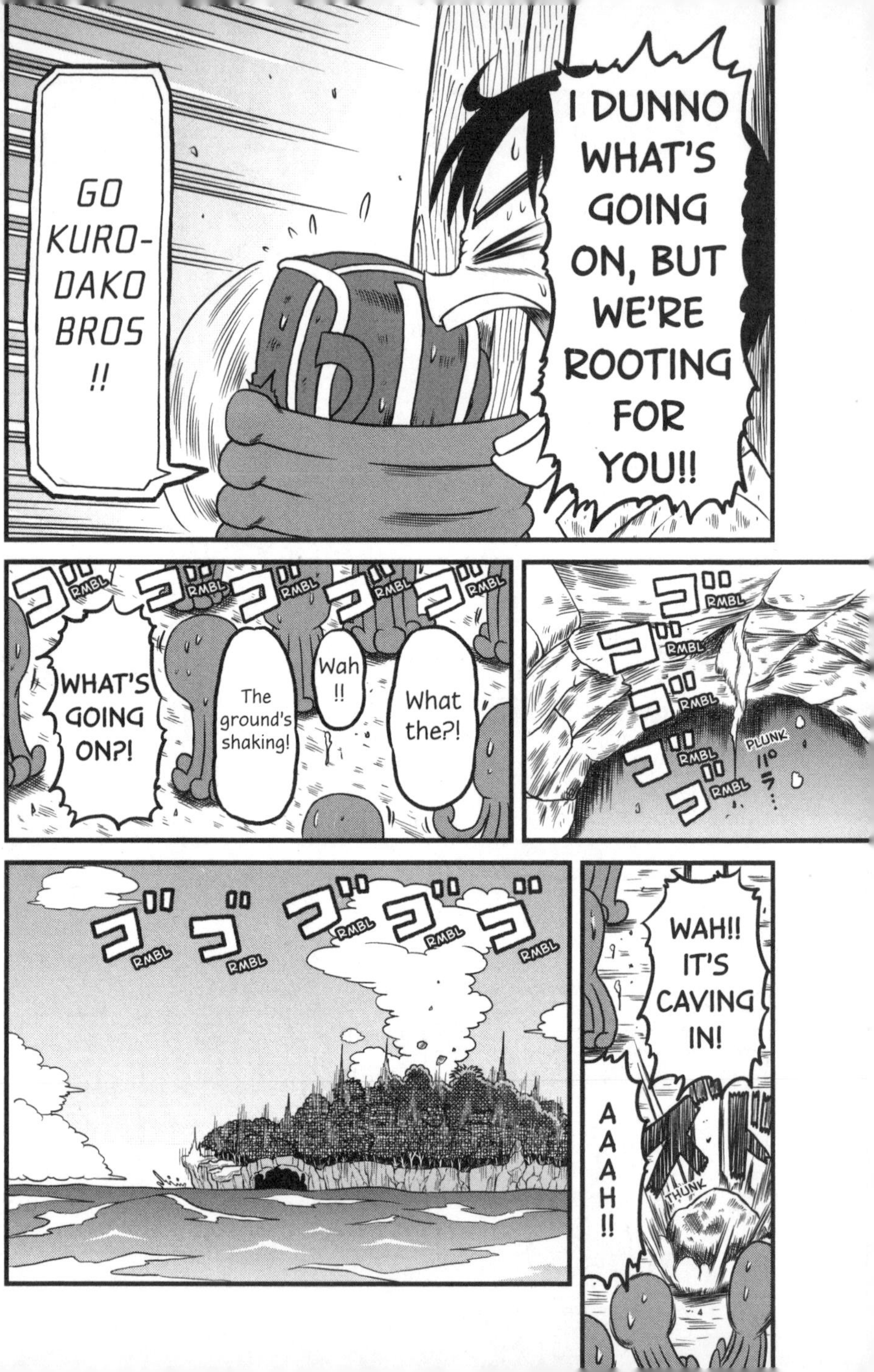
I DUNNO WHAT'S GOING ON, BUT WE'RE ROOTING FOR YOU!!
GO KURO-DAKO BROS!!
RMBL RMBL RMBL RMBL
PLUNK
RMBL RMBL RMBL RMBL RMBL
What the?!
Wah!!
The ground's shaking!
WHAT'S GOING ON?!
WAH!! IT'S CAVING IN!
THUNK
AAAH!!
RMBL RMBL RMBL RMBL RMBL

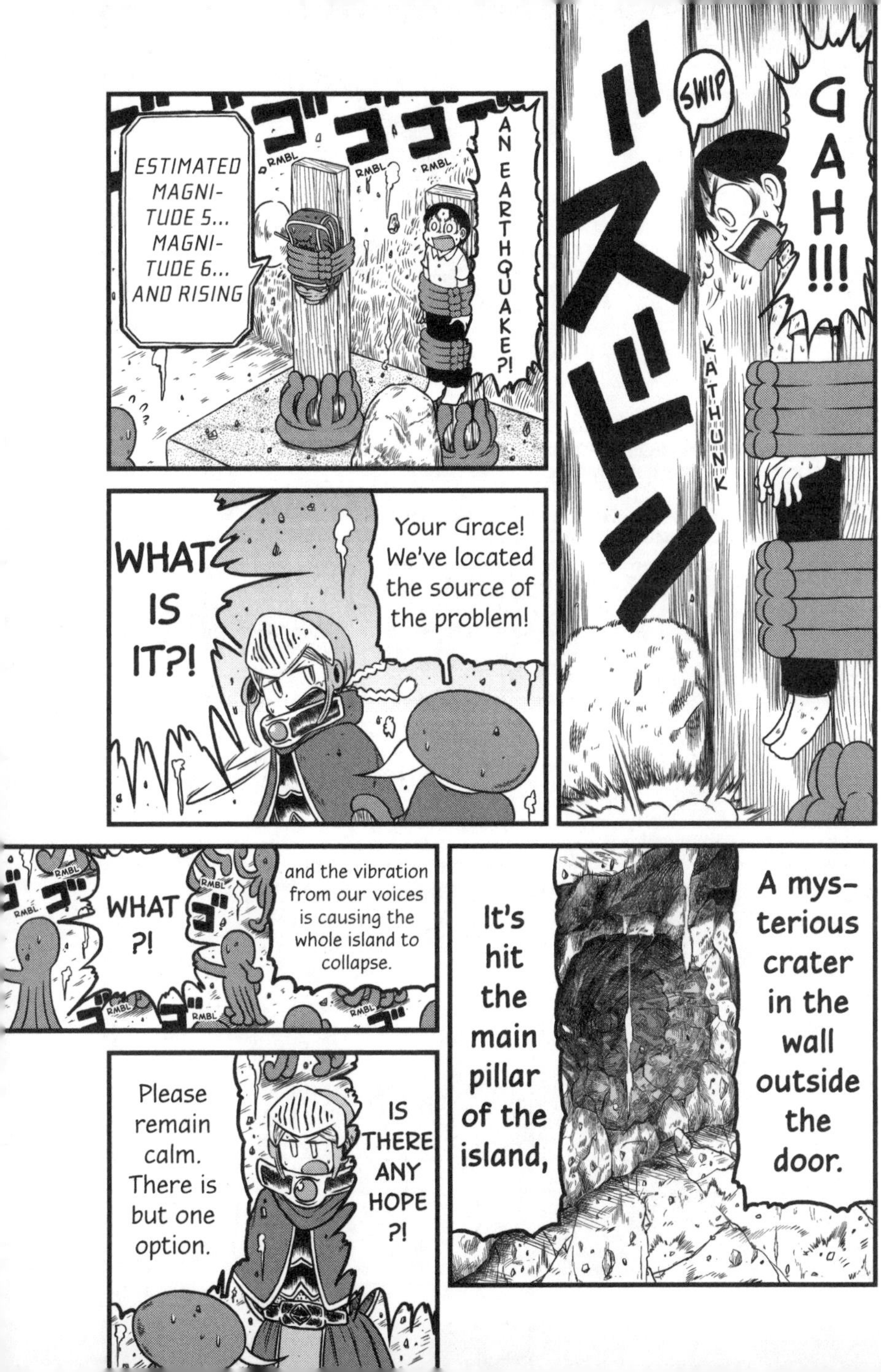

GAH!!!
SWIP
KATHUNK
AN EARTHQUAKE?!
RMBL
RMBL
RMBL
ESTIMATED MAGNITUDE 5... MAGNITUDE 6... AND RISING
Your Grace! We've located the source of the problem!
WHAT IS IT?!
A mysterious crater in the wall outside the door.
It's hit the main pillar of the island,
and the vibration from our voices is causing the whole island to collapse.
RMBL
RMBL
WHAT?!
RMBL
RMBL
RMBL
RMBL
IS THERE ANY HOPE?!
Please remain calm. There is but one option.

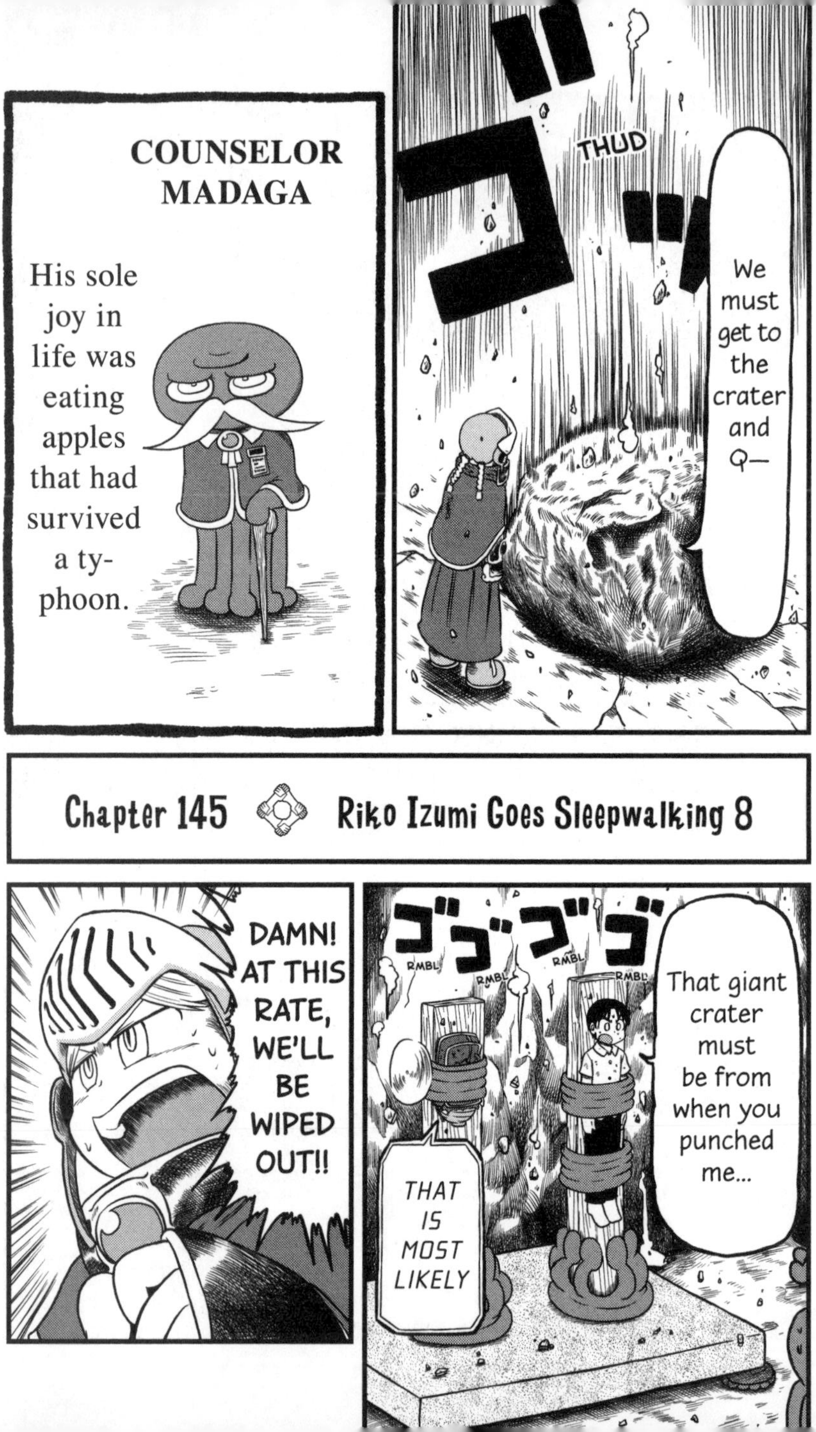
THUD
We must get to the crater and Q—
COUNSELOR MADAGA
His sole joy in life was eating apples that had survived a ty-phoon.
Chapter 145 Riko Izumi Goes Sleepwalking 8
RMBL RMBL RMBL RMBL
That giant crater must be from when you punched me...
THAT IS MOST LIKELY
DAMN! AT THIS RATE, WE'LL BE WIPED OUT!!

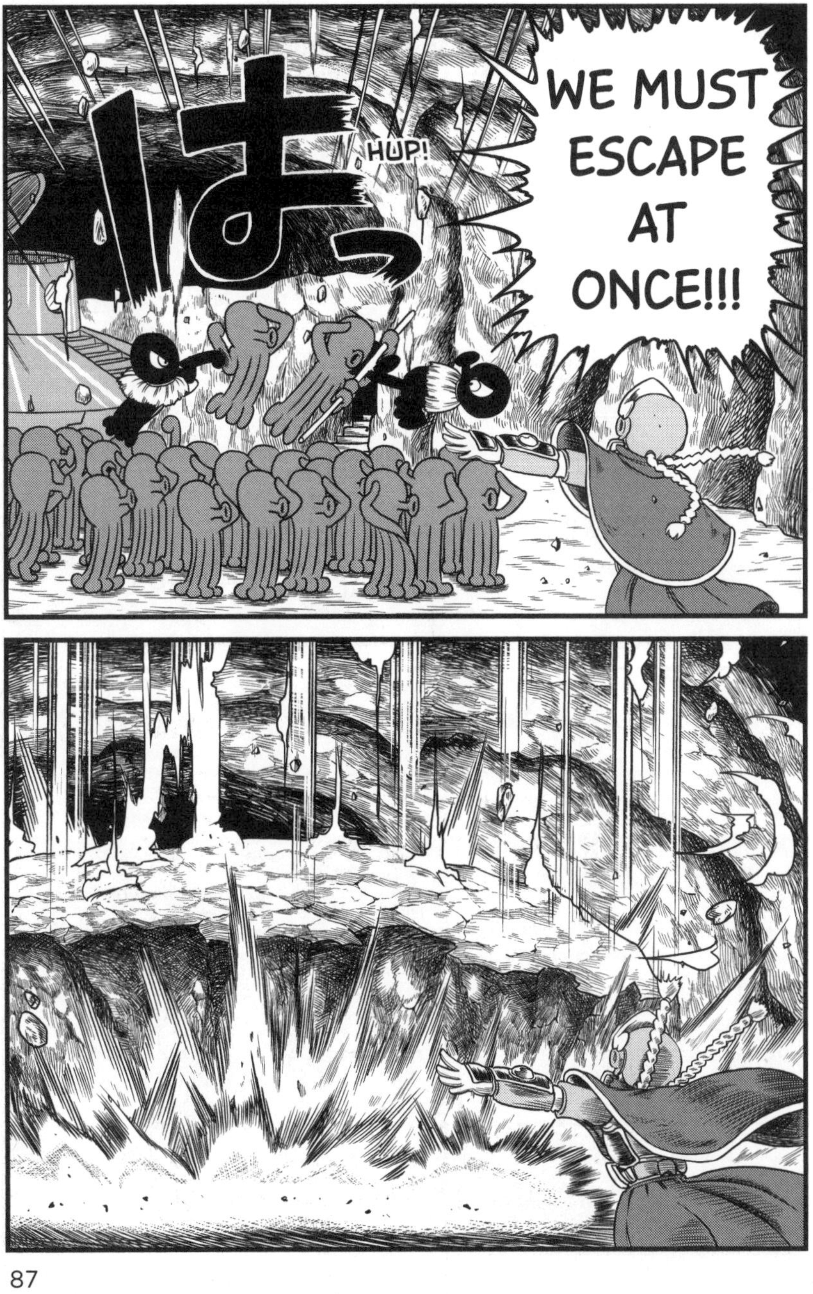
WE MUST ESCAPE AT ONCE!!!
はっ
HUP!

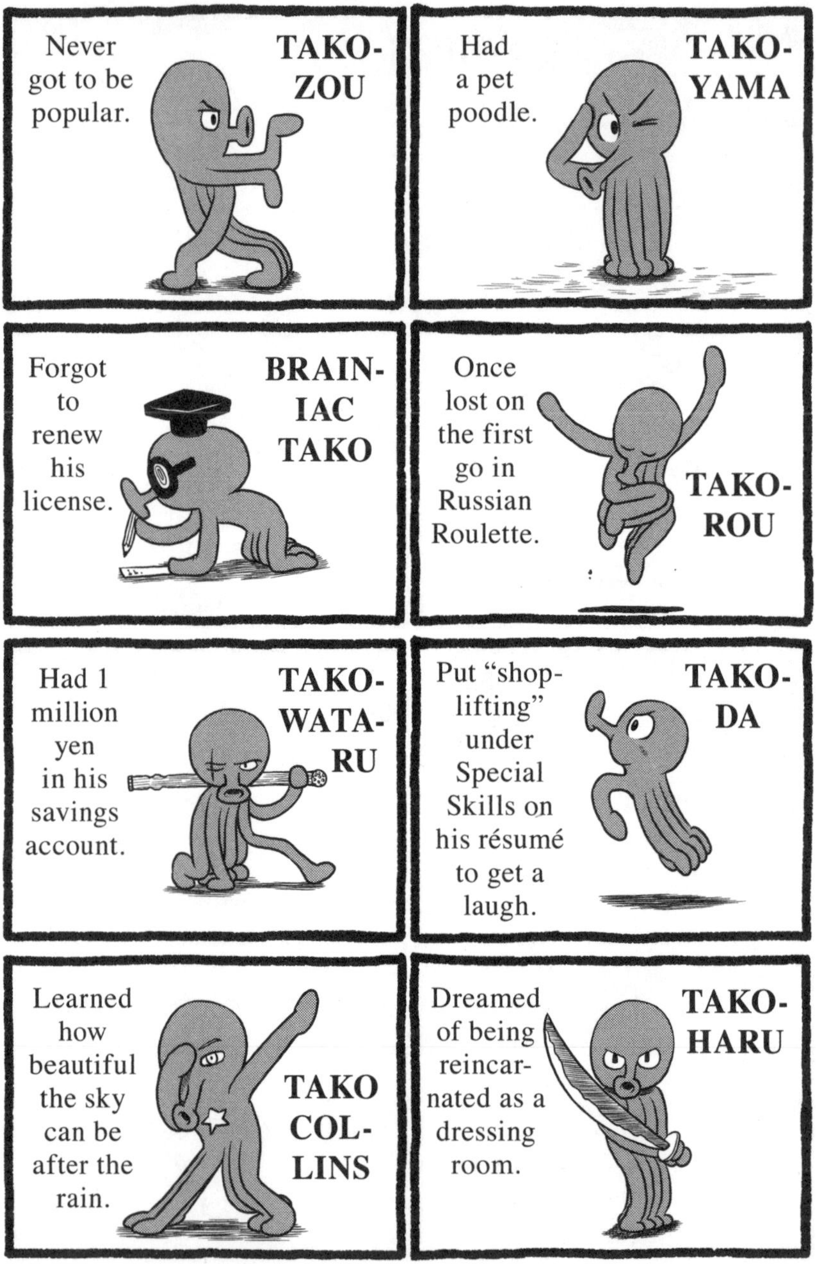
TAKO-YAMA
Had a pet poodle.
TAKO-ZOU
Never got to be popular.
TAKO-ROU
Once lost on the first go in Russian Roulette.
BRAIN-IAC TAKO
Forgot to renew his license.
TAKO-DA
Put "shop-lifting" under Special Skills on his résumé to get a laugh.
TAKO-WATA-RU
Had 1 million yen in his savings account.
TAKO-HARU
Dreamed of being reincar-nated as a dressing room.
TAKO COL-LINS
Learned how beautiful the sky can be after the rain.

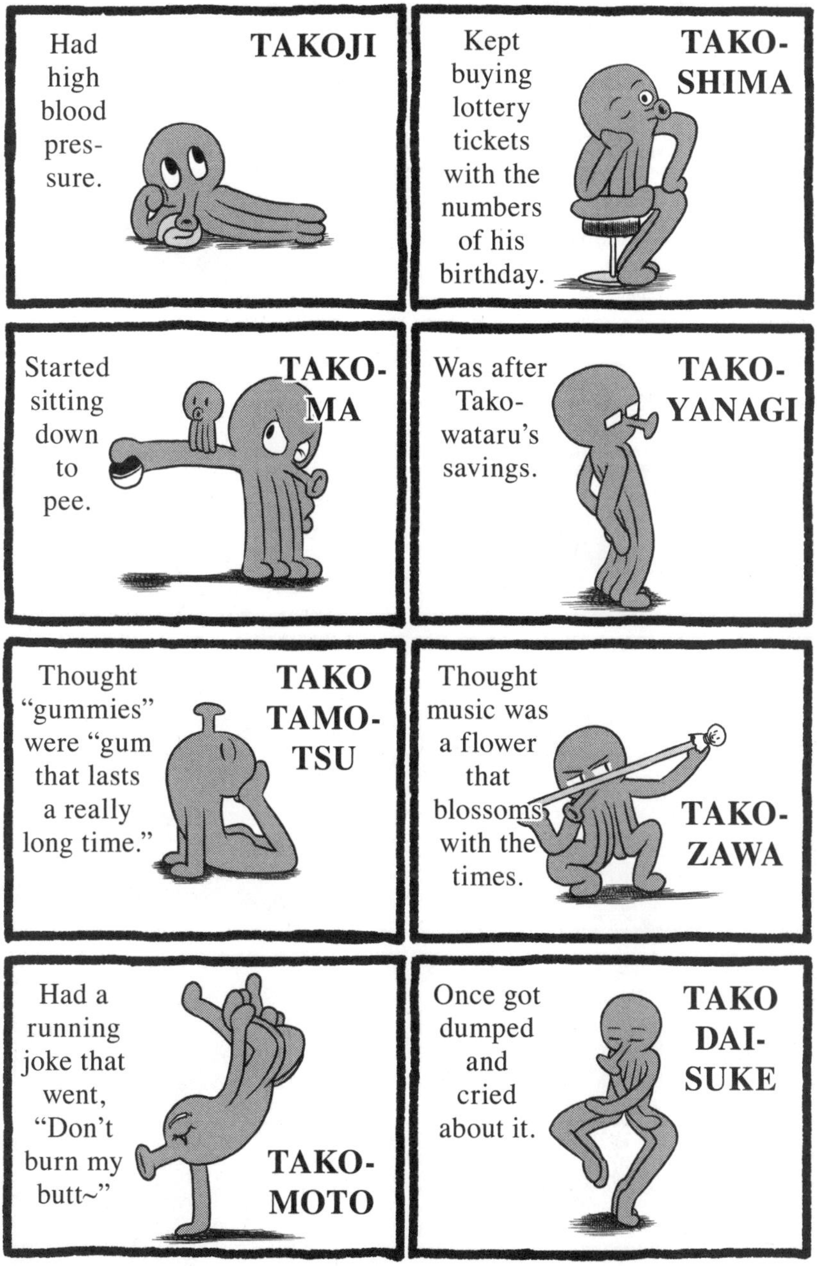
TAKO-SHIMA
Kept buying lottery tickets with the numbers of his birthday.
TAKOJI
Had high blood pres-sure.
TAKO-YANAGI
Was after Tako-wataru's savings.
TAKO-MA
Started sitting down to pee.
Thought music was a flower that blossoms with the times.
TAKO-ZAWA
TAKO TAMO-TSU
Thought "gummies" were "gum that lasts a really long time."
TAKO DAI-SUKE
Once got dumped and cried about it.
Had a running joke that went, "Don't burn my butt~"
TAKO-MOTO

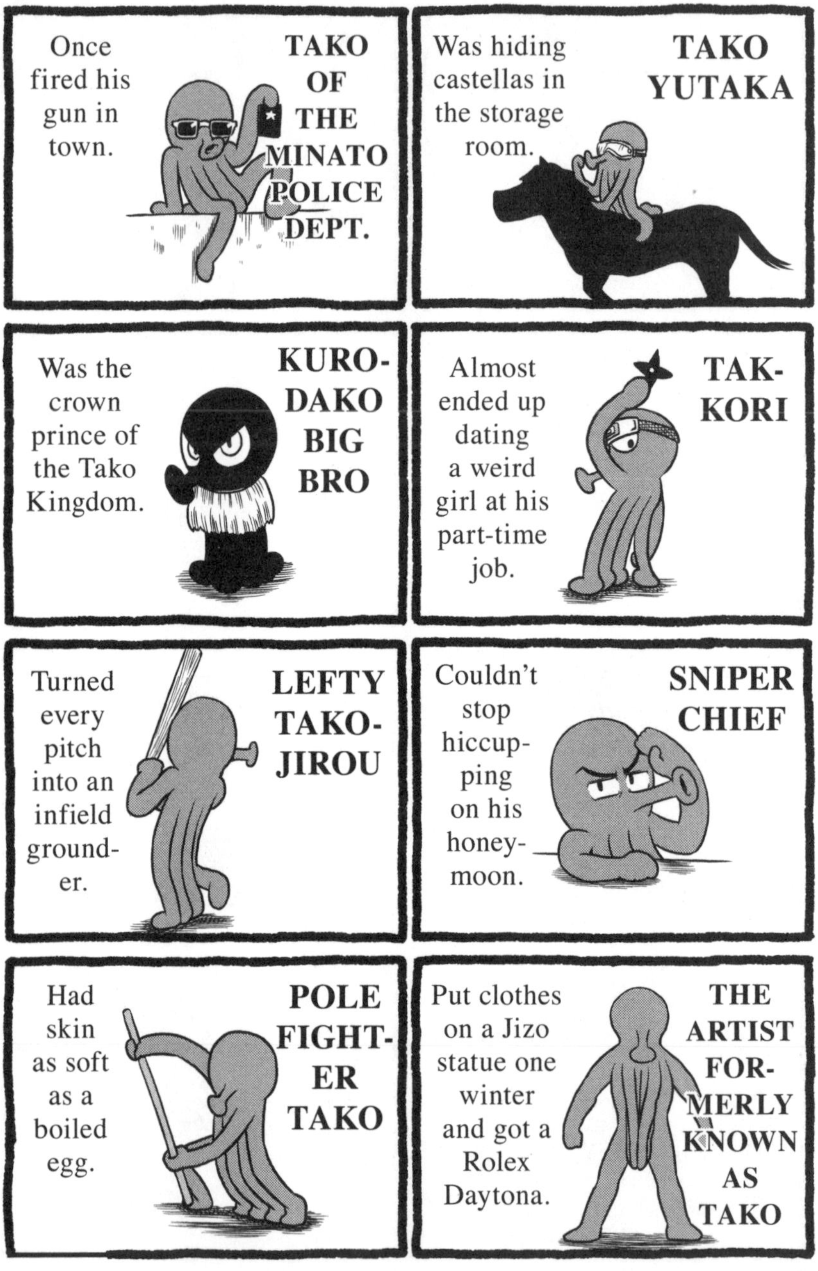
TAKO YUTAKA
Was hiding castellas in the storage room.
TAKO OF THE MINATO POLICE DEPT.
Once fired his gun in town.
TAK-KORI
Almost ended up dating a weird girl at his part-time job.
KURO-DAKO BIG BRO
Was the crown prince of the Tako Kingdom.
SNIPER CHIEF
Couldn't stop hiccup-ping on his honey-moon.
LEFTY TAKO-JIROU
Turned every pitch into an infield ground-er.
THE ARTIST FOR-MERLY KNOWN AS TAKO
Put clothes on a Jizo statue one winter and got a Rolex Daytona.
POLE FIGHT-ER TAKO
Had skin as soft as a boiled egg.

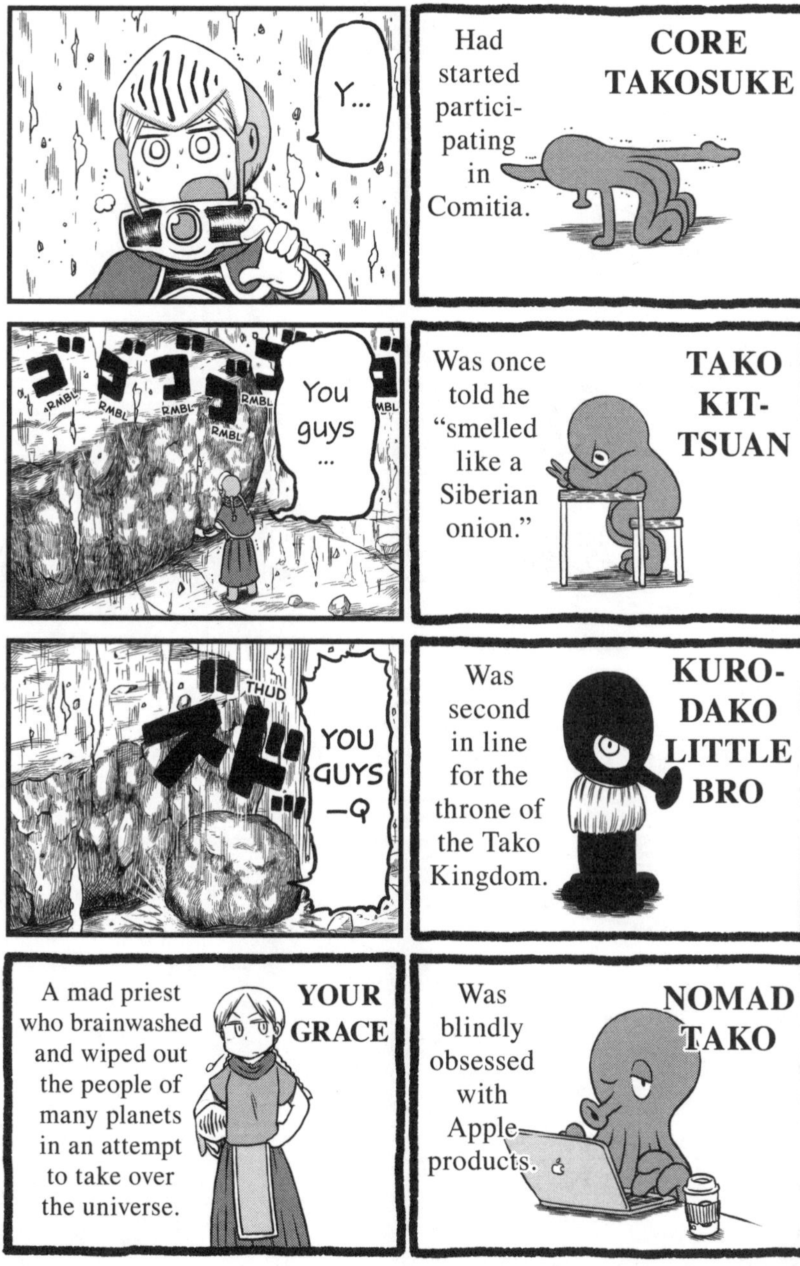
CORE TAKOSUKE
Had started partici-pating in Comitia.
TAKO KIT-TSUAN
Was once told he "smelled like a Siberian onion."
KURO-DAKO LITTLE BRO
Was second in line for the throne of the Tako Kingdom.
NOMAD TAKO
Was blindly obsessed with Apple products.
Y...
You guys ...
RMBL RMBL RMBL RMBL RMBL RMBL
YOU GUYS —Q
THUD
YOUR GRACE
A mad priest who brainwashed and wiped out the people of many planets in an attempt to take over the universe.

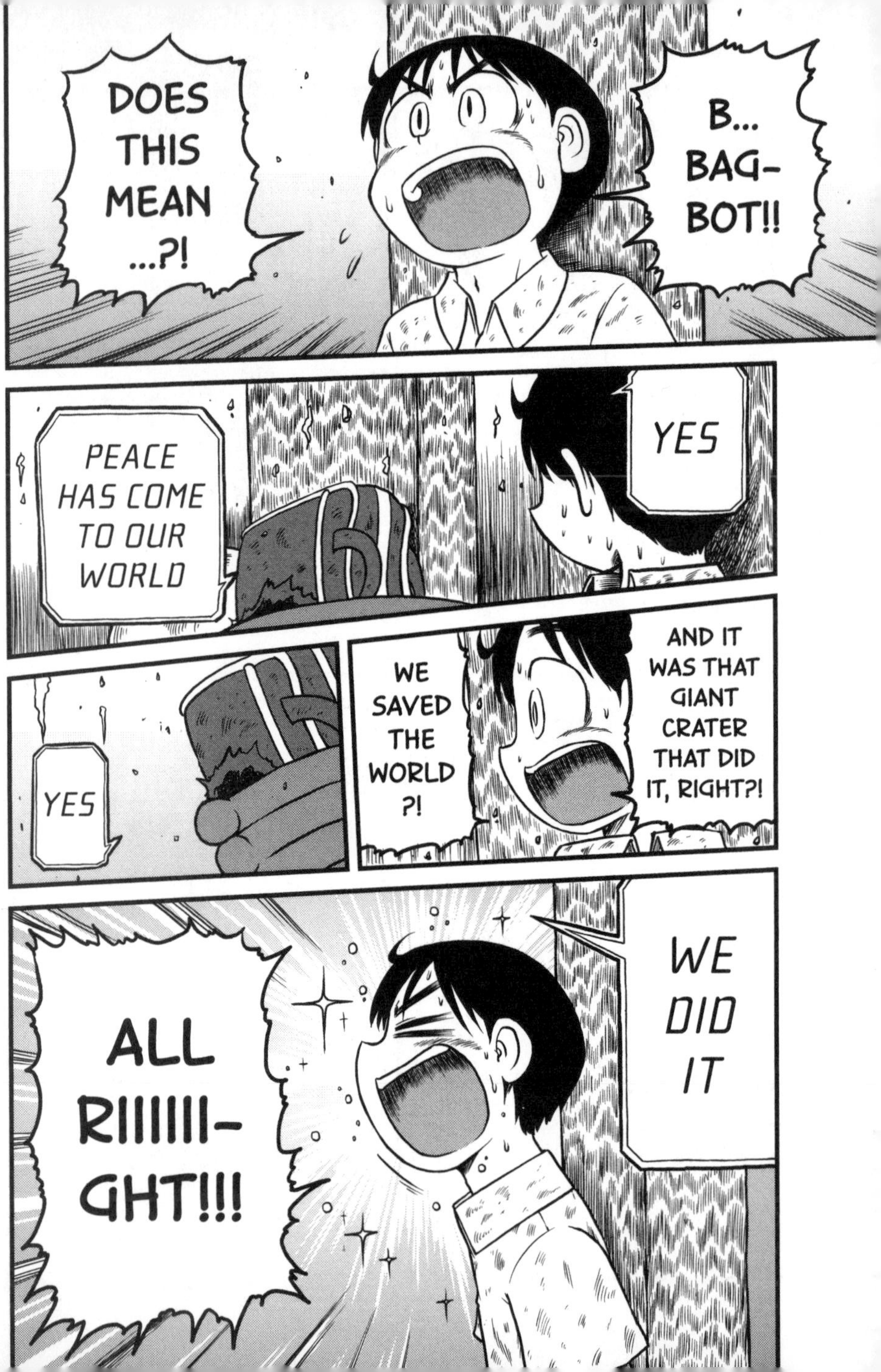
B... BAG-BOT!!
DOES THIS MEAN ...?!
YES
PEACE HAS COME TO OUR WORLD
AND IT WAS THAT GIANT CRATER THAT DID IT, RIGHT?!
WE SAVED THE WORLD ?!
YES
WE DID IT
ALL RIIIIII-GHT!!!

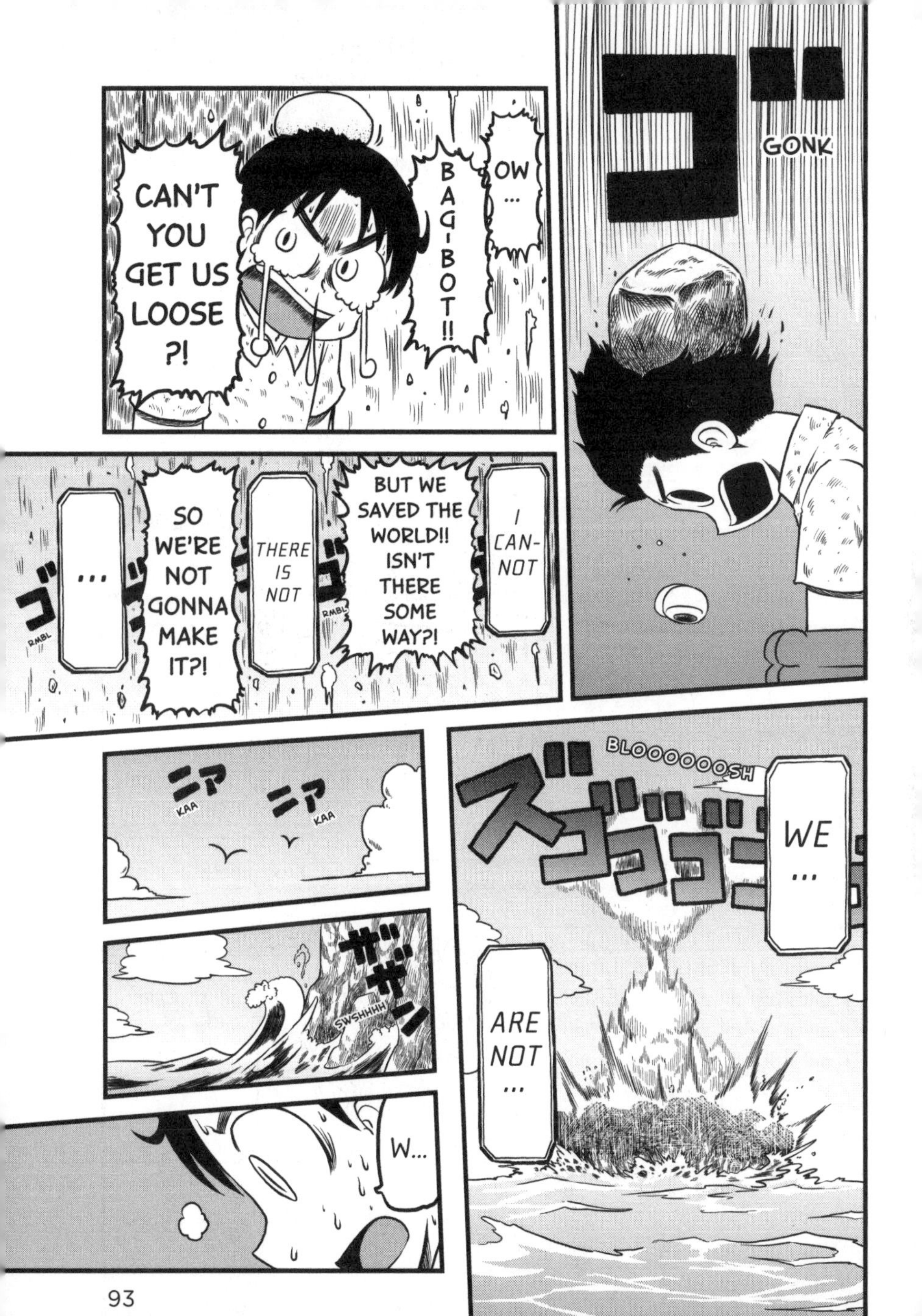
ゴ
GONK
OW ...
BAGI-BOT!!
CAN'T YOU GET US LOOSE ?!
I CAN-NOT
BUT WE SAVED THE WORLD!! ISN'T THERE SOME WAY?!
ゴ
RMBL
THERE IS NOT
SO WE'RE NOT GONNA MAKE IT?!
...
ゴ
RMBL
ズゴゴゴゴ
BLOOOOOOOSH
WE ...
ARE NOT ...
ニア
KAA
ニア
KAA
ザザーン
SWSHHHH
W...

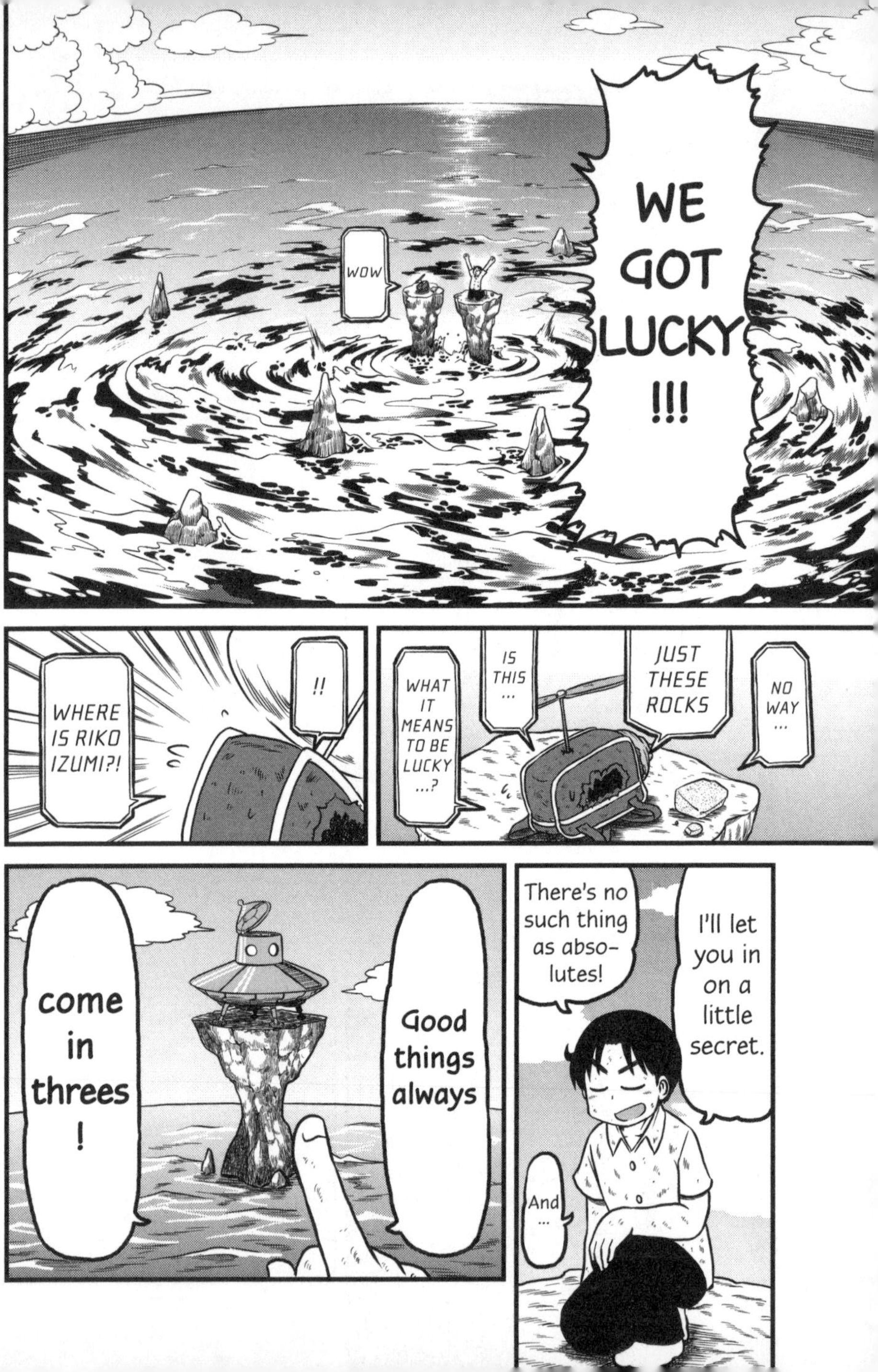
WE GOT LUCKY !!!
WOW
NO WAY ...
JUST THESE ROCKS
IS THIS ...
WHAT IT MEANS TO BE LUCKY ...?
!!
WHERE IS RIKO IZUMI?!
I'll let you in on a little secret.
There's no such thing as abso-lutes!
And ...
Good things always
come in threes
!

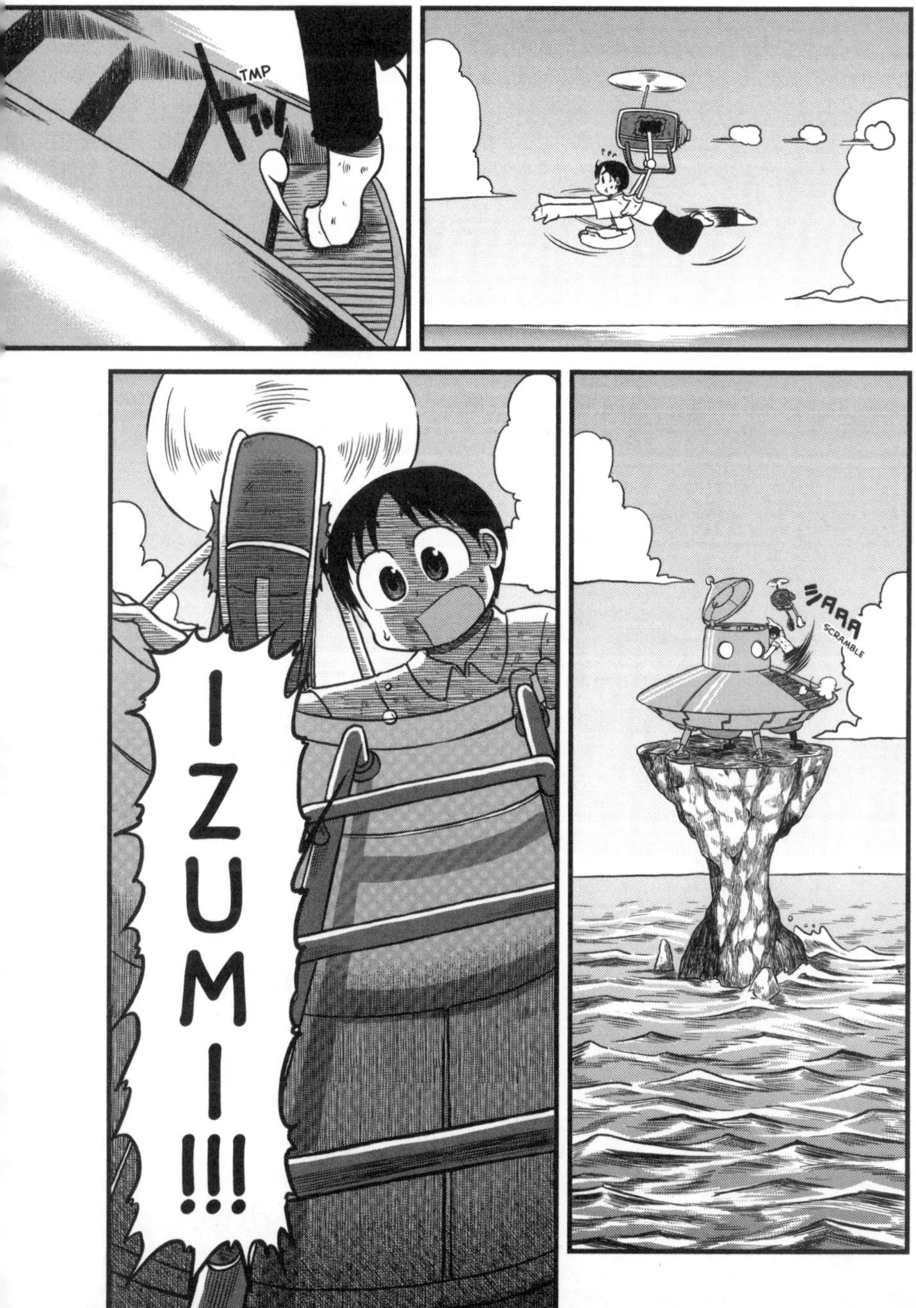
TMP
ドッ
シャアア
SCRAMBLE
IZUMI!!!

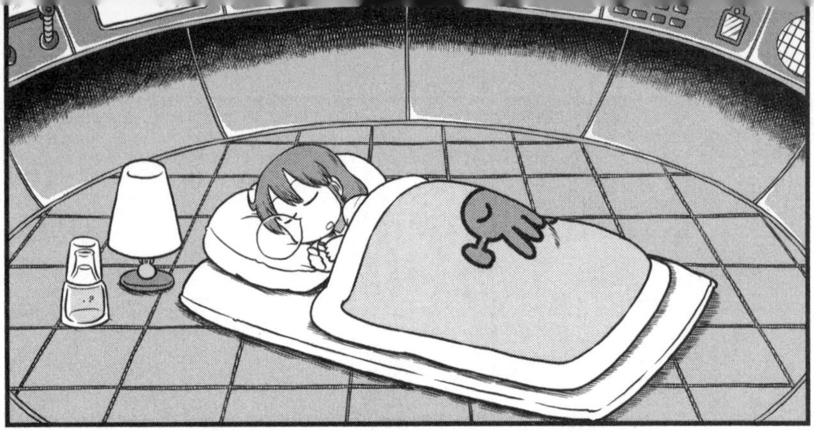

Chapter 146 Riko Izumi Goes Sleepwalking 9

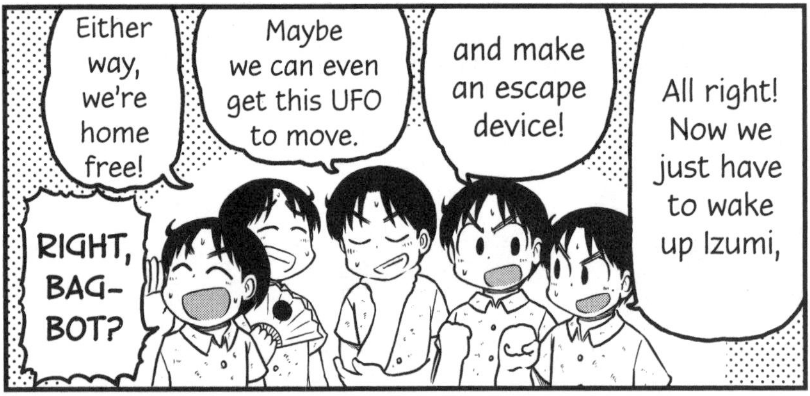
All right! Now we just have to wake up Izumi,
and make an escape device!
Maybe we can even get this UFO to move.
Either way, we're home free!
RIGHT, BAG-BOT?

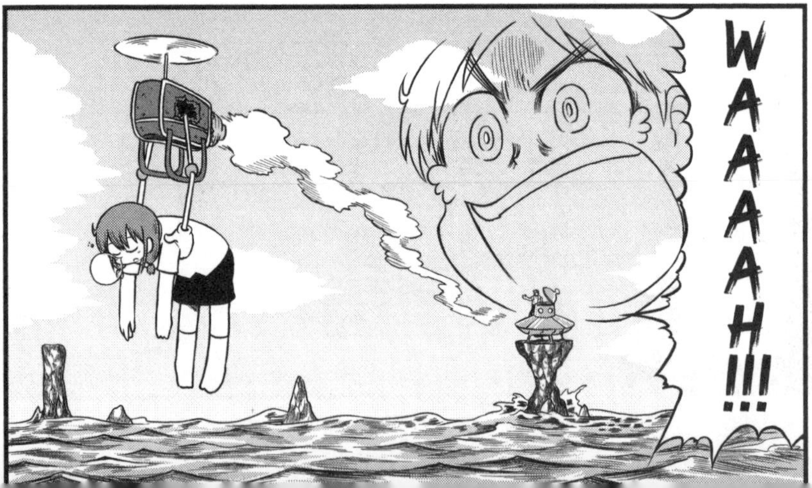
WAAAAAH!!!

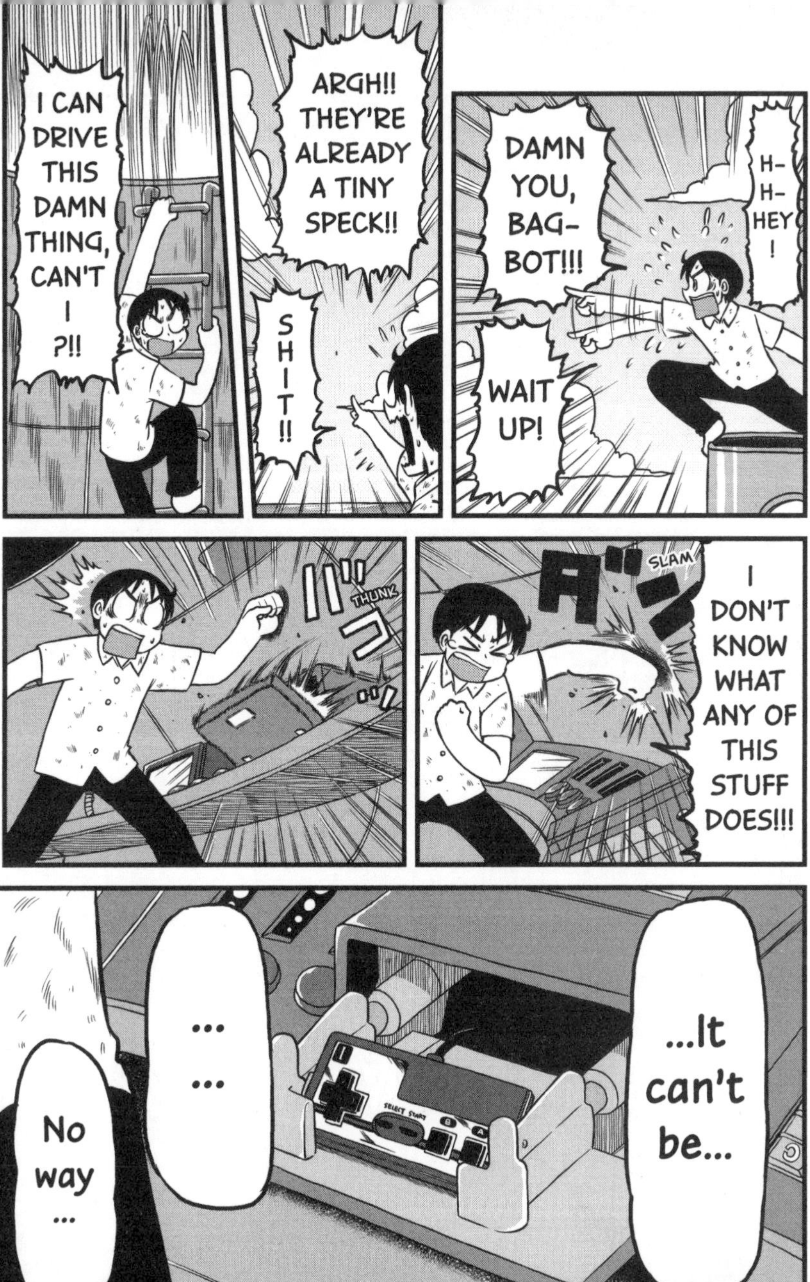
H-H-HEY!
DAMN YOU, BAG-BOT!!!
WAIT UP!
ARGH!! THEY'RE ALREADY A TINY SPECK!!
SHIT!!
I CAN DRIVE THIS DAMN THING, CAN'T I?!!
SLAM
I DON'T KNOW WHAT ANY OF THIS STUFF DOES!!!
THUNK
...It can't be...
......
No way...
SELECT START
B
A

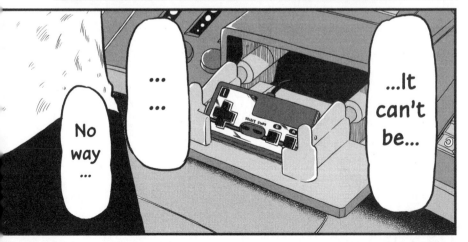

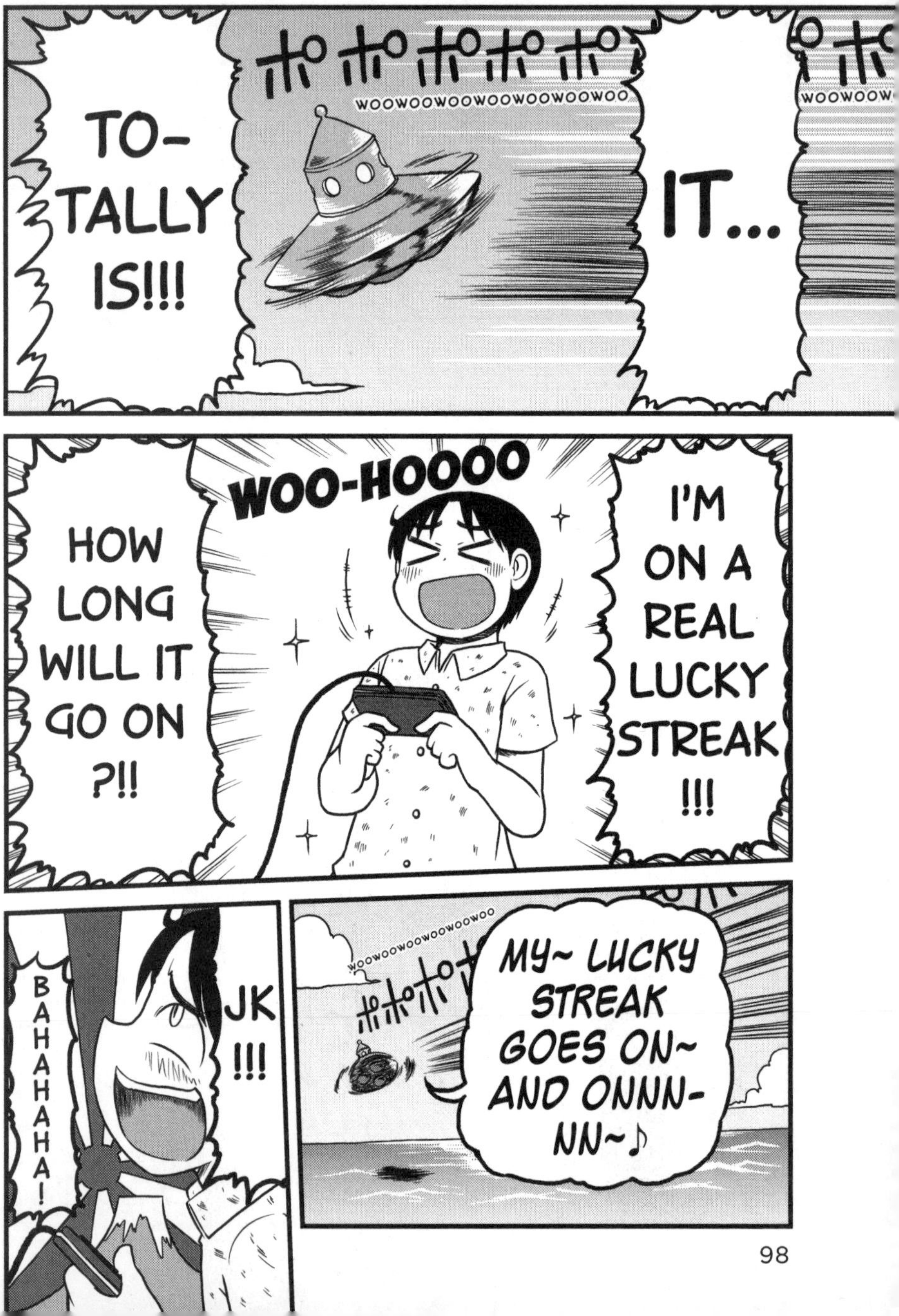

ポポ
WOOWOOW
IT...
ポポポポポ
WOOWOOWOOWOOWOOWOOWOO
TO-TALLY IS!!!
I'M ON A REAL LUCKY STREAK!!!
WOO-HOOOO
HOW LONG WILL IT GO ON?!!
MY~ LUCKY STREAK GOES ON~ AND ONNNN-NN~♪
ポポポ
WOOWOOWOOWOOWOOWOO
JK!!!
BAHAHAHAHA!

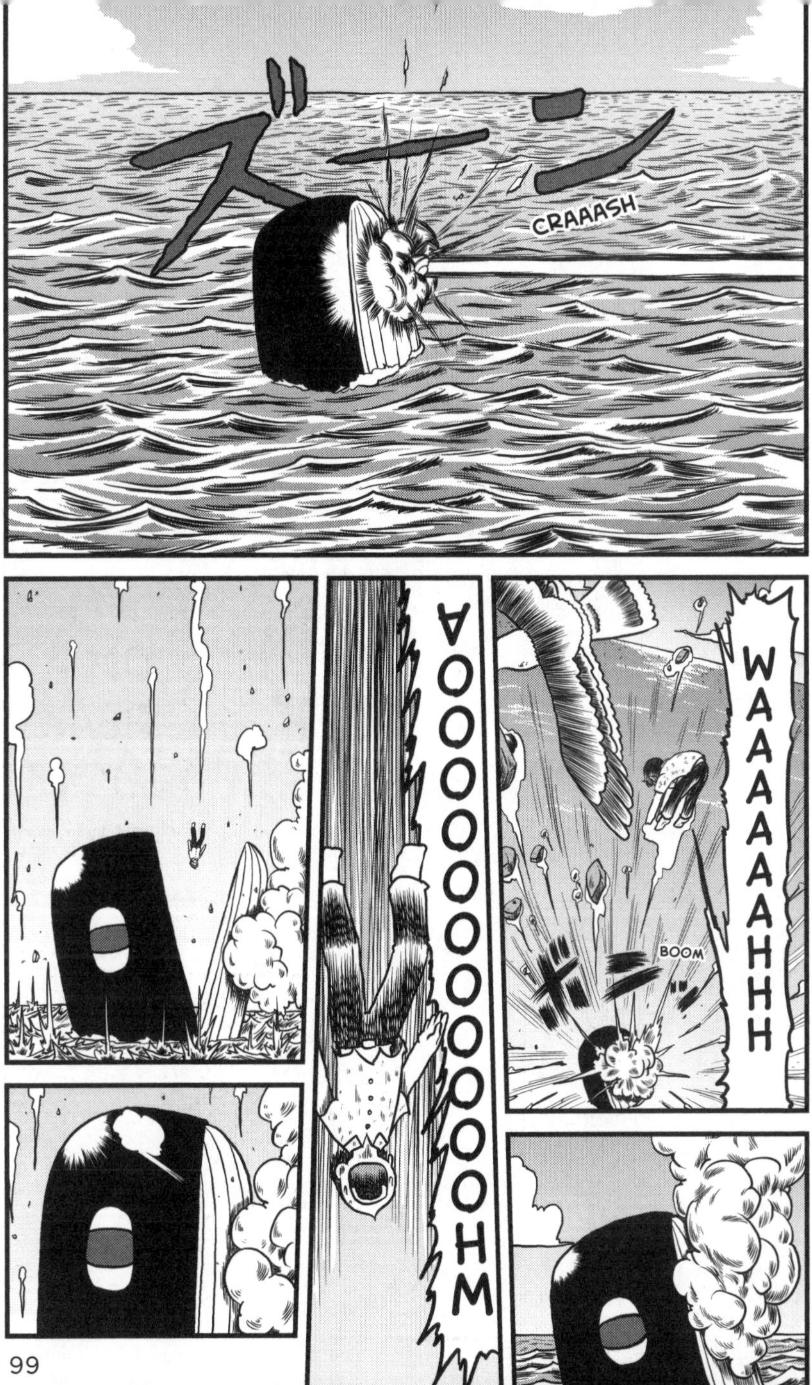
ズー
CRAAASH
WAAAAAAAHHH
ドー
BOOM
WHOOOOOOOOOOOOA

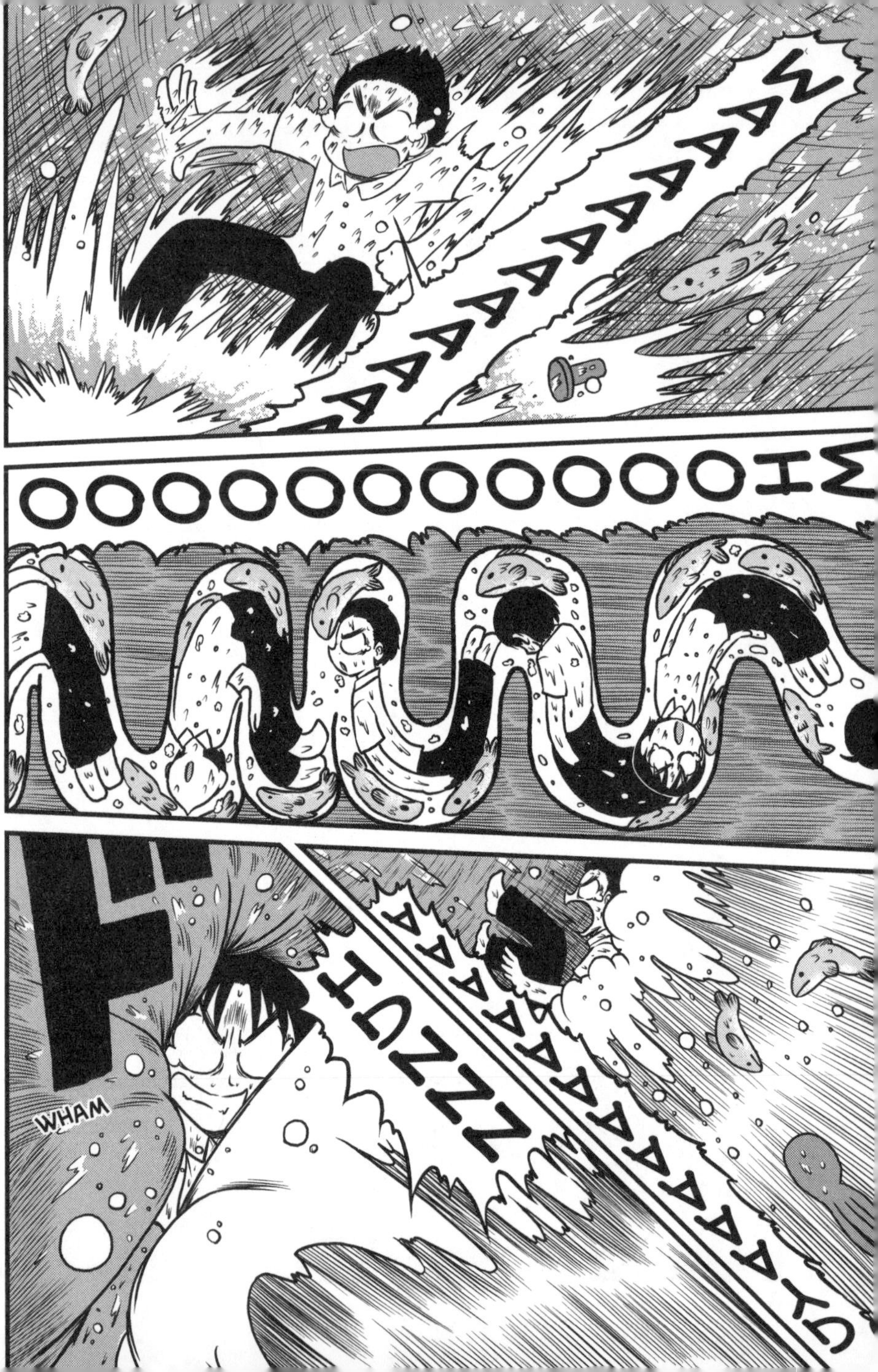
WAAAAAAAAAAAA
WHOOOOOOOOOO
GYAAAAAAAAAAAAA
ZZZZIT
WHAM

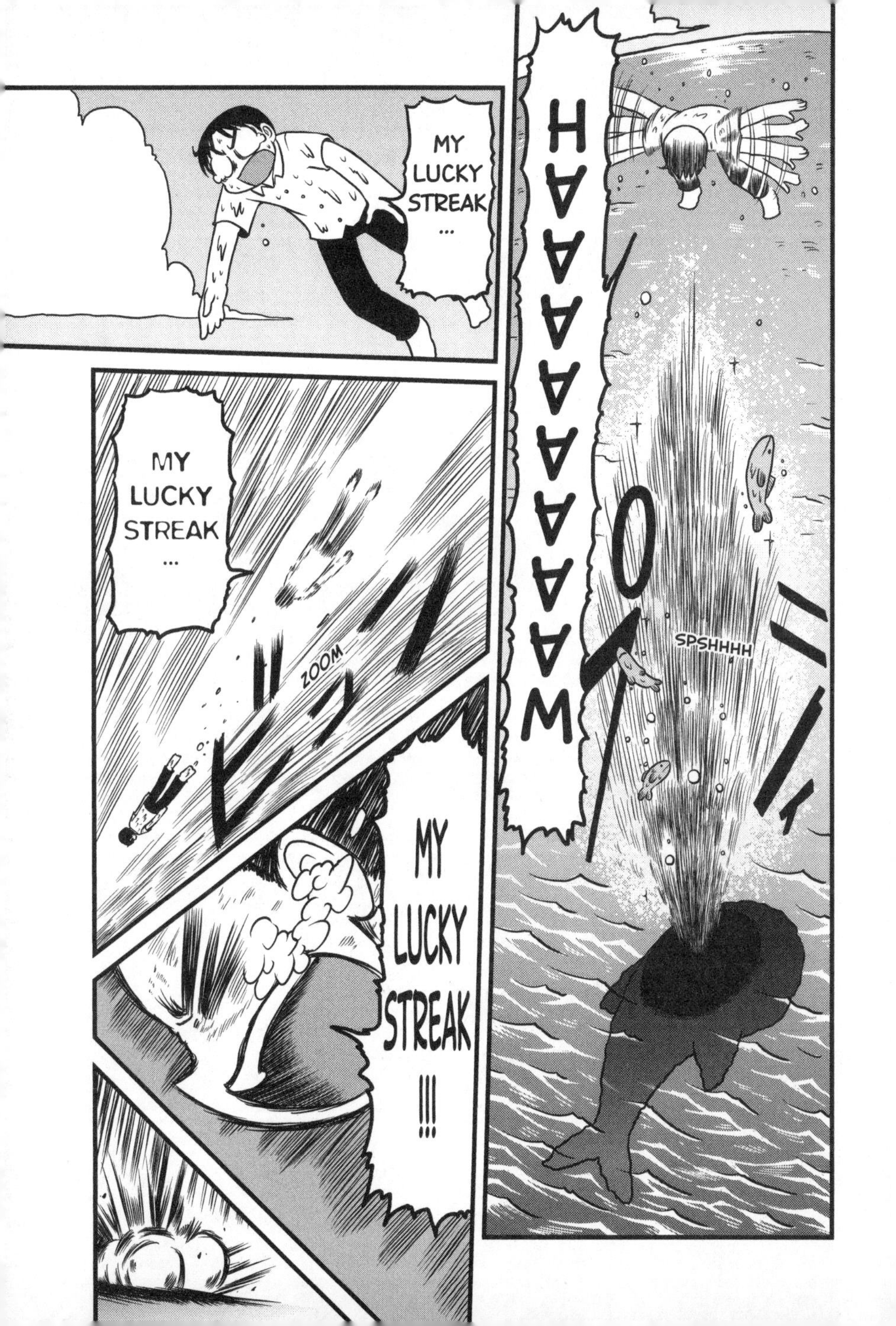
WAAAAAAAAAH
SPSHHHH
MY LUCKY STREAK ...
MY LUCKY STREAK ...
ZOOM
MY LUCKY STREAK !!!

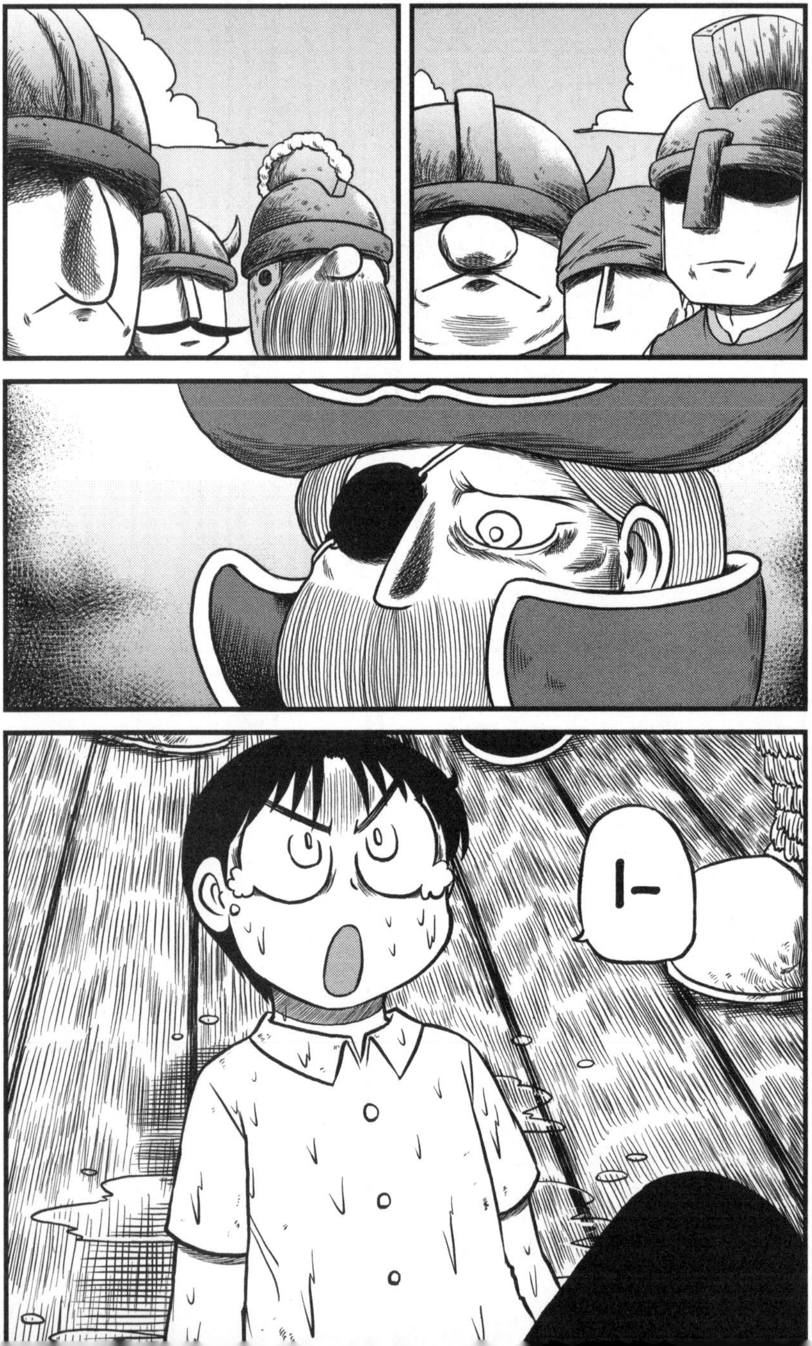
I–

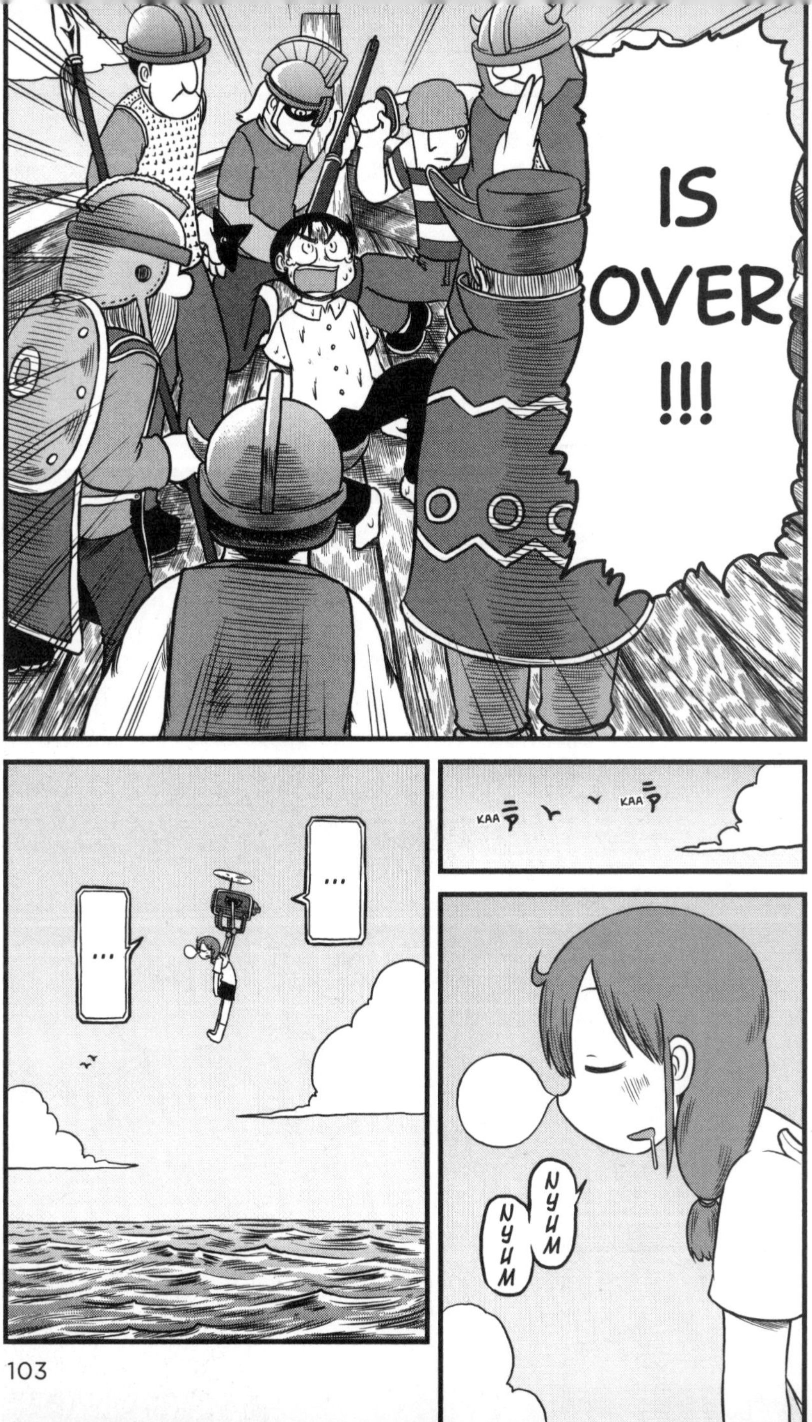
IS OVER !!!
KAA KAA
NYUM NYUM
...
...

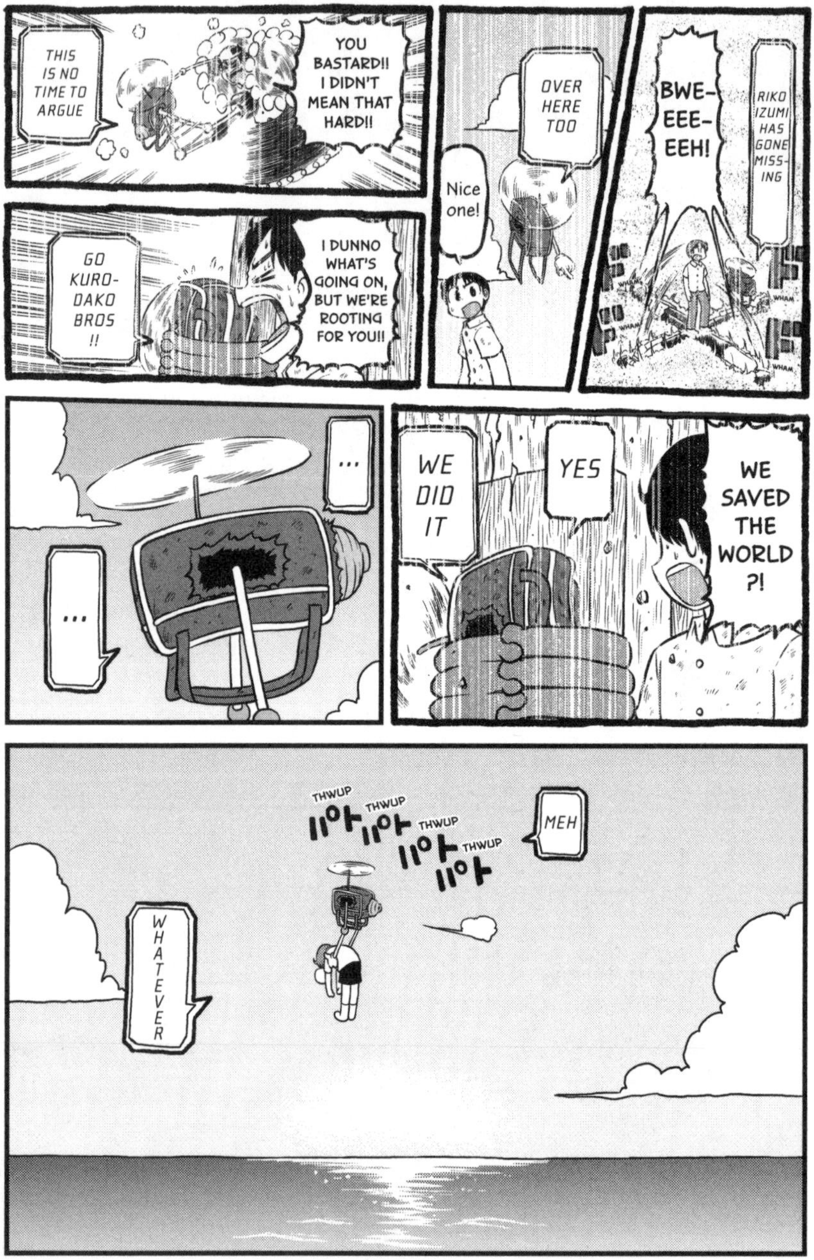
RIKO IZUMI HAS GONE MISSING
BWE-EEE-EEH!
WHAM
WHAM
WHAM
OVER HERE TOO
Nice one!
YOU BASTARD!! I DIDN'T MEAN THAT HARD!!
THIS IS NO TIME TO ARGUE
I DUNNO WHAT'S GOING ON, BUT WE'RE ROOTING FOR YOU!!
GO KURO-DAKO BROS !!
WE SAVED THE WORLD ?!
YES
WE DID IT
...
...
THWUP
THWUP
THWUP
THWUP
MEH
WHATEVER

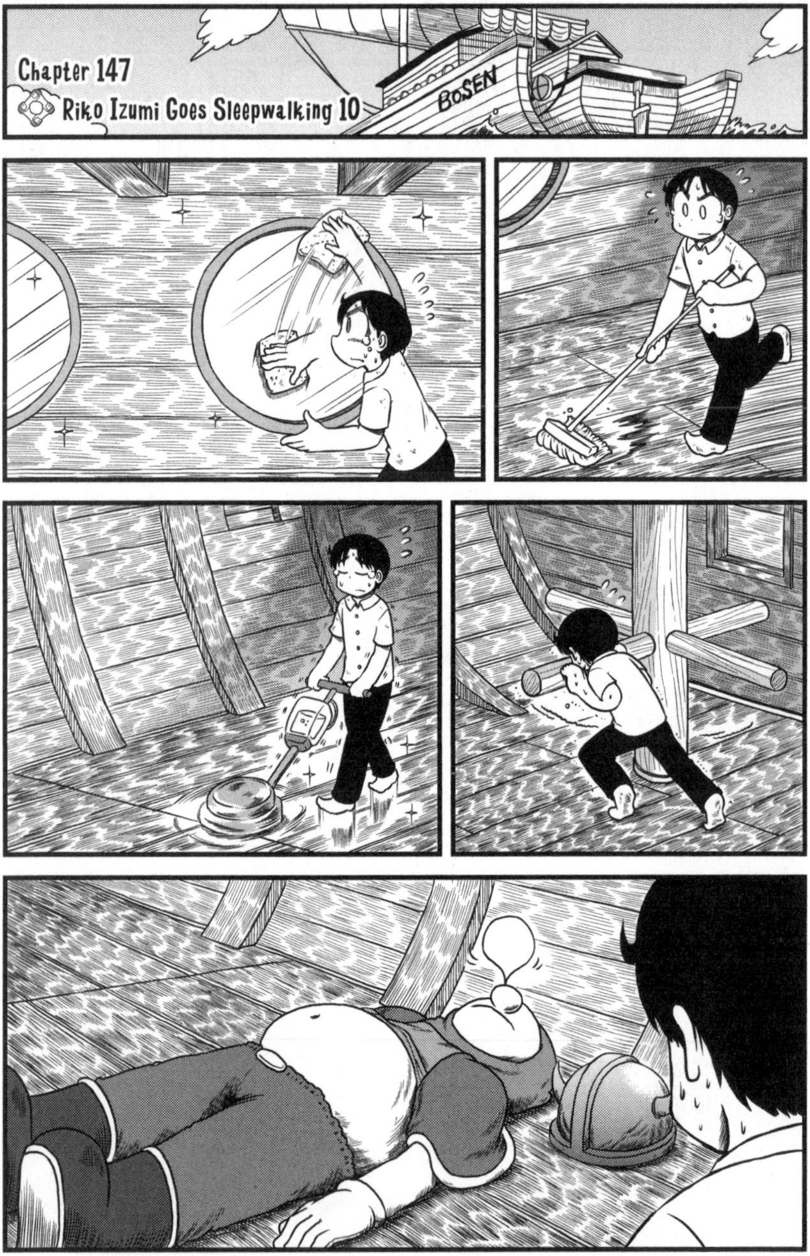
Chapter 147
Riko Izumi Goes Sleepwalking 10
BOSEN

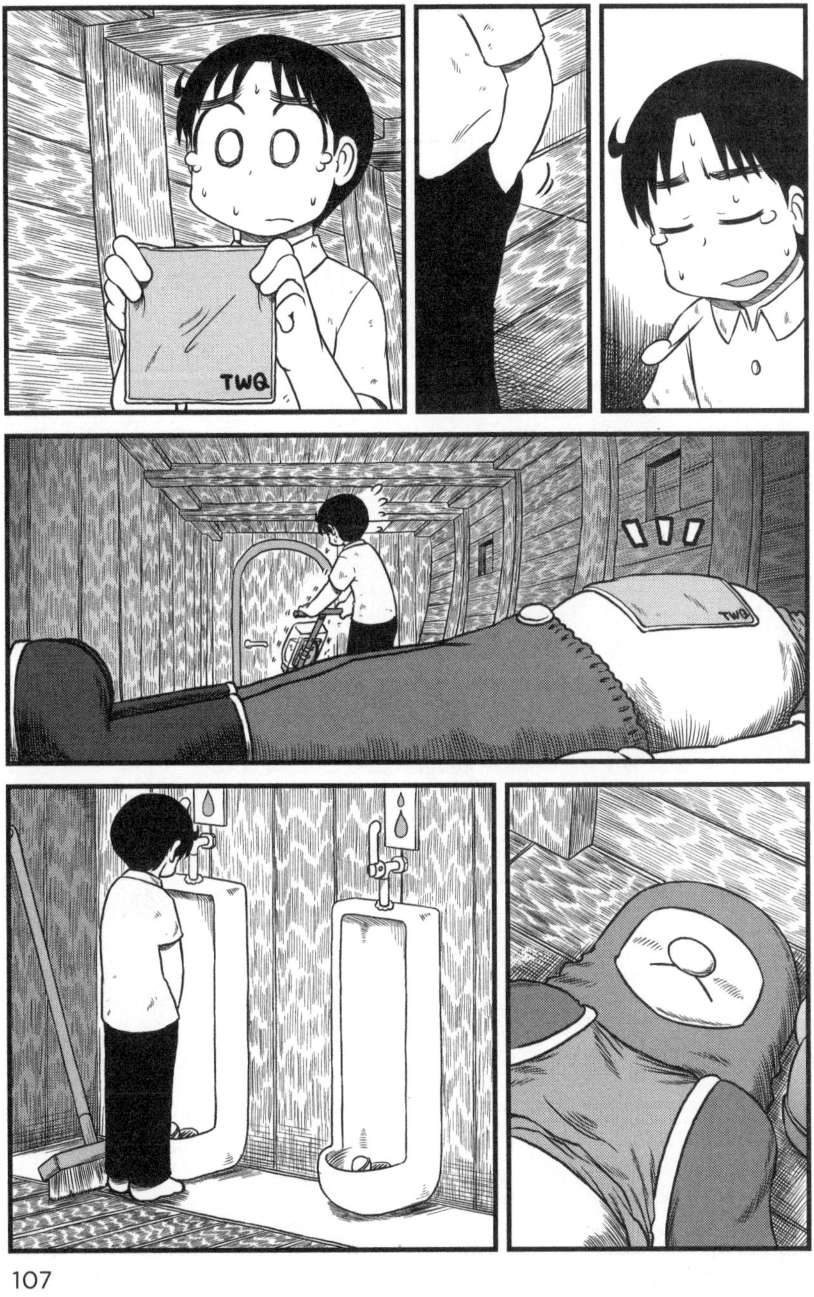
TWQ
TWQ

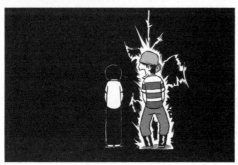

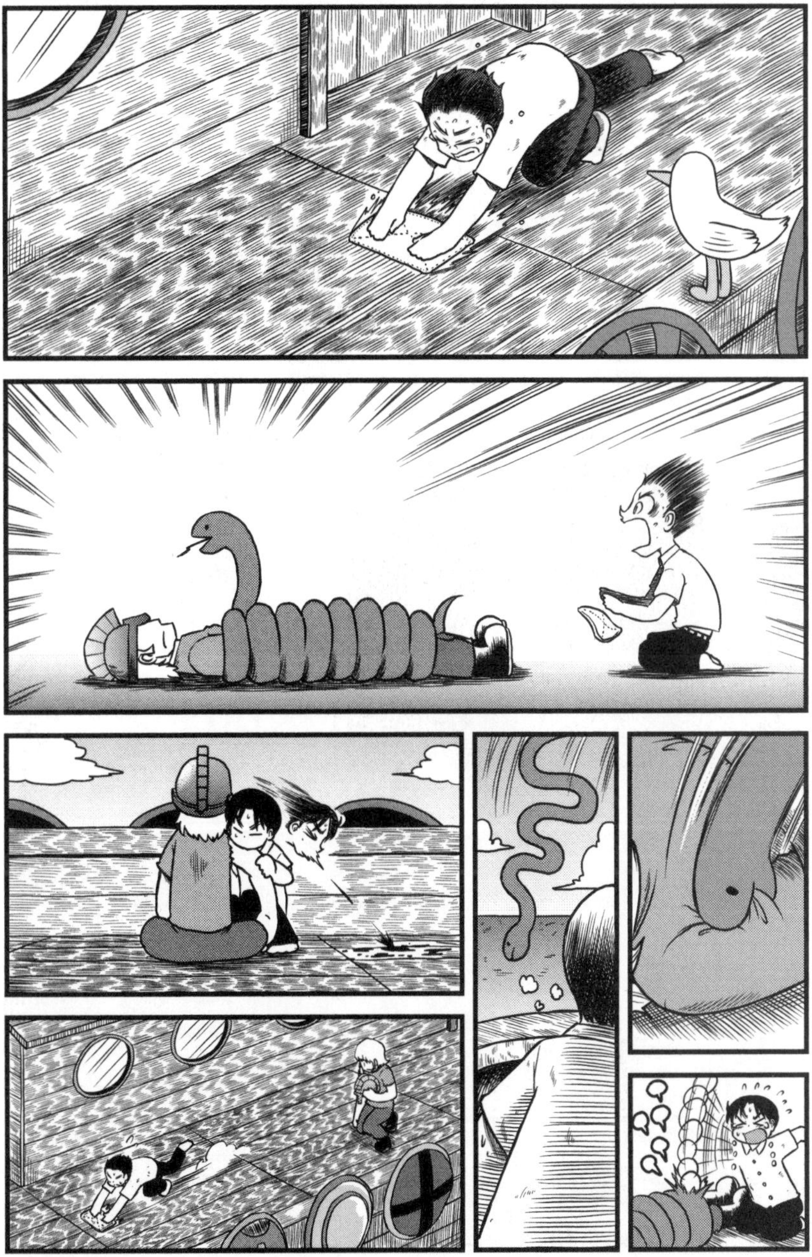

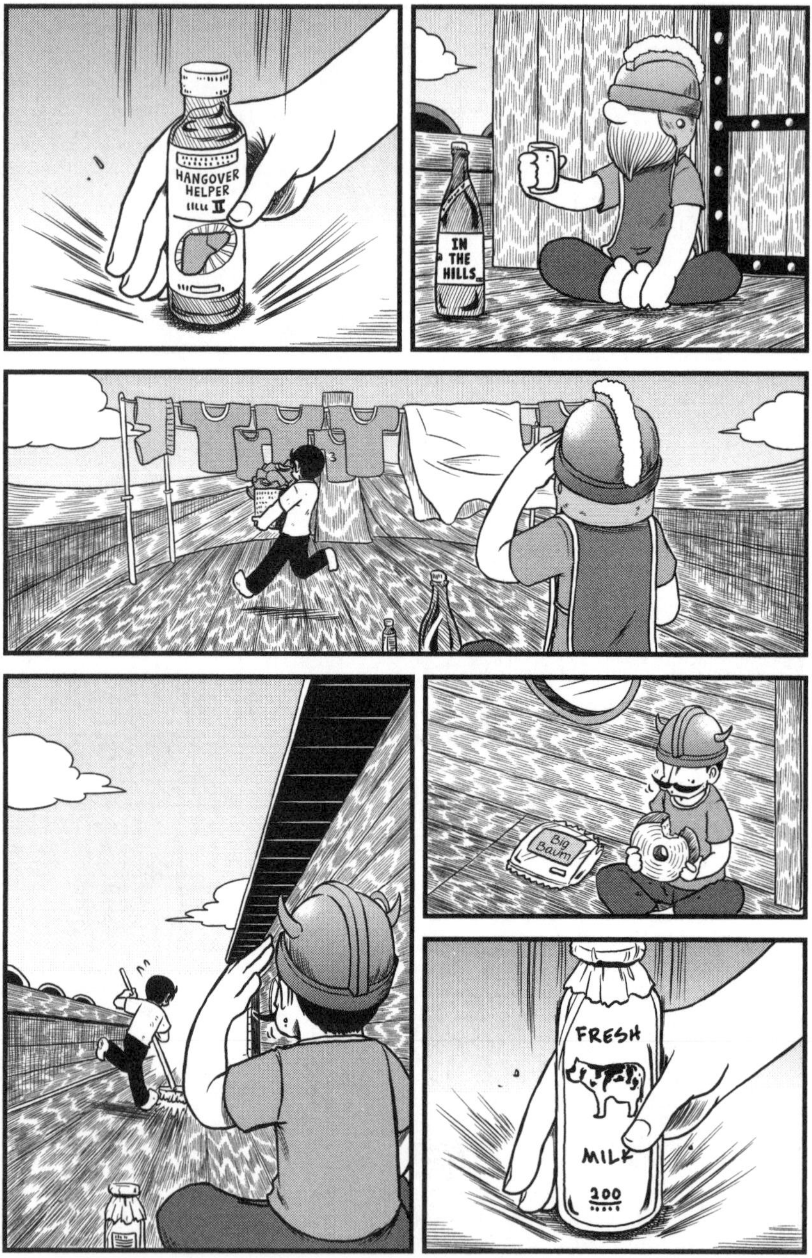
IN THE HILLS
HANGOVER HELPER
Big Baum
FRESH
MILK
200

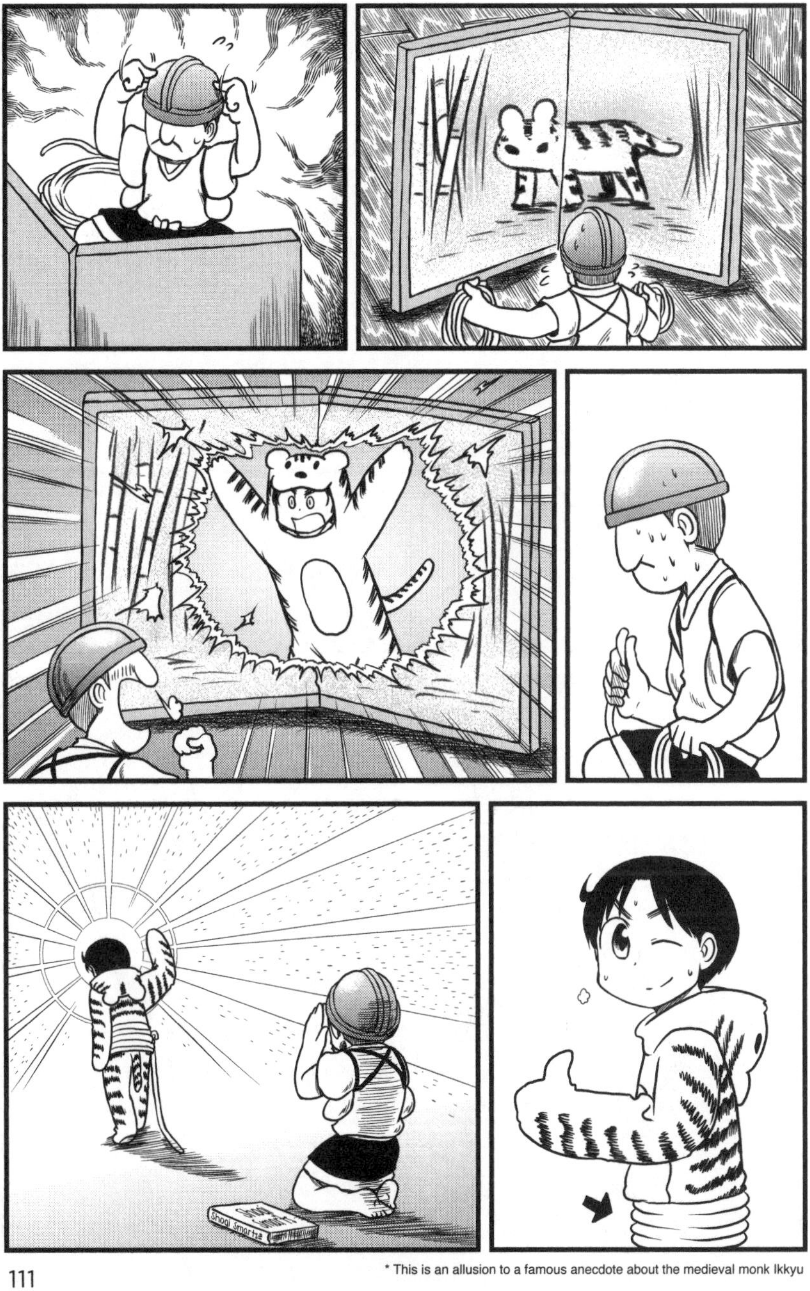
Shogi Smarts

* This is an allusion to a famous anecdote about the medieval monk Ikkyu

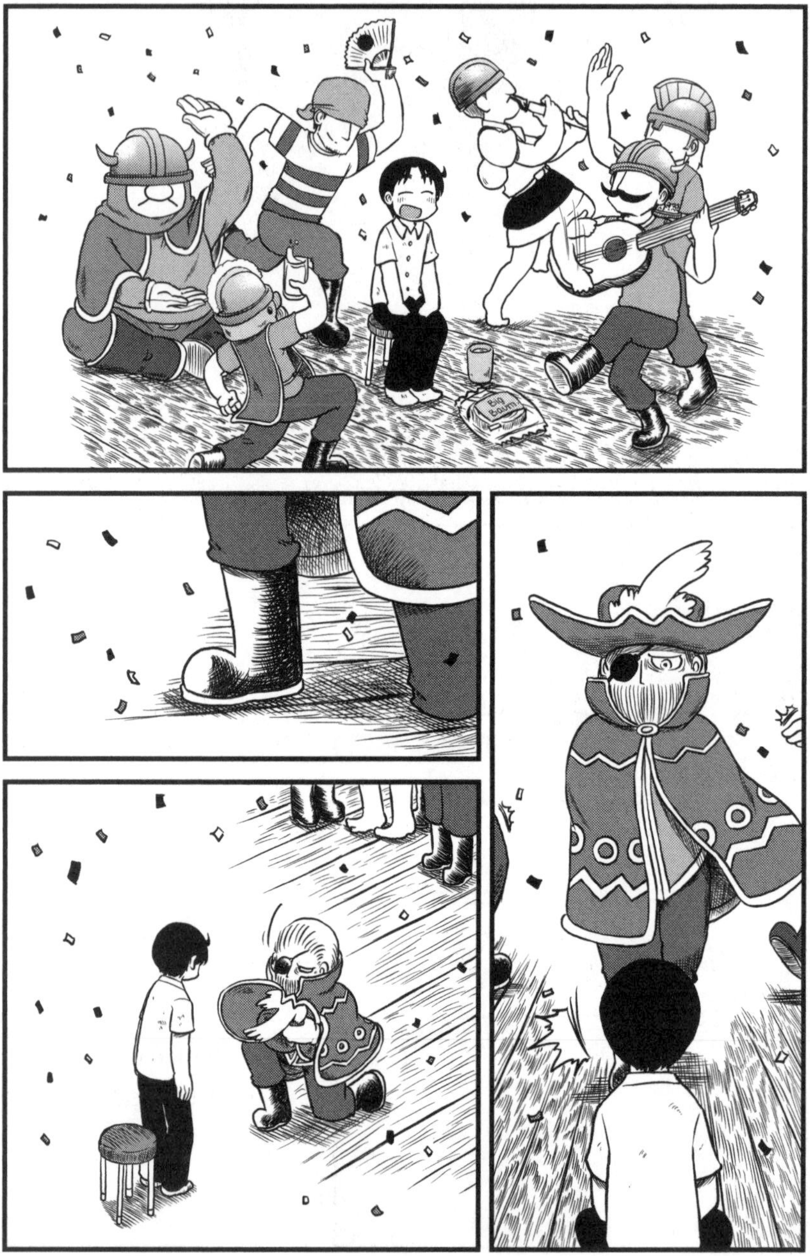
Big Baum

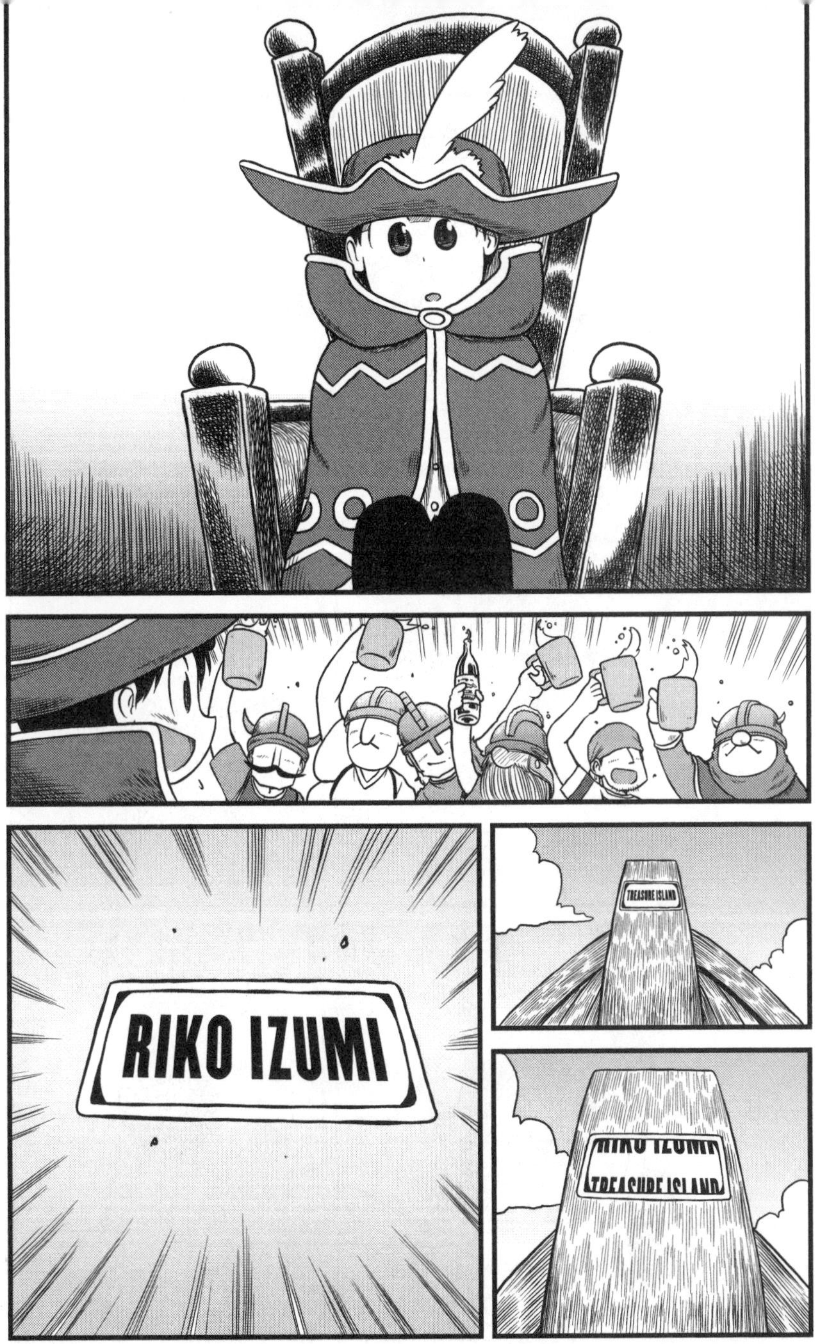
TREASURE ISLAND
RIKO IZUMI

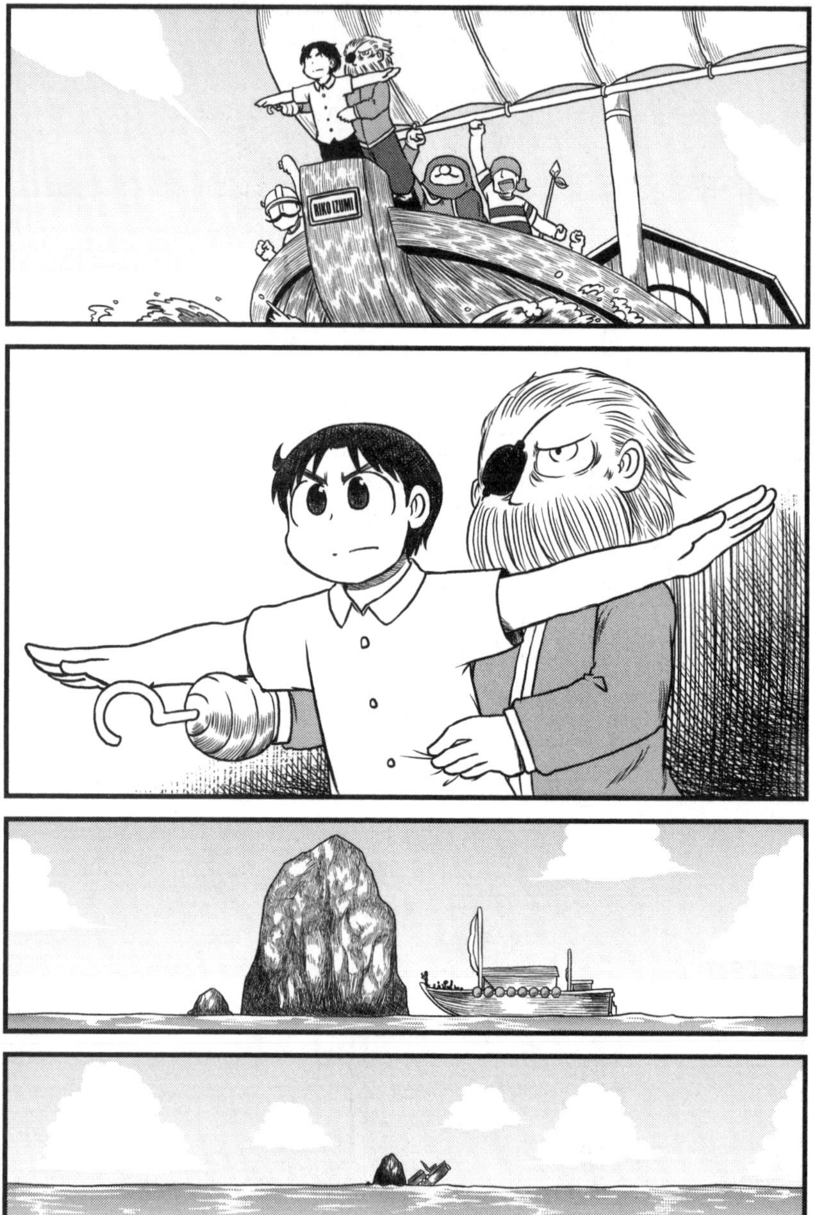
RIKO IZUMI

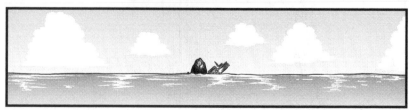

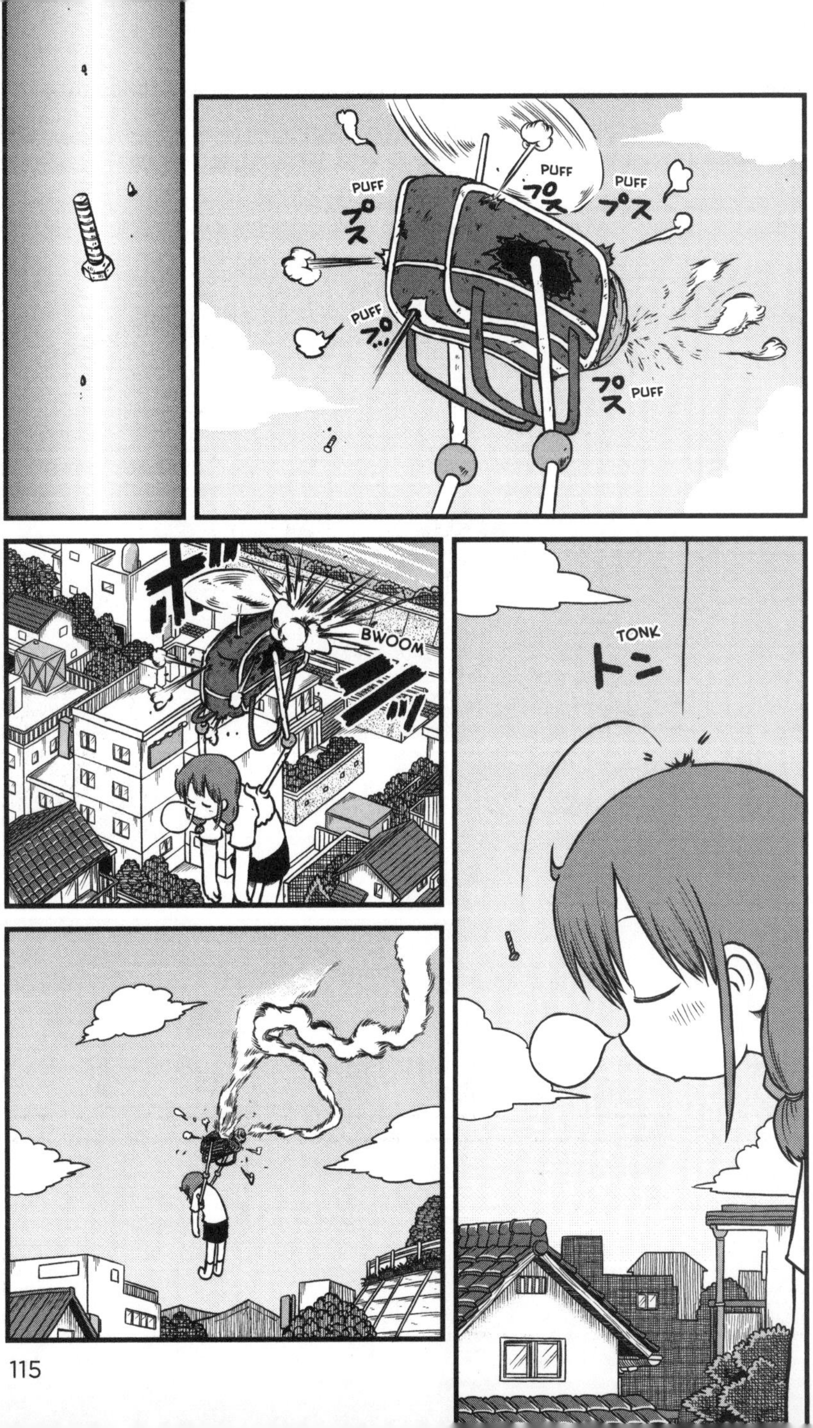
PUFF
プス
PUFF
プス
PUFF
プス
PUFF
プッ
プス
PUFF
TONK
トン
BWOOM

Chapter 148 ◇ Riko Izumi Goes Sleepwalking 11

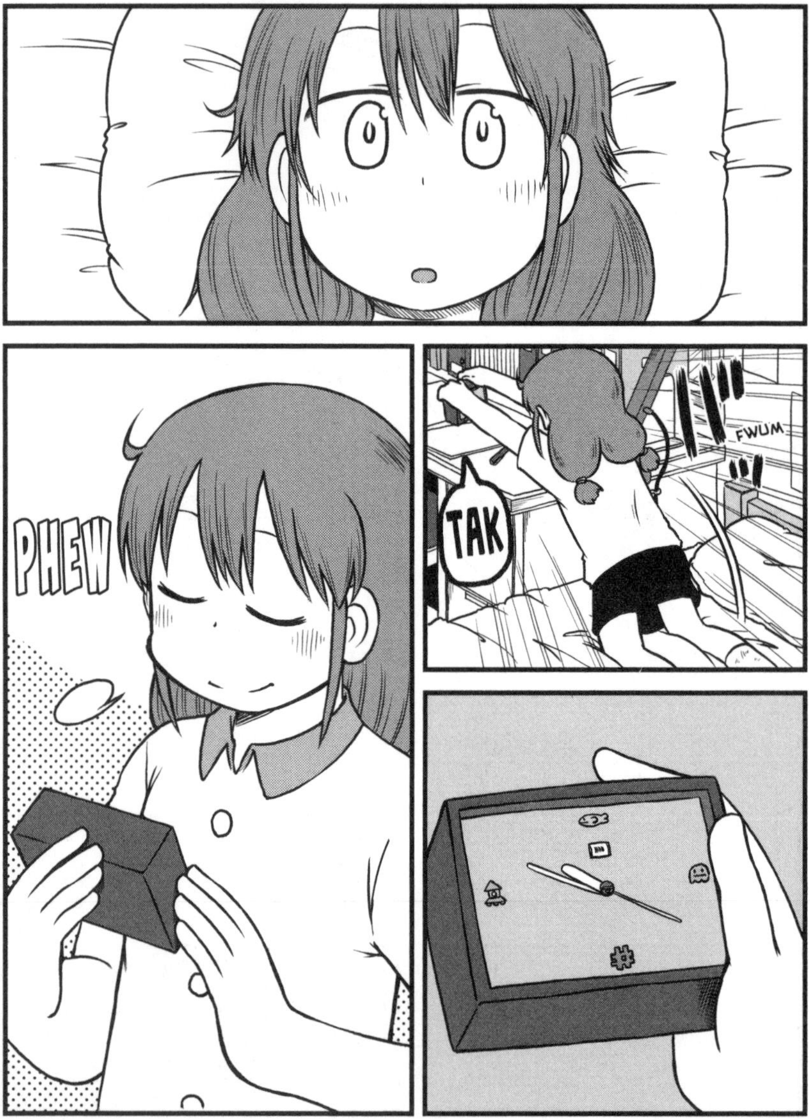
FWUM
TAK
PHEW

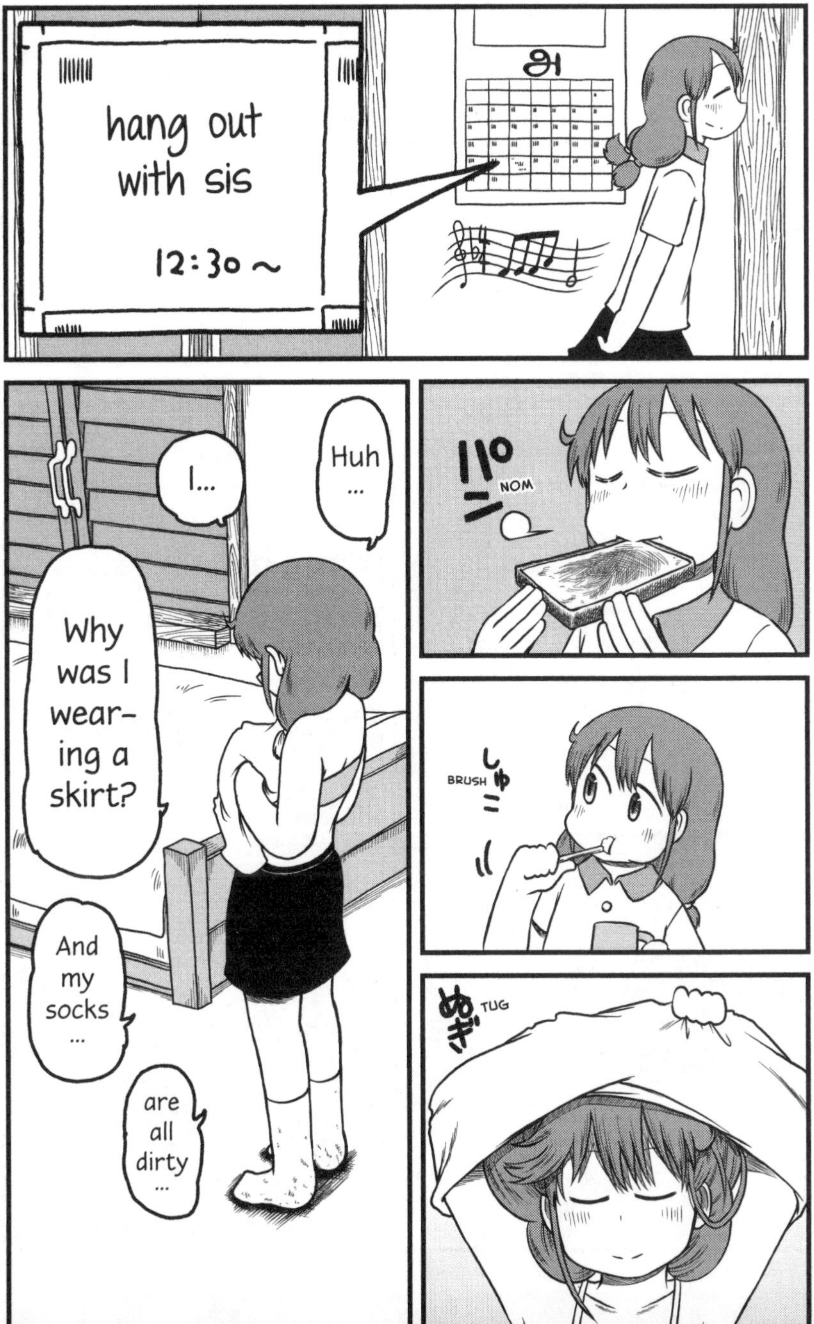
hang out with sis
12:30 ~
NOM
BRUSH
TUG
Huh ...
I...
Why was I wear-ing a skirt?
And my socks ...
are all dirty ...

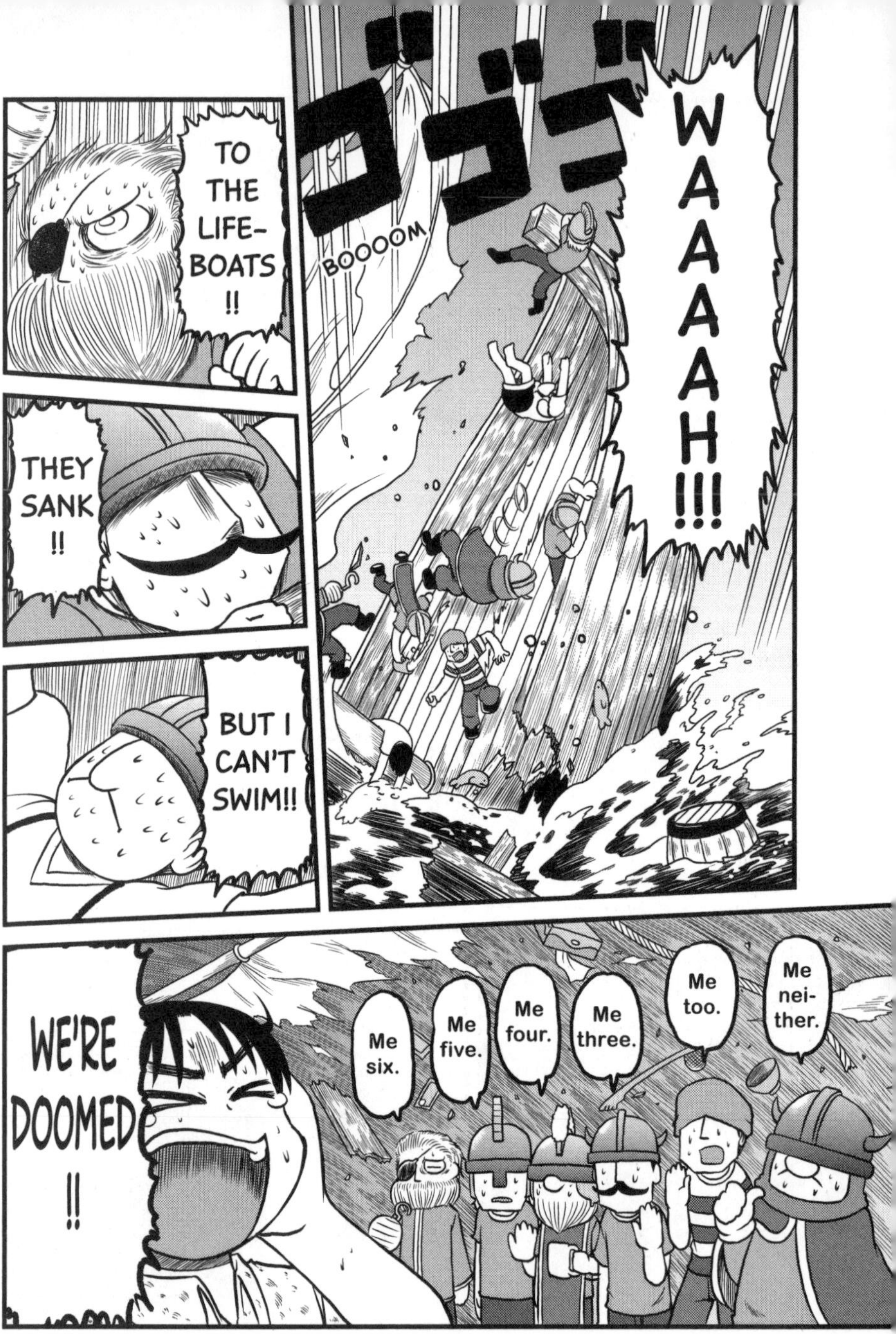

ゴゴゴ
WAAAAAH!!!
BOOOOM
TO THE LIFE-BOATS!!
THEY SANK!!
BUT I CAN'T SWIM!!
Me neither.
Me too.
Me three.
Me four.
Me five.
Me six.
WE'RE DOOMED!!

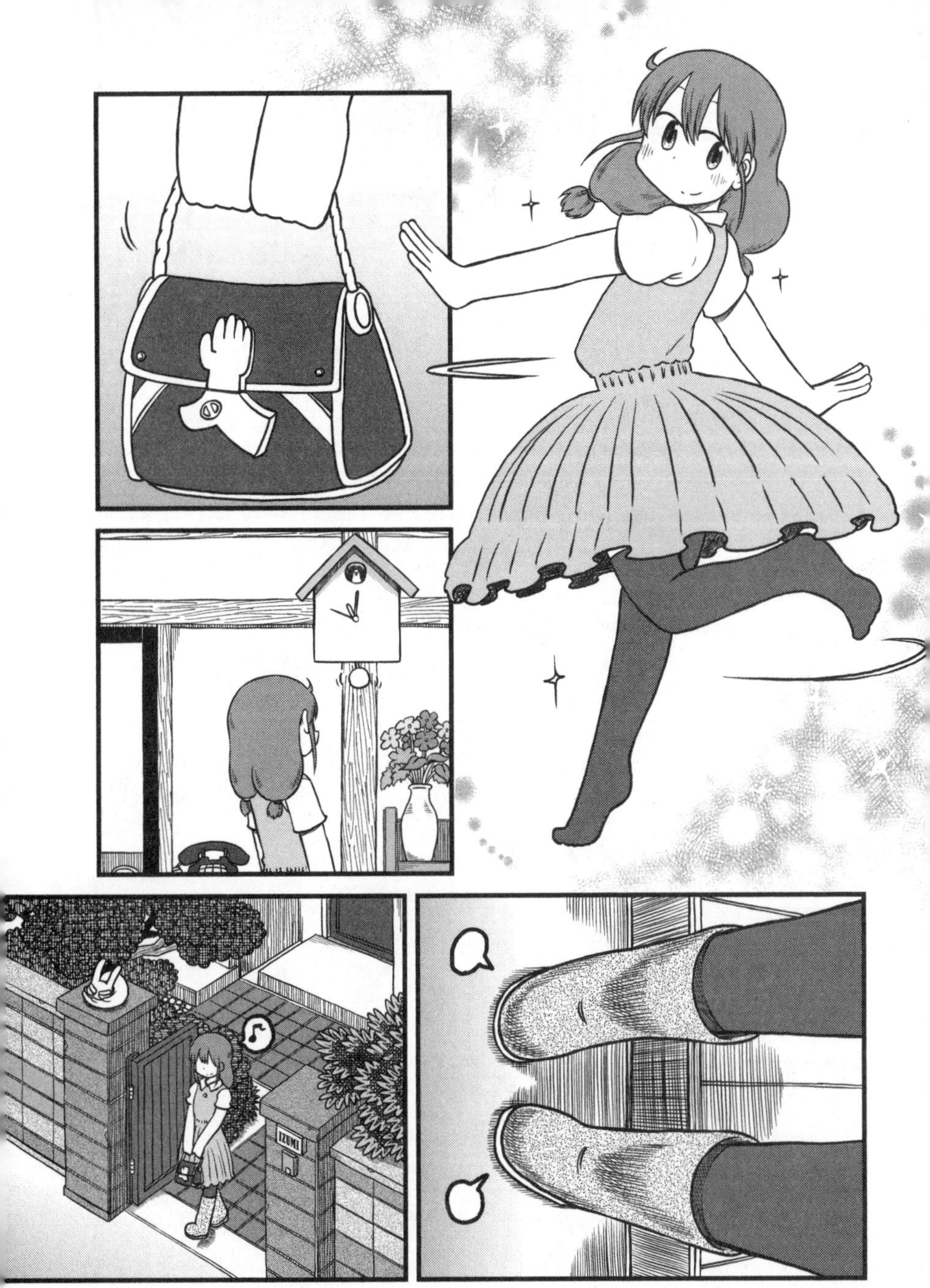
IZUMI

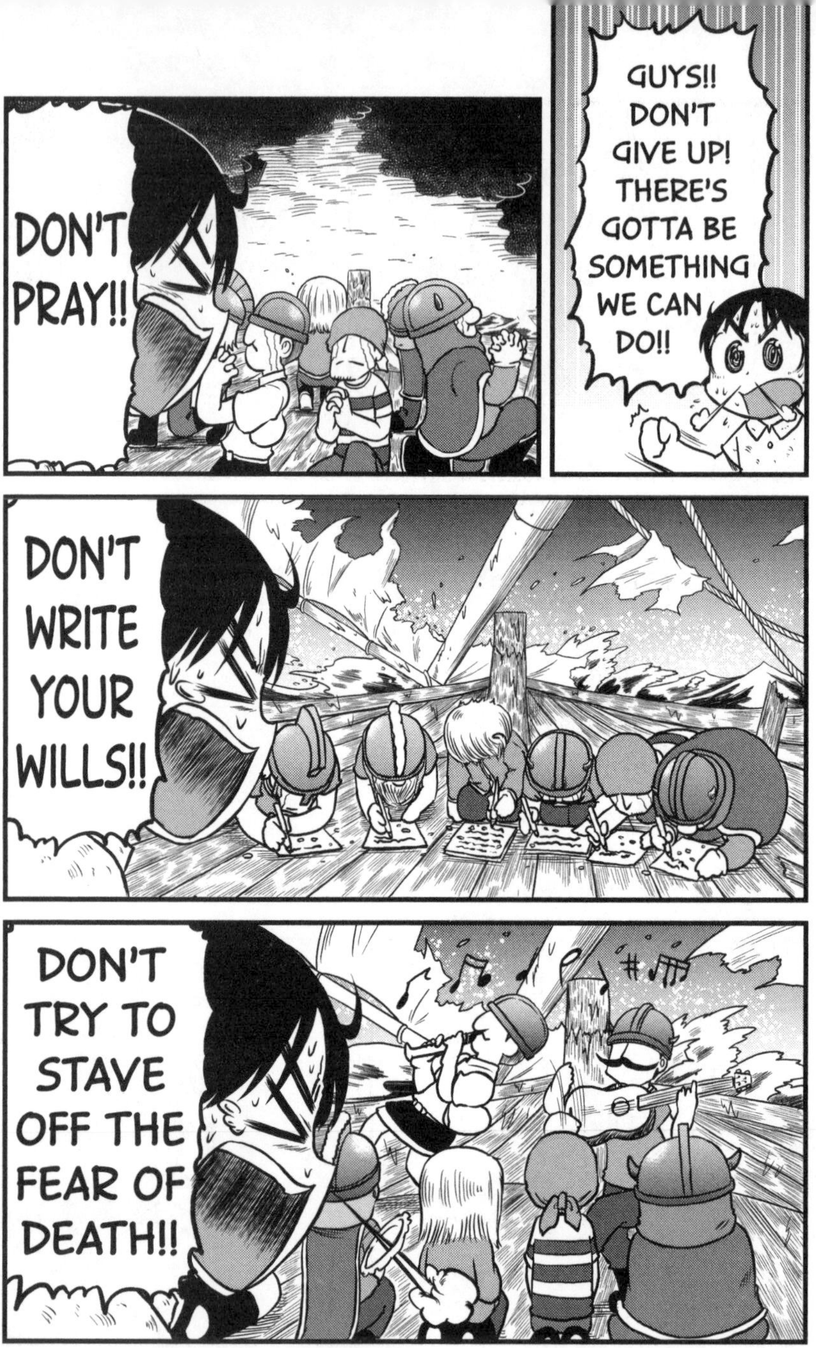
GUYS!! DON'T GIVE UP! THERE'S GOTTA BE SOMETHING WE CAN DO!!
DON'T PRAY!!
DON'T WRITE YOUR WILLS!!
DON'T TRY TO STAVE OFF THE FEAR OF DEATH!!

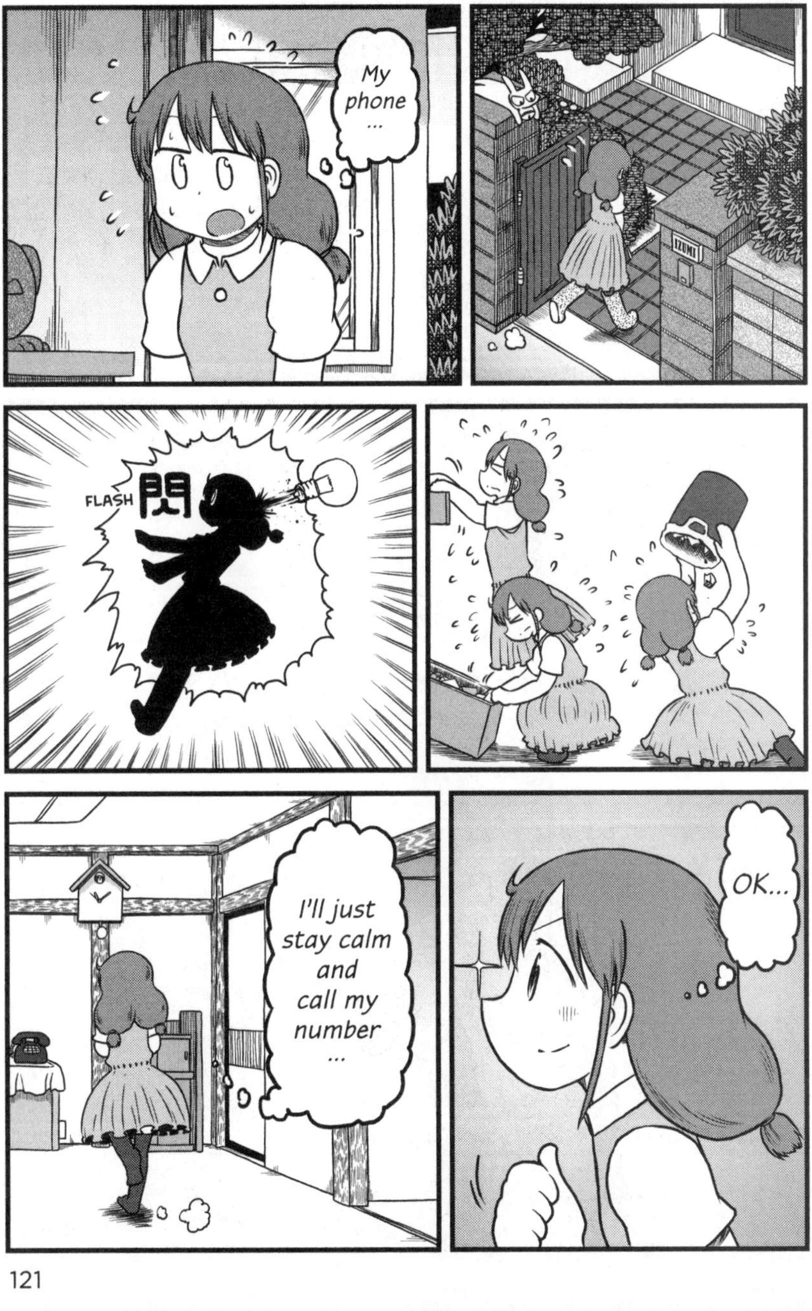
IZUMI
My phone ...
FLASH 閃
OK...
I'll just stay calm and call my number ...

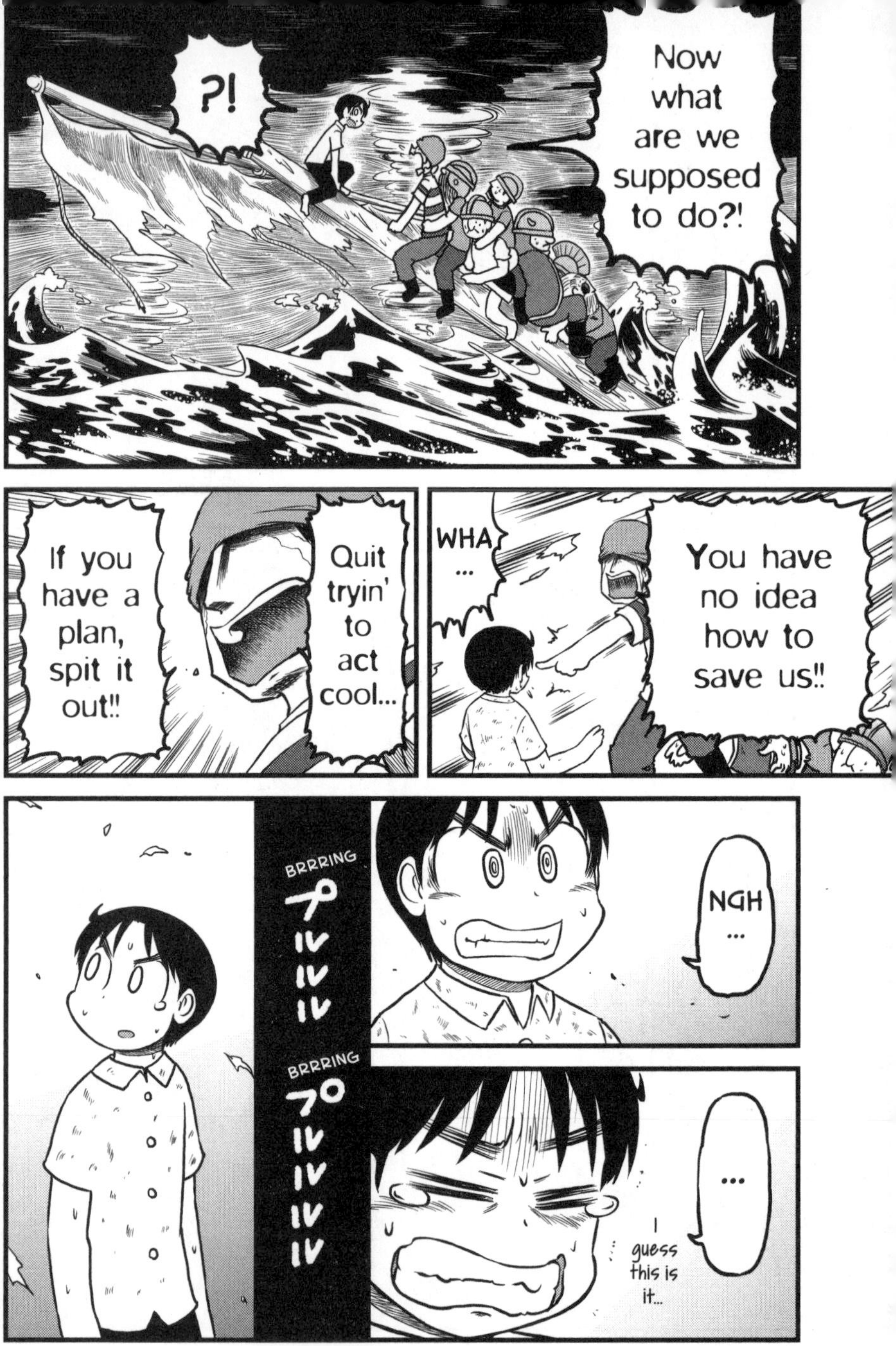
Now what are we supposed to do?!
?!
You have no idea how to save us!!
WHA...
Quit tryin' to act cool...
If you have a plan, spit it out!!
NGH...
BRRRING
プルルルル
BRRRING
プルルルルル
...
I guess this is it..

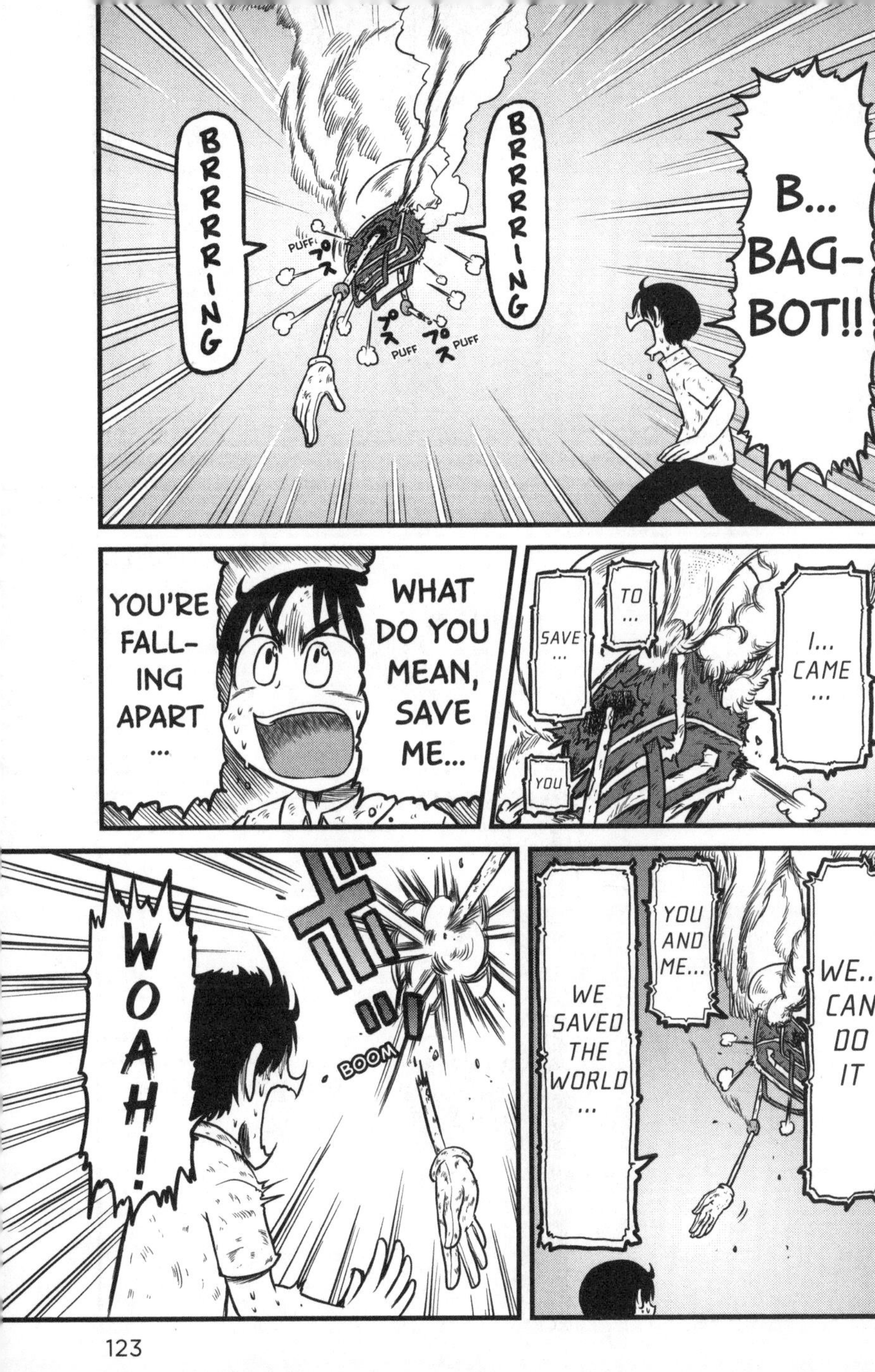
B... BAG-BOT!!
BRRRRING
PUFF プス
PUFF プス
PUFF プス
BRRRRING
I... CAME ...
TO ...
SAVE ...
YOU
WHAT DO YOU MEAN, SAVE ME...
YOU'RE FALL-ING APART ...
WE... CAN DO IT
YOU AND ME...
WE SAVED THE WORLD ...
BOOM
WOAH!

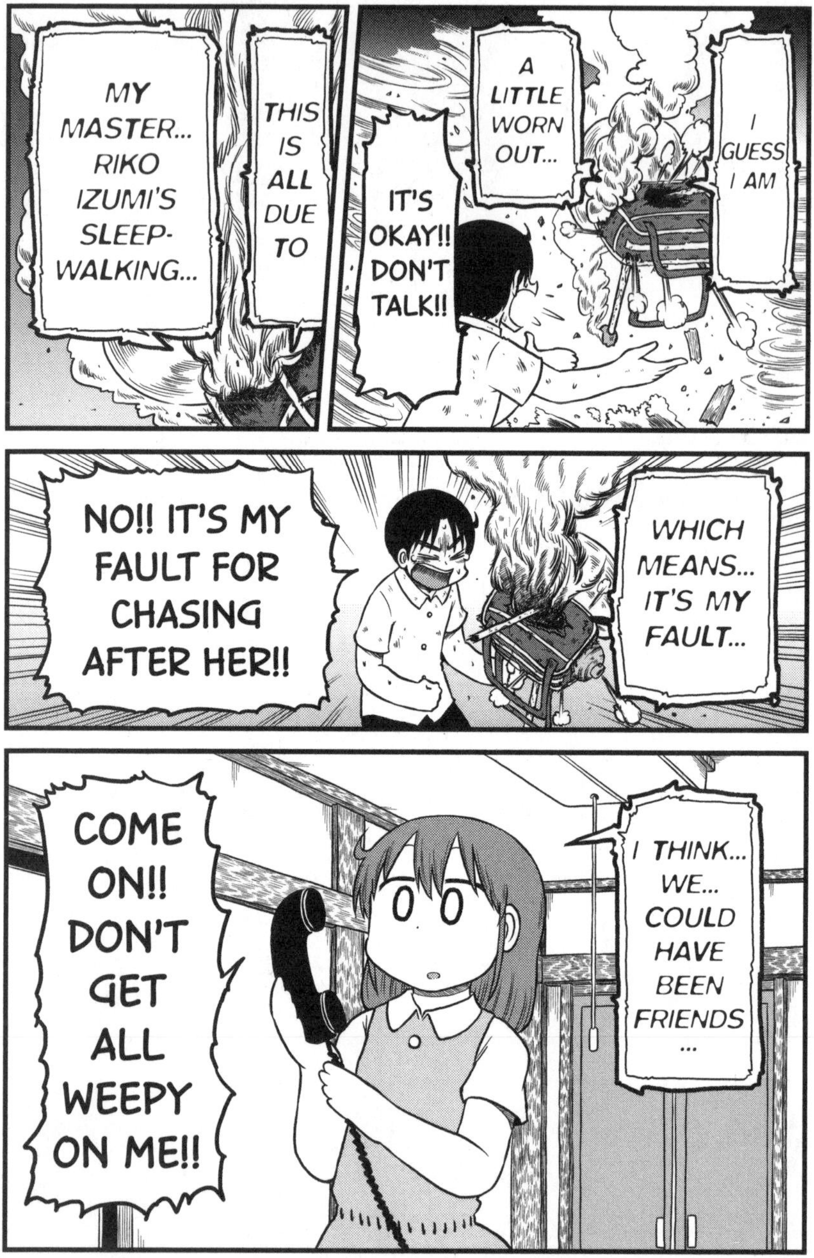
I GUESS I AM
A LITTLE WORN OUT...
IT'S OKAY!! DON'T TALK!!
THIS IS ALL DUE TO
MY MASTER... RIKO IZUMI'S SLEEP-WALKING...
WHICH MEANS... IT'S MY FAULT...
NO!! IT'S MY FAULT FOR CHASING AFTER HER!!
I THINK... WE... COULD HAVE BEEN FRIENDS ...
COME ON!! DON'T GET ALL WEEPY ON ME!!

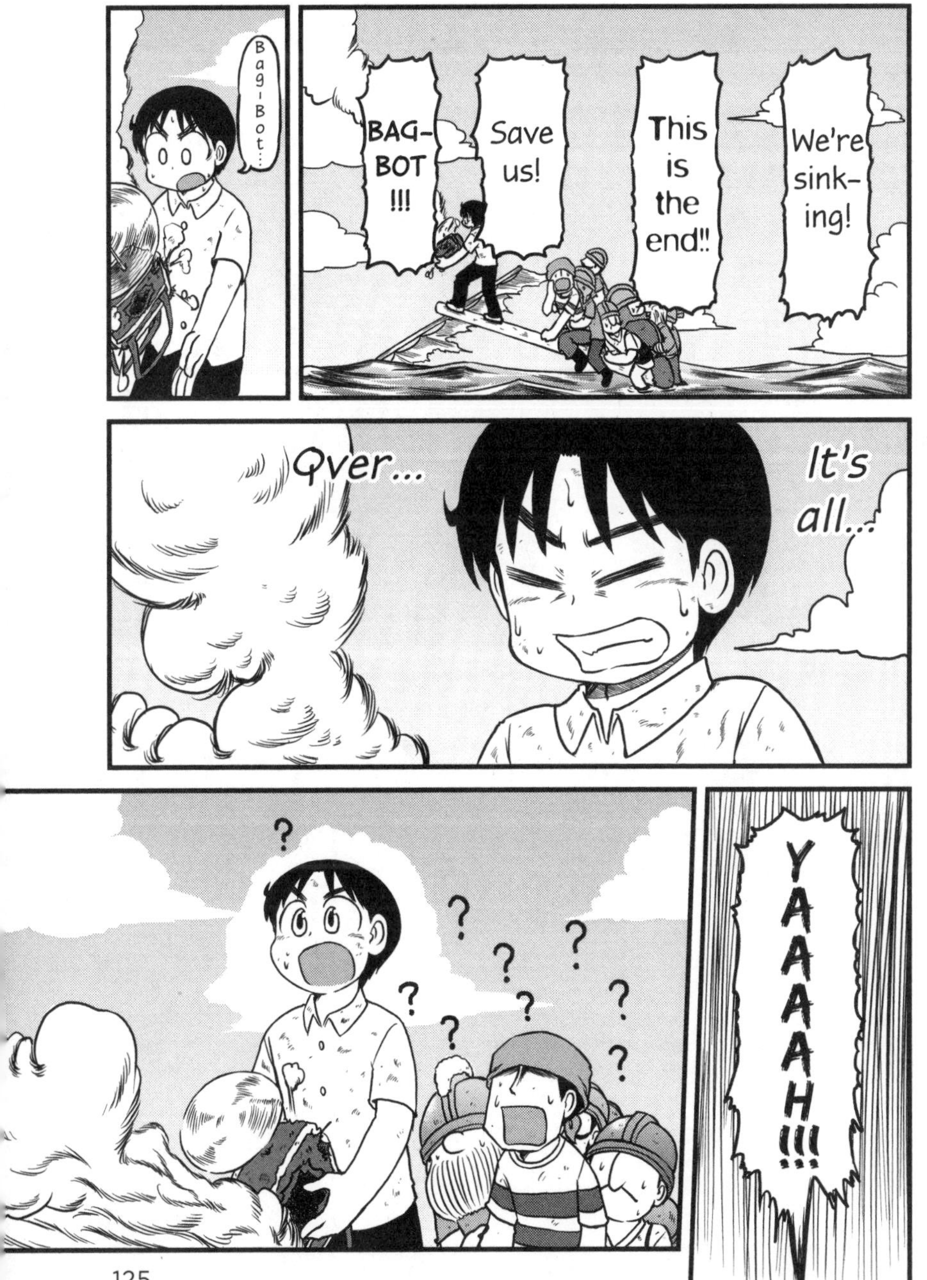
We're sinking!
This is the end!!
Save us!
BAG-BOT!!!
Bag-Bot...
It's all...
Over...
YAAAAAH!!!

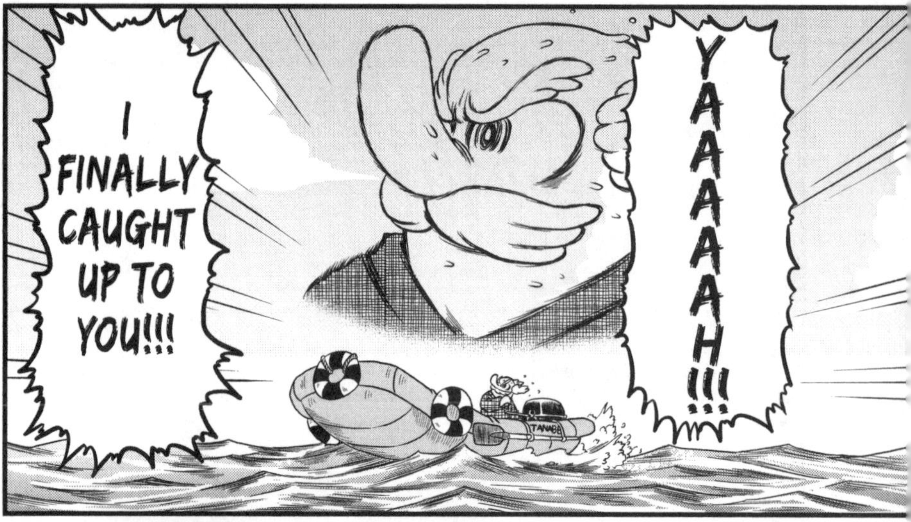
YAAAAAH!!!
I FINALLY CAUGHT UP TO YOU!!!

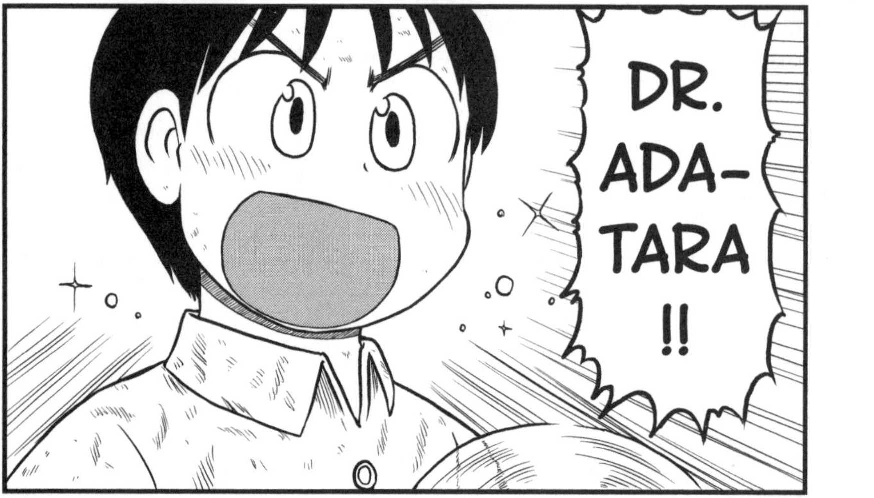
DR. ADA-TARA!!

Chapter 149 Riko Izumi Goes Sleepwalking 12

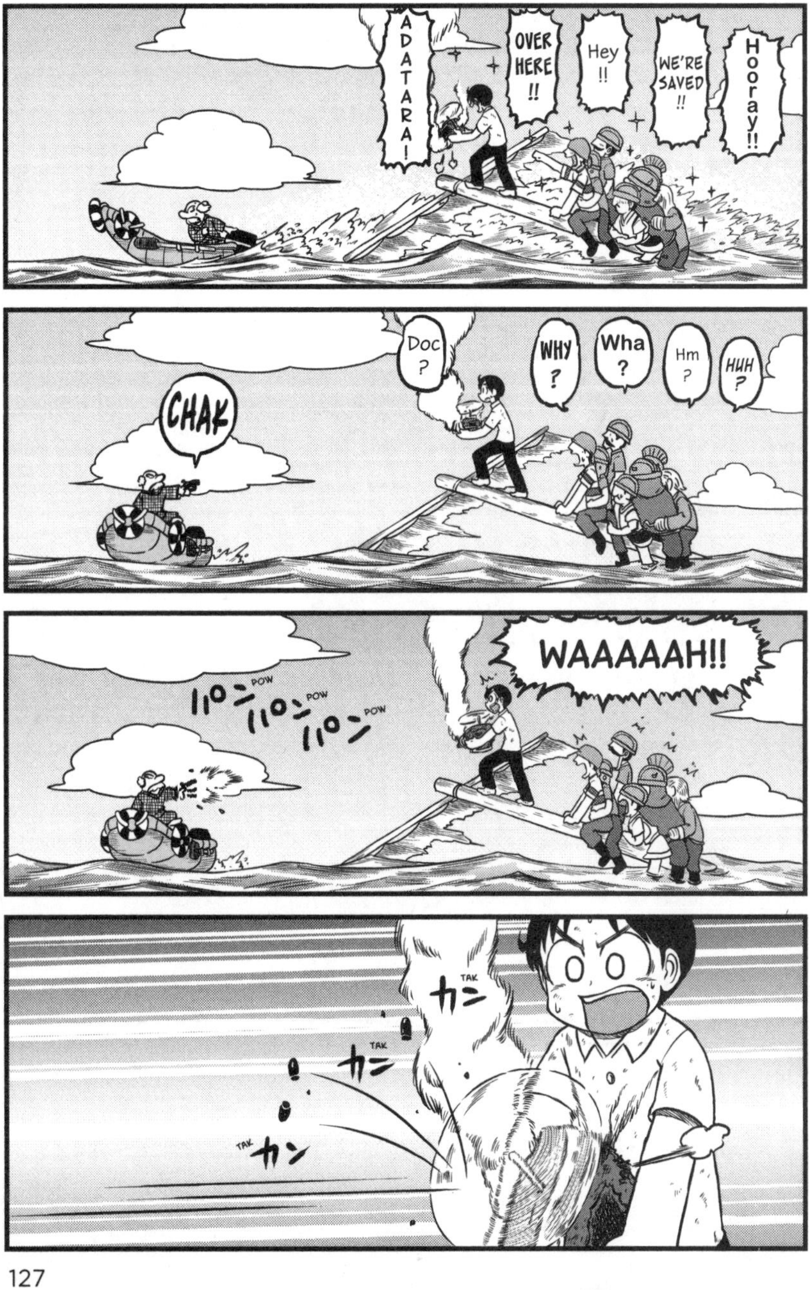
Hooray!!
WE'RE SAVED!!
Hey!!
OVER HERE!!
ADATARA!
HUH?
Hm?
Wha?
WHY?
Doc?
CHAK
WAAAAAH!!
パン POW
パン POW
パン POW
カン TAK
カン TAK
カン TAK

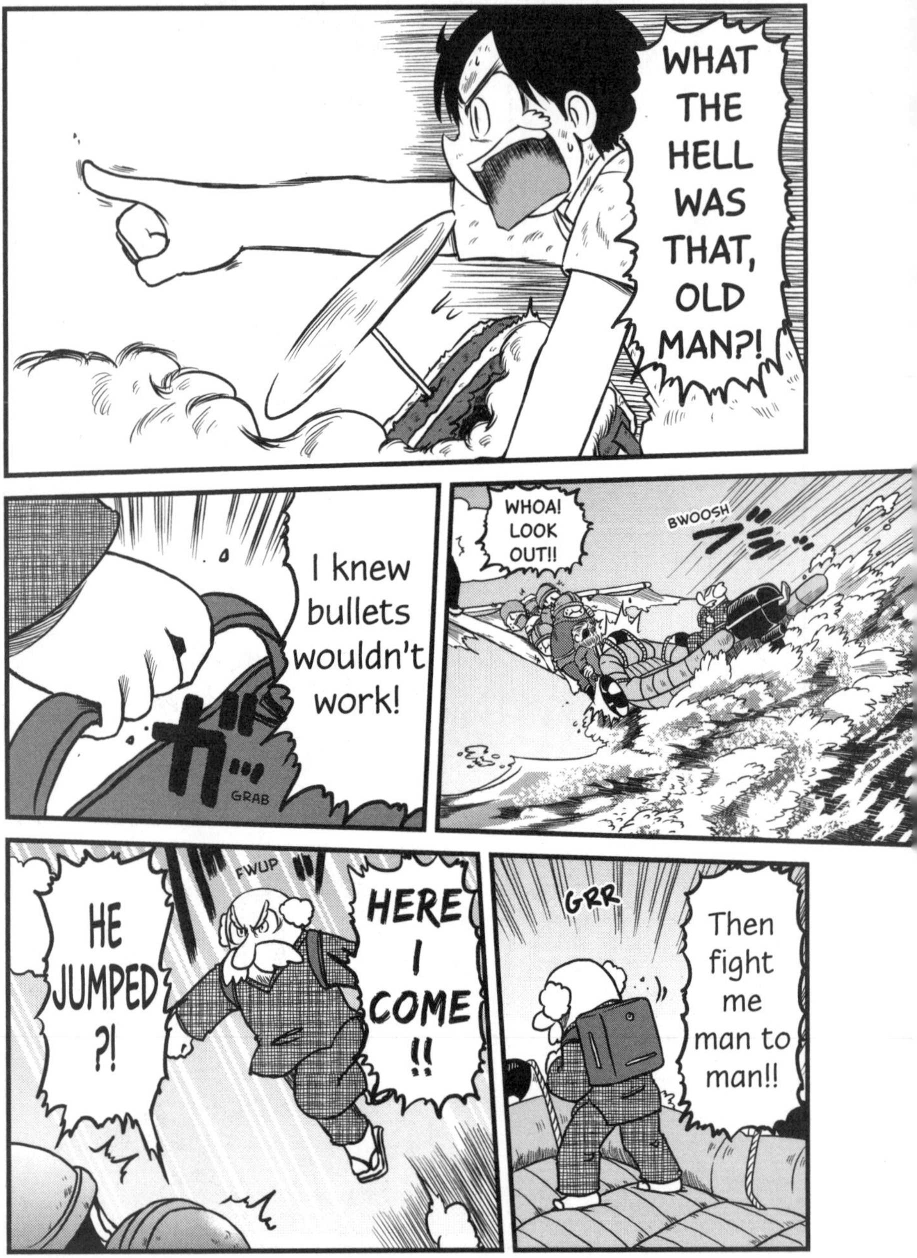
WHAT THE HELL WAS THAT, OLD MAN?!
WHOA! LOOK OUT!!
BWOOSH
I knew bullets wouldn't work!
GRAB
GRR
Then fight me man to man!!
FWUP
HERE I COME!!
HE JUMPED?!

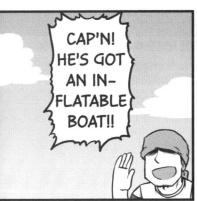

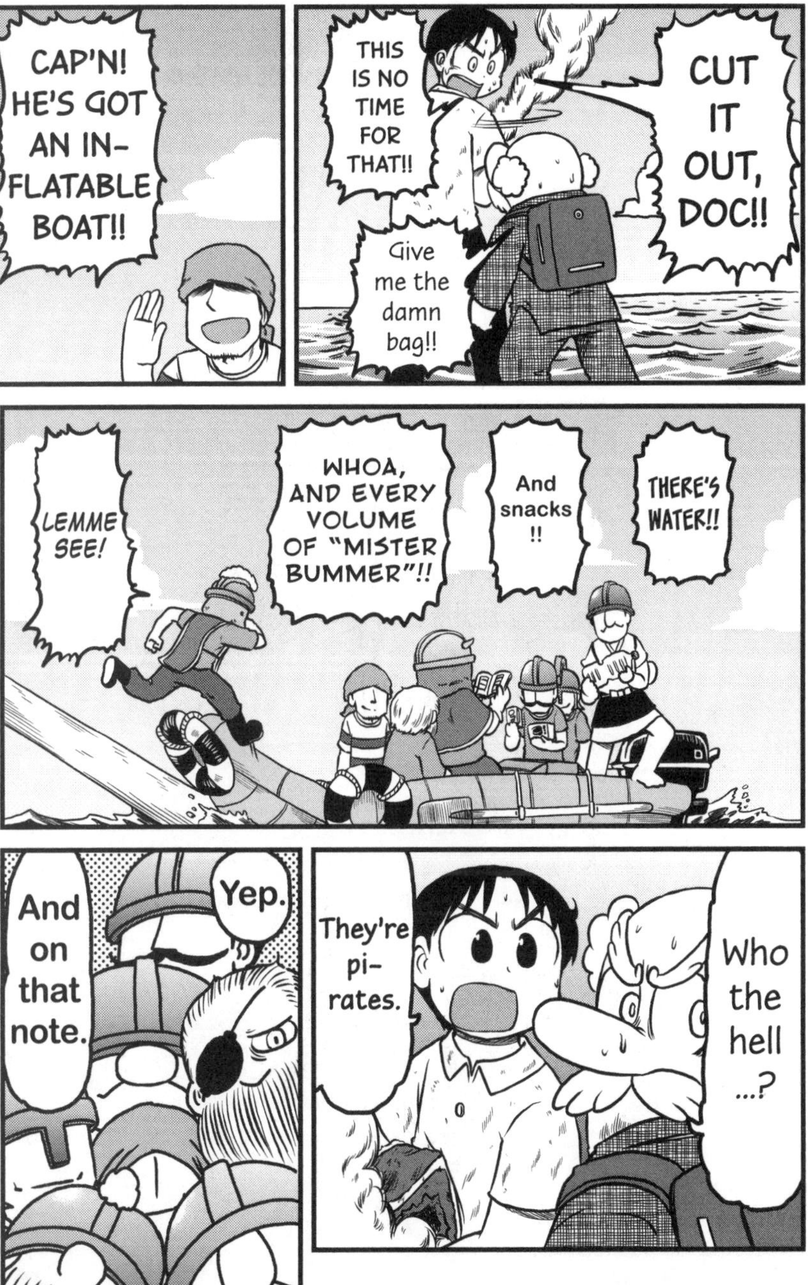
CUT IT OUT, DOC!!
THIS IS NO TIME FOR THAT!!
Give me the damn bag!!
CAP'N! HE'S GOT AN IN-FLATABLE BOAT!!
THERE'S WATER!!
And snacks!!
WHOA, AND EVERY VOLUME OF "MISTER BUMMER"!!
LEMME SEE!
Who the hell...?
They're pi-rates.
Yep.
And on that note.

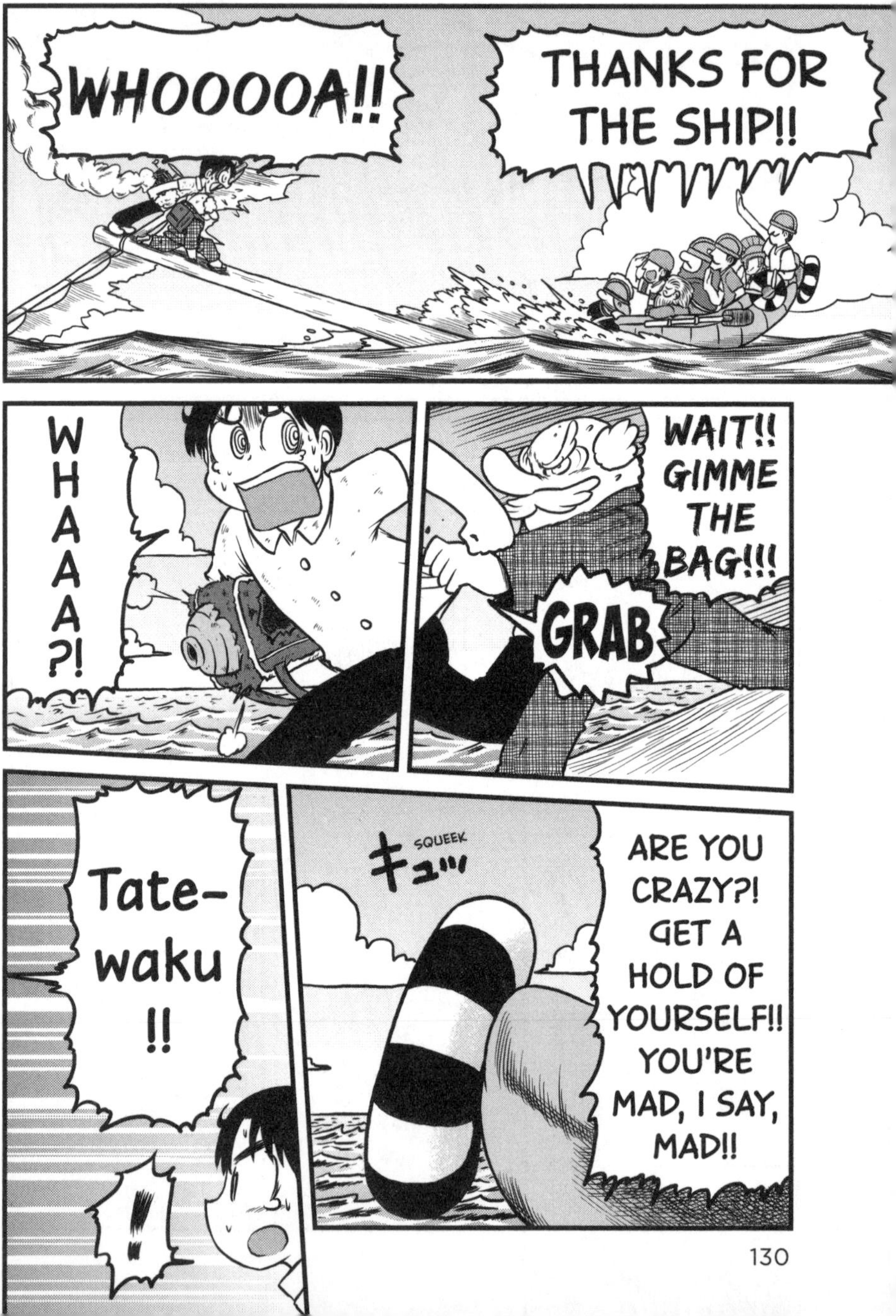
THANKS FOR THE SHIP!!
WHOOOOA!!
WAIT!! GIMME THE BAG!!!
GRAB
WHAAAA?!
キュッ SQUEEK
ARE YOU CRAZY?! GET A HOLD OF YOURSELF!! YOU'RE MAD, I SAY, MAD!!
Tate-waku !!
!

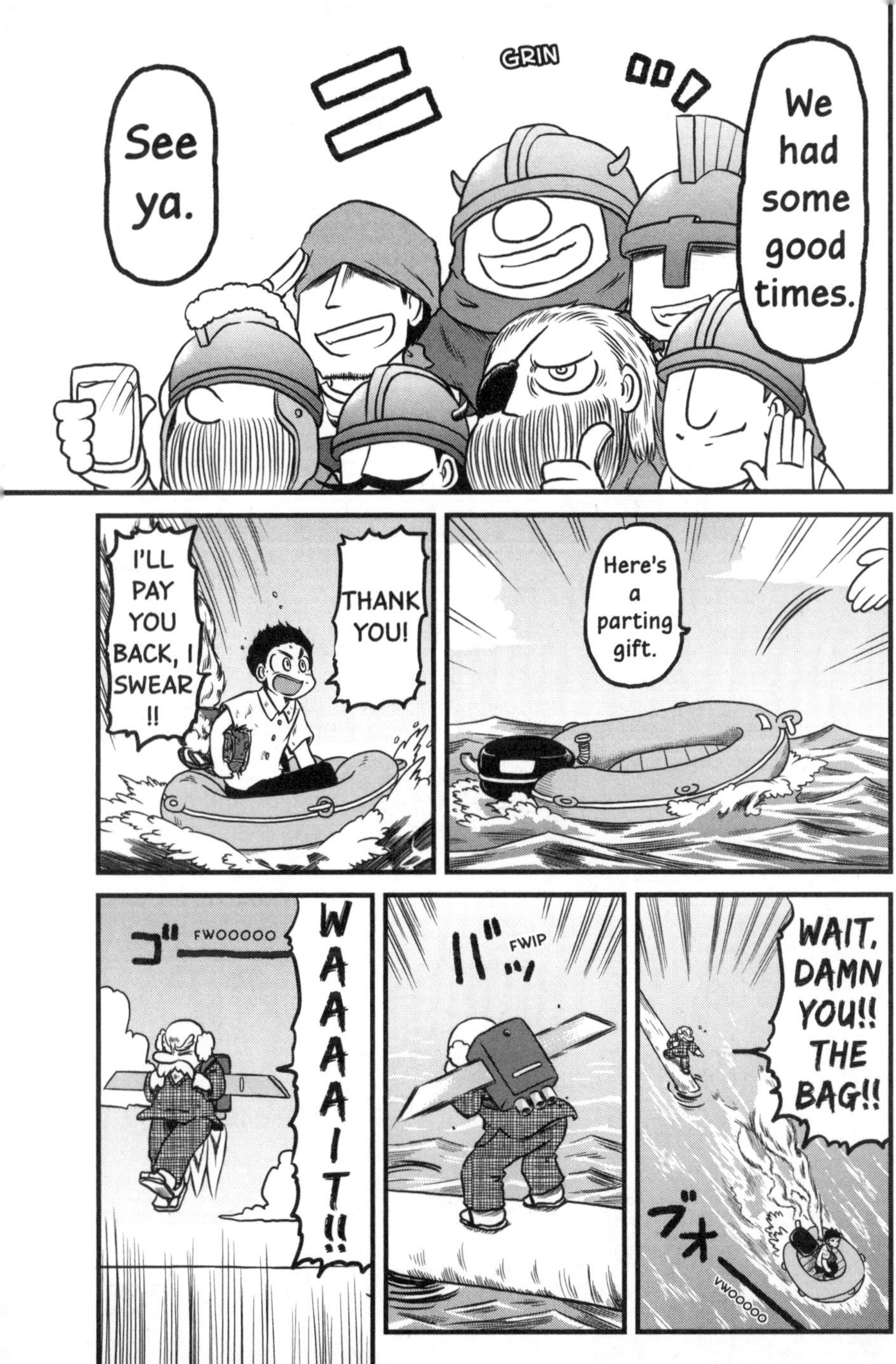
We had some good times.
GRIN
See ya.
Here's a parting gift.
THANK YOU!
I'LL PAY YOU BACK, I SWEAR!!
WAIT, DAMN YOU!! THE BAG!!
ブオ
VWOOOOO
バッ
FWIP
WAAAAAIT!!
ゴー
FWOOOOO

Soaking my bare feet in a cool fountain
Gazing up at the skyscrapers
Just wearing my favorite clothes
I'm not doing anything wrong

Cruising around town with a golden steering wheel
Hooked on having fun
I want to see the sights
The boob tube will never show me

Hang on to the way your heart beats
The moment the needle drops
It's a great collection
But I want to keep on adding to it

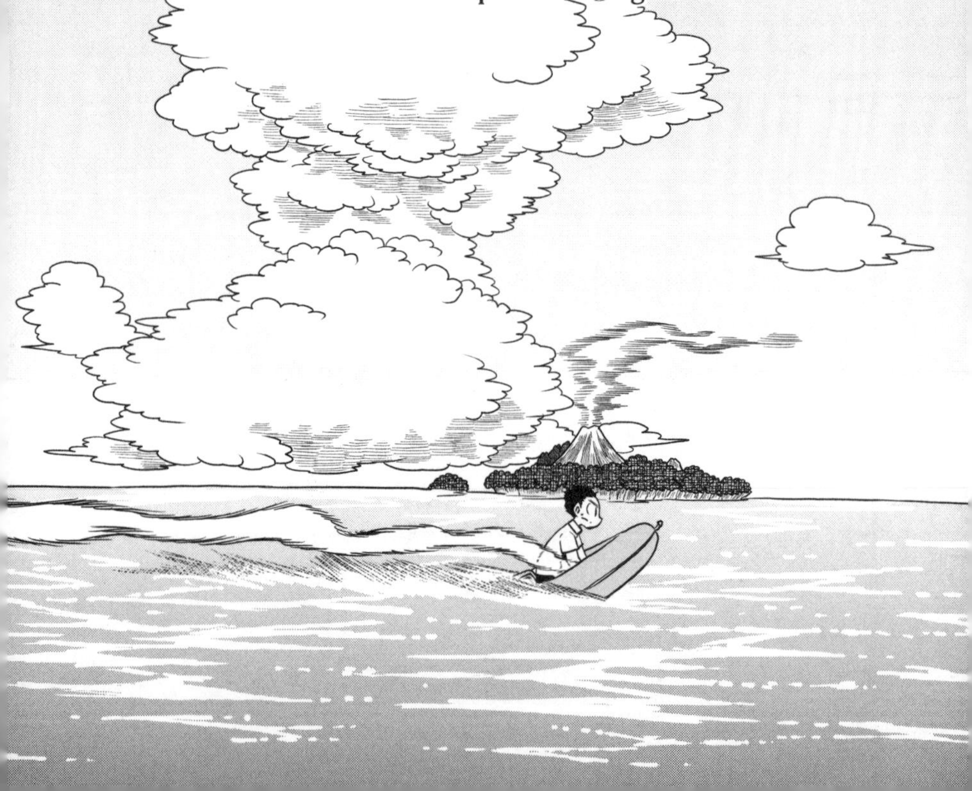

Even if I'm sleepy
Even if they hate me
Even when I'm old
I'll never stop, I just can't stop

They're diamonds
AH, AH, these little scenes
AH, AH, I don't know how to put it into words
But they're my treasures

I felt it in my bones that day
AH, AH, that hunch was the real thing
AH, it's those feelings
That keep me going now

BGM: "Diamond" by Princess Princess

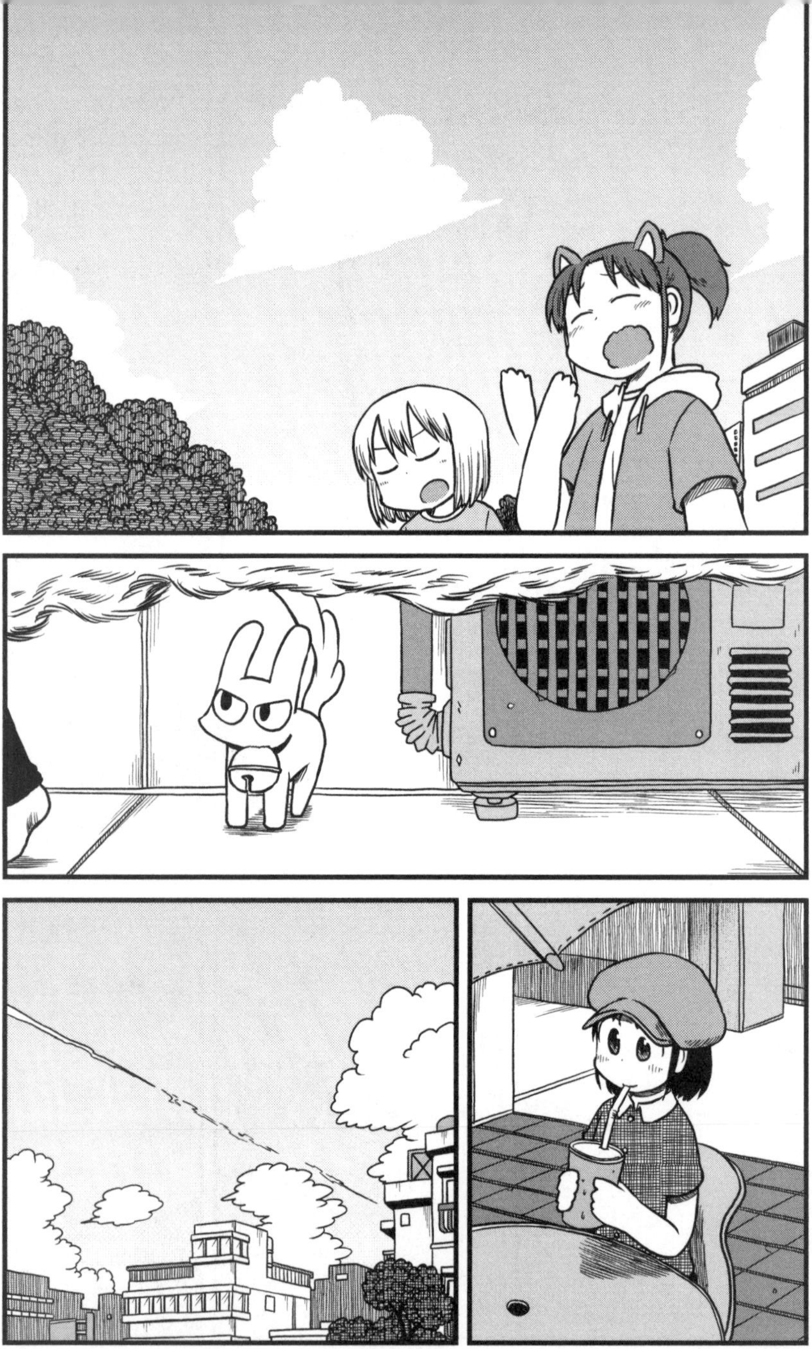

ding-dong

IZUMI

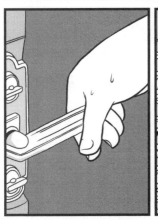

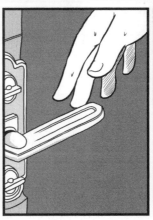

135

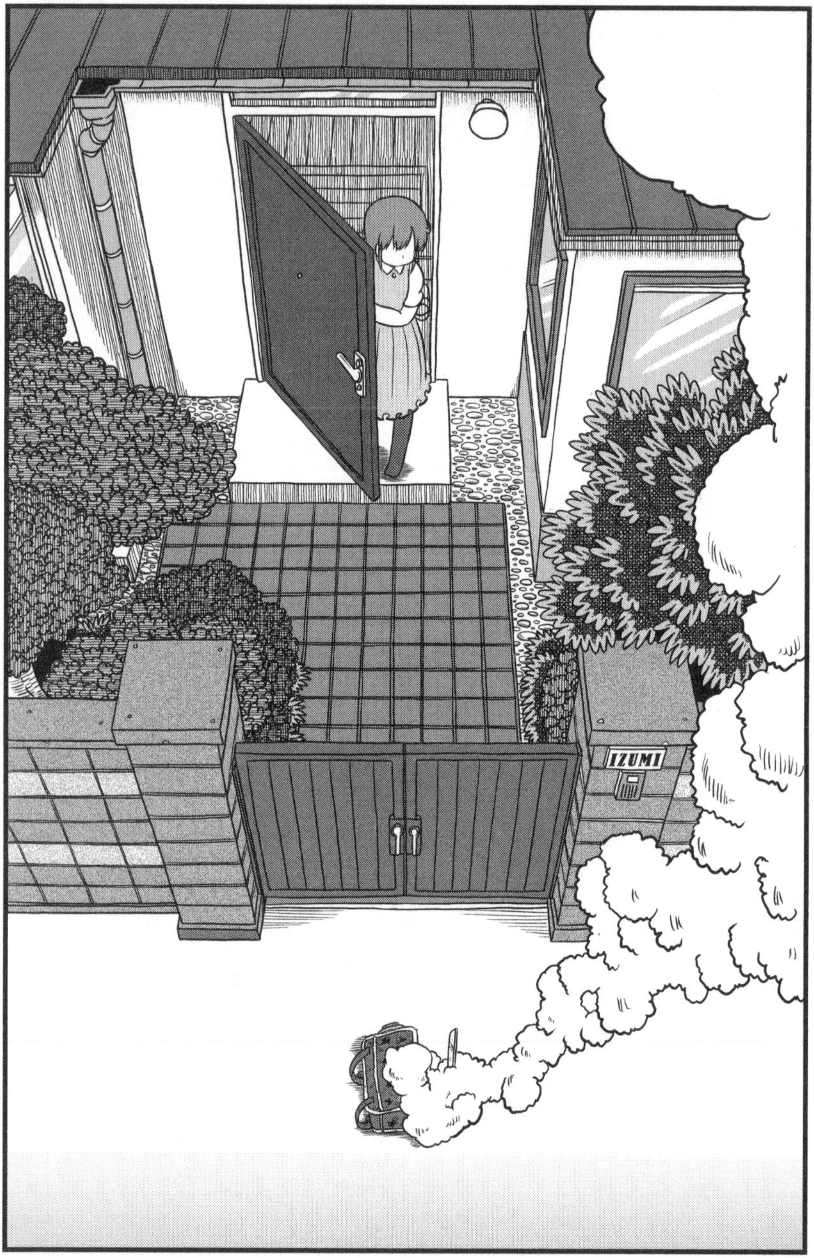
IZUMI

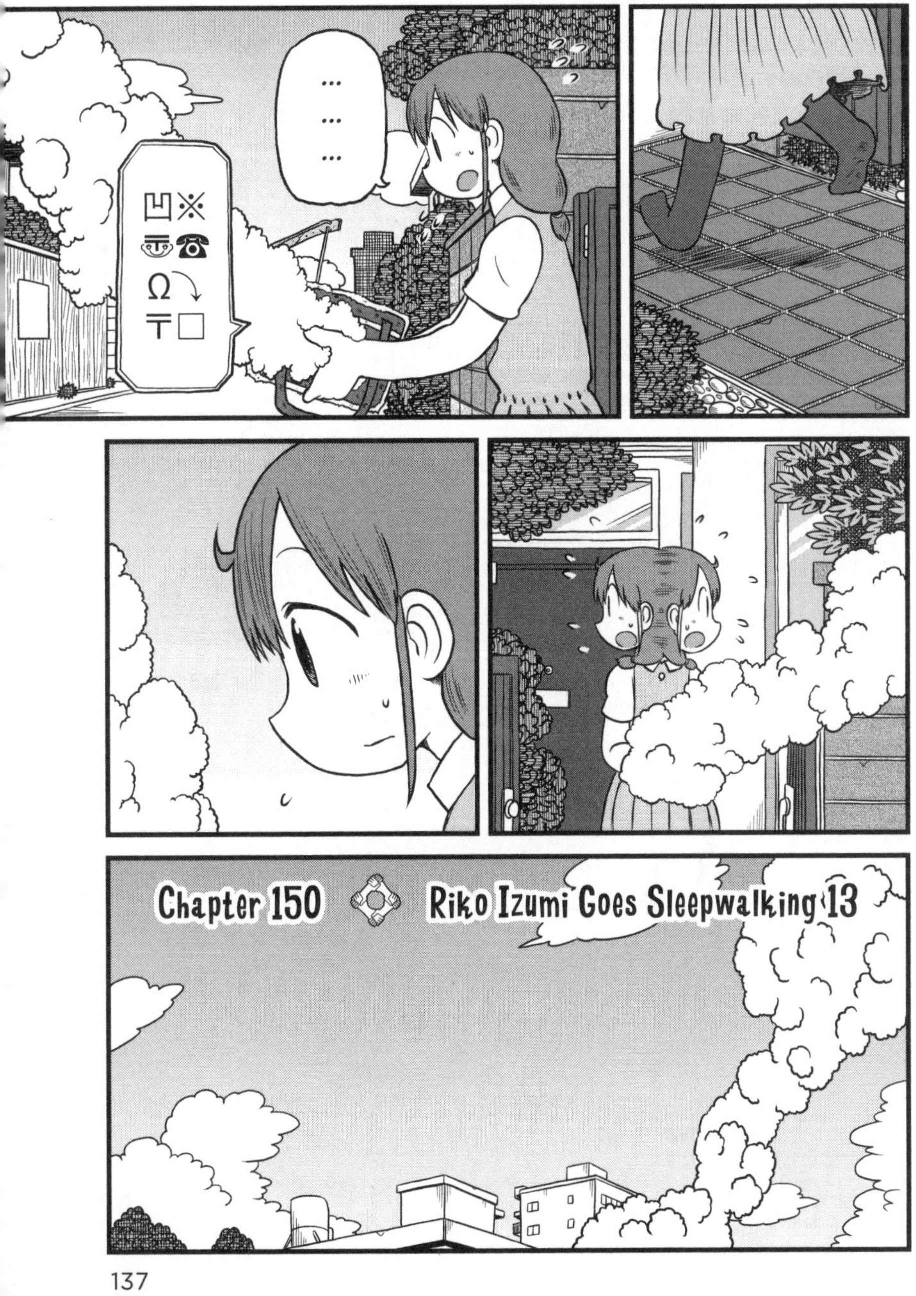
… … …
凹※ 〒☎ Ω↷ 〒□
Chapter 150 Riko Izumi Goes Sleepwalking 13

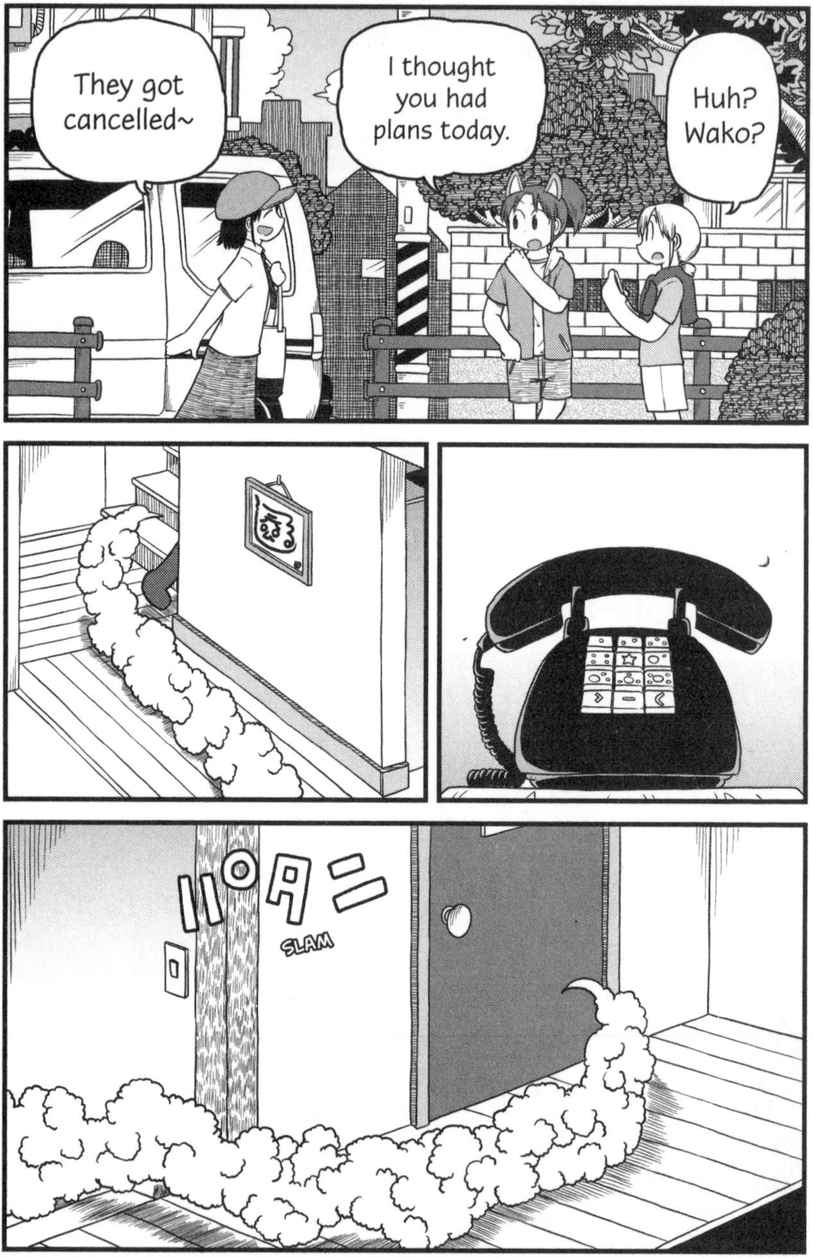
Huh? Wako?
I thought you had plans today.
They got cancelled~
SLAM

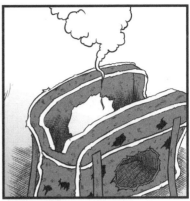

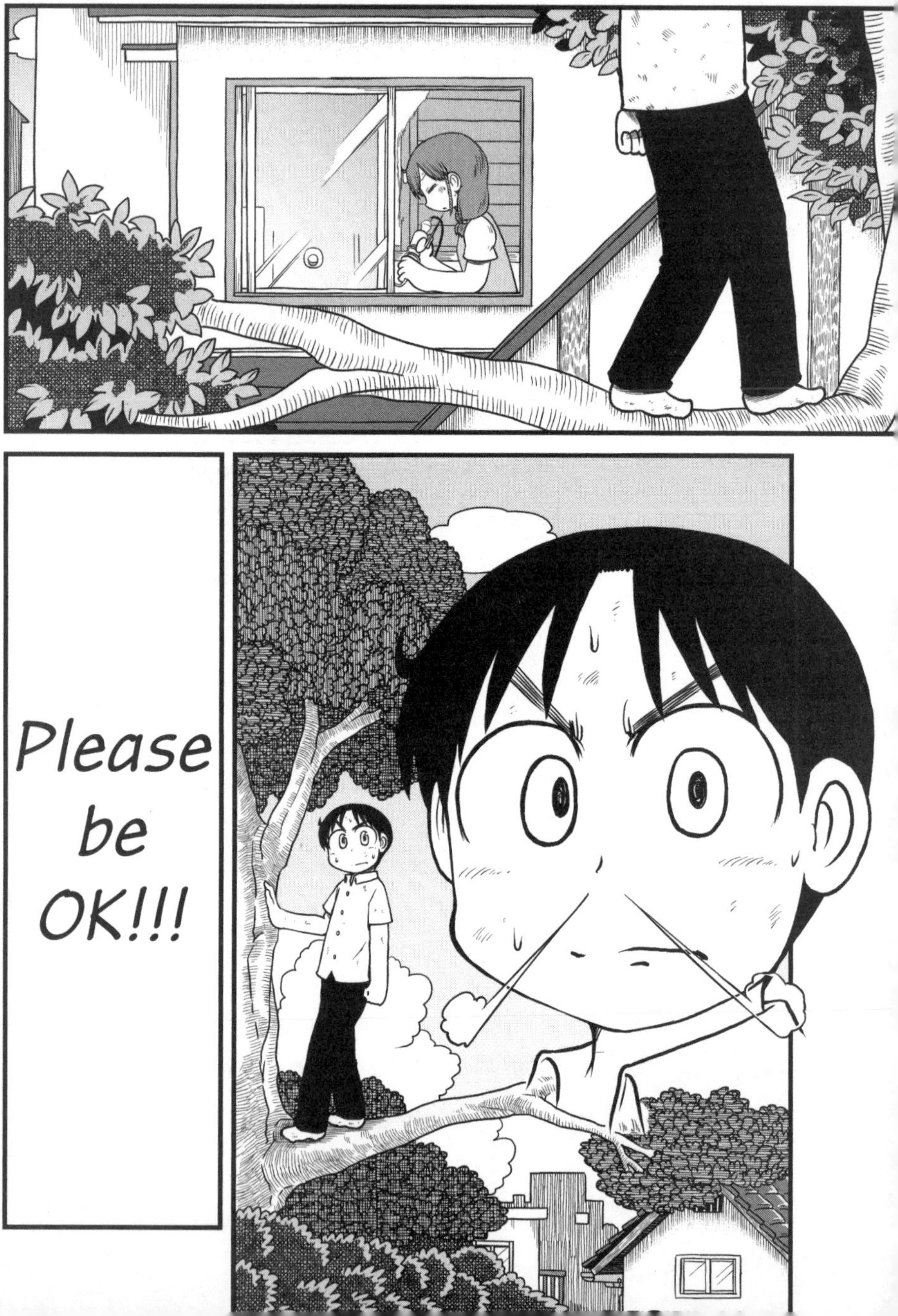
Please be OK!!!

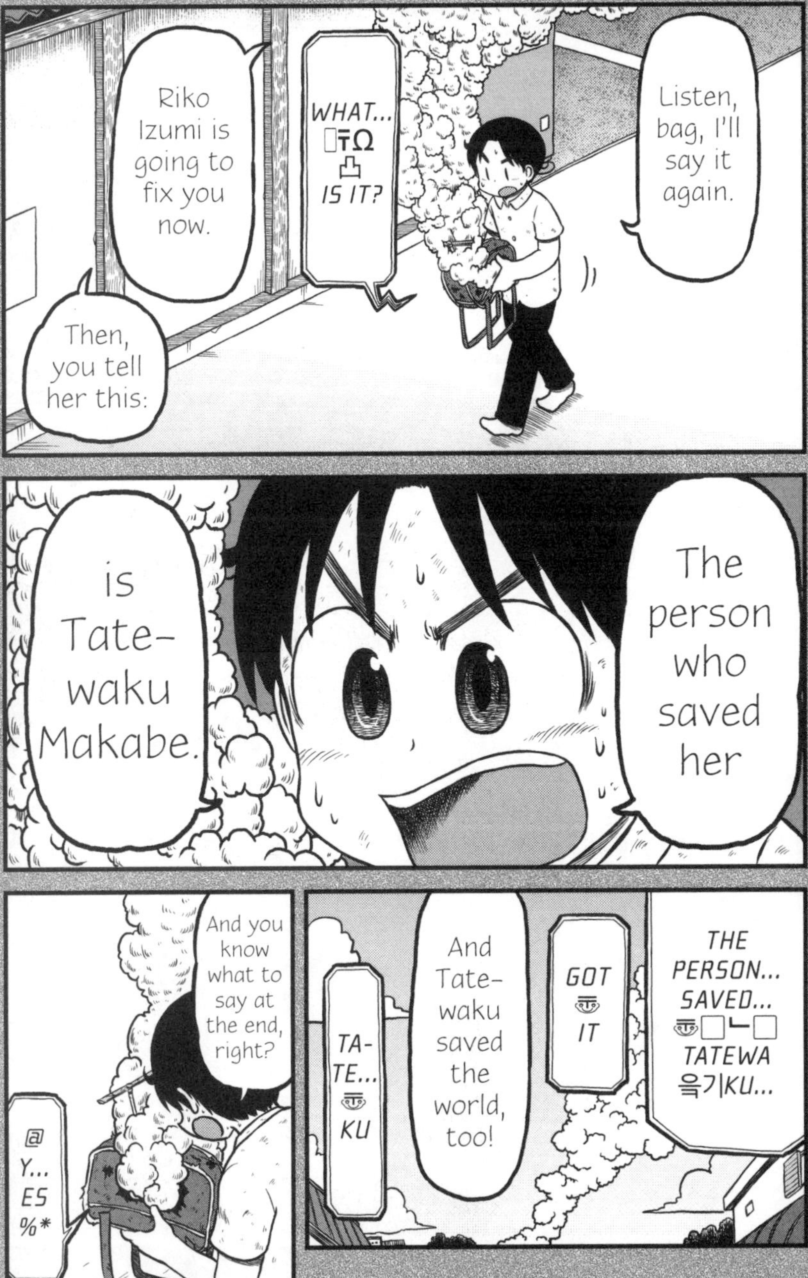
Listen, bag, I'll say it again.
WHAT... IS IT?
Riko Izumi is going to fix you now.
Then, you tell her this:
The person who saved her
is Tate-waku Makabe.
THE PERSON... SAVED... TATEWA KU...
GOT IT
And Tate-waku saved the world, too!
TA-TE... KU
And you know what to say at the end, right?
@ Y... ES %*

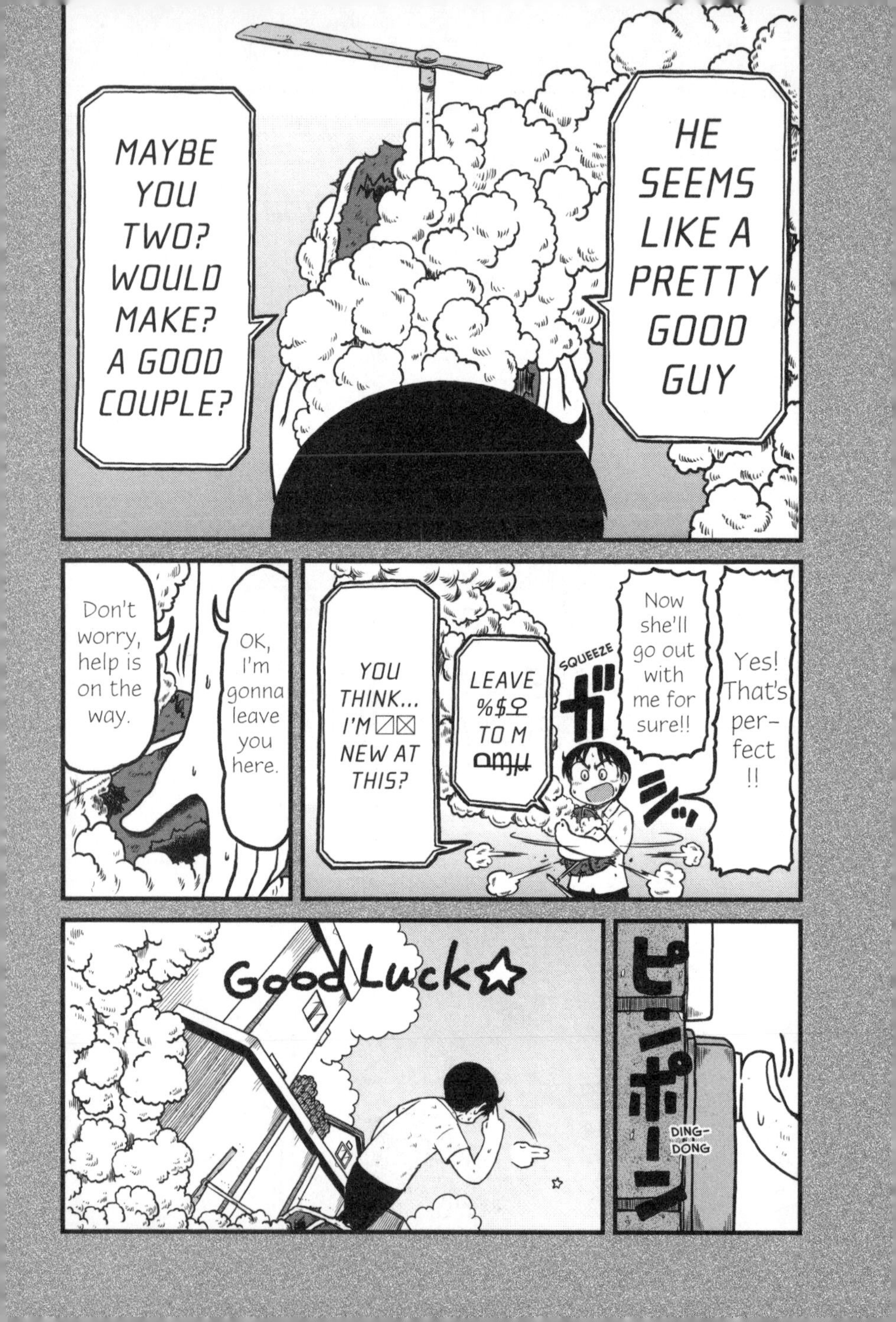
HE SEEMS LIKE A PRETTY GOOD GUY
MAYBE YOU TWO? WOULD MAKE? A GOOD COUPLE?
Yes! That's per-fect!!
Now she'll go out with me for sure!!
SQUEEZE
LEAVE %$오 TO M
YOU THINK... I'M ⊠⊠ NEW AT THIS?
OK, I'm gonna leave you here.
Don't worry, help is on the way.
DING-DONG
Good Luck☆

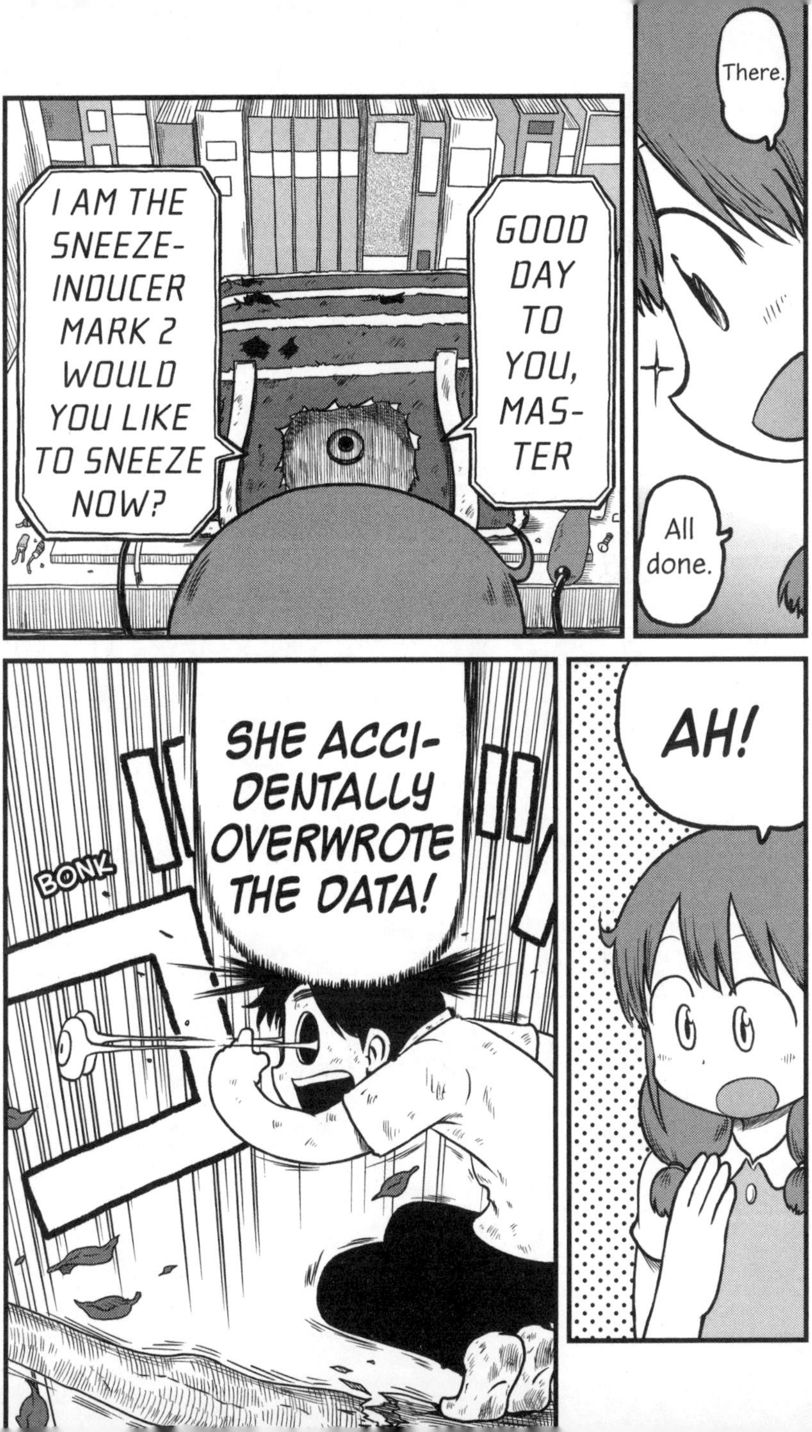
There.
All done.
GOOD DAY TO YOU, MAS-TER
I AM THE SNEEZE-INDUCER MARK 2 WOULD YOU LIKE TO SNEEZE NOW?
AH!
SHE ACCI-DENTALLY OVERWROTE THE DATA!
BONK

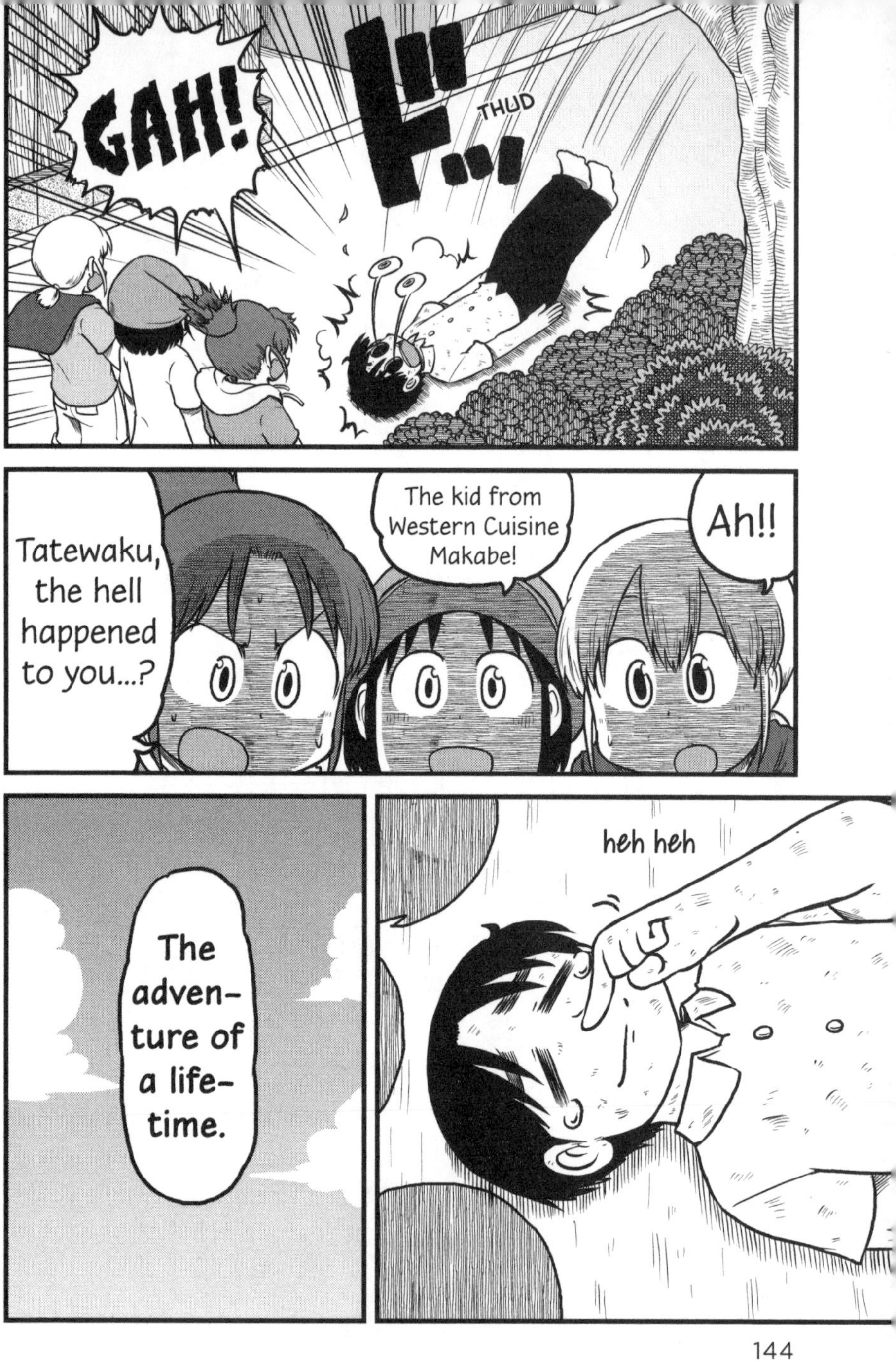
THUD
GAH!
Ah!!
The kid from Western Cuisine Makabe!
Tatewaku, the hell happened to you...?
heh heh
The adventure of a lifetime.

CITY

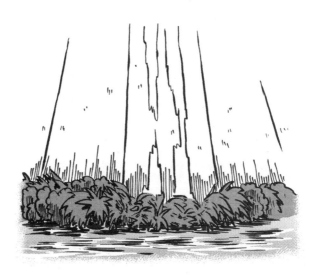

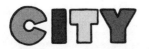

CONTENTS

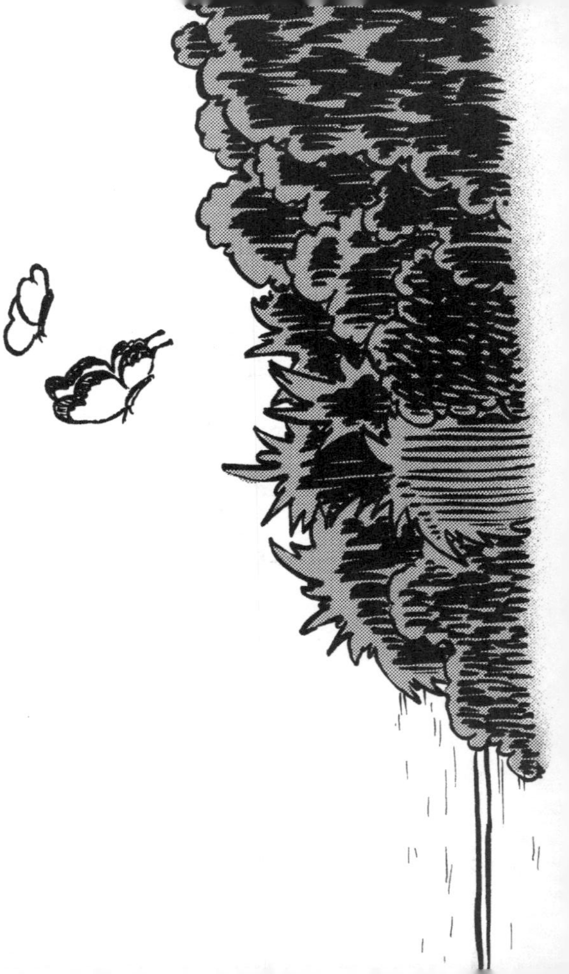

CITY

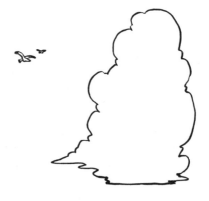

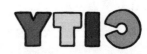

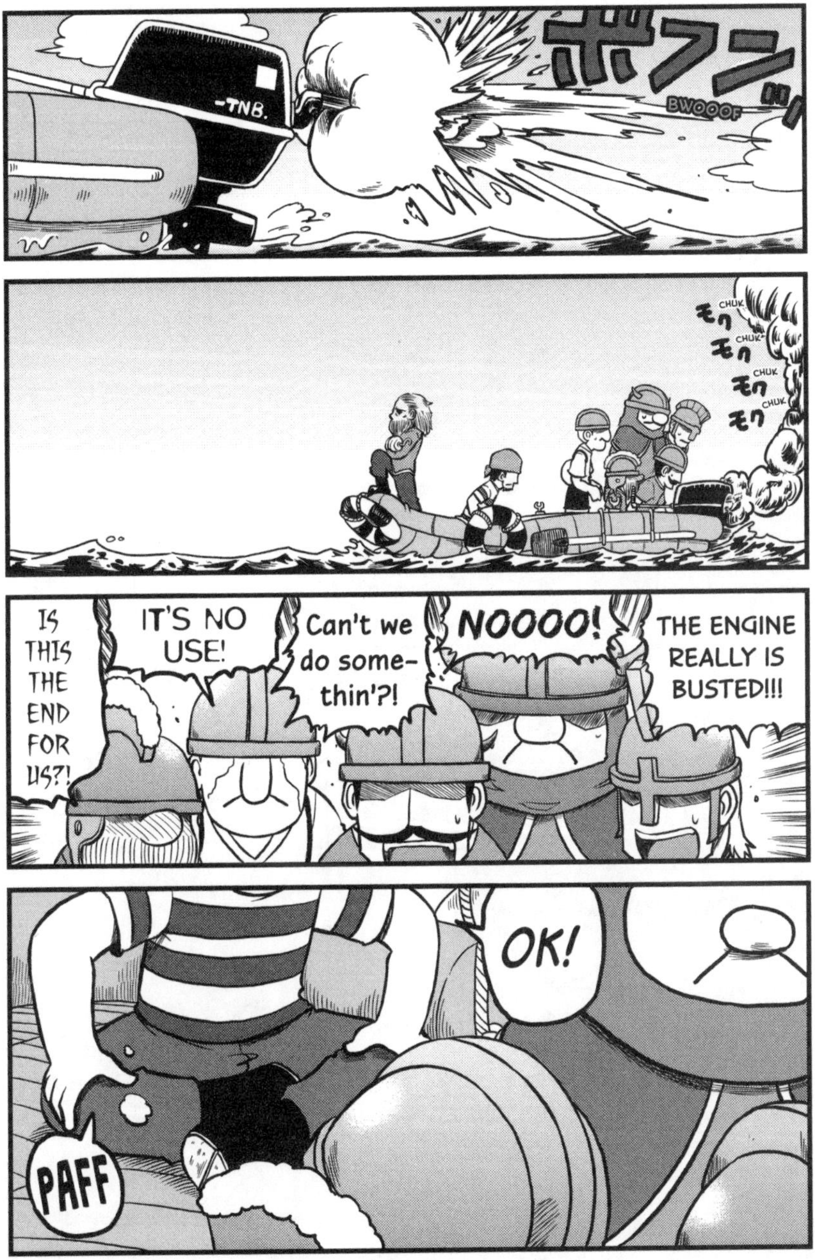
ボフン
BWOOOF
モク
CHUK
モク
CHUK
モク
CHUK
モク
CHUK
THE ENGINE REALLY IS BUSTED!!!
NOOOO!
Can't we do some-thin'?!
IT'S NO USE!
IS THIS THE END FOR US?!
OK!
PAFF

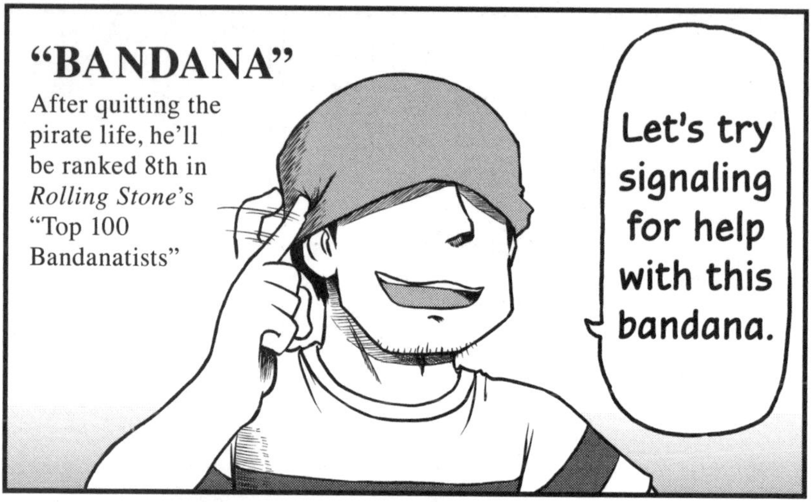
Let's try signaling for help with this bandana.
"BANDANA"
After quitting the pirate life, he'll be ranked 8th in *Rolling Stone*'s "Top 100 Bandanatists"

Chapter 151 Pirate Epilogue

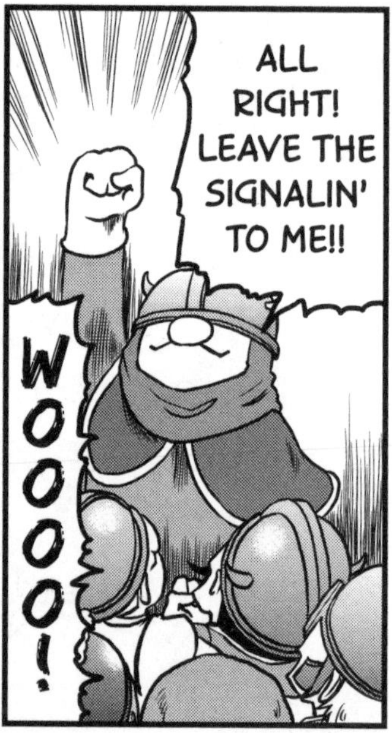
ALL RIGHT! LEAVE THE SIGNALIN' TO ME!!
WOOOOO!

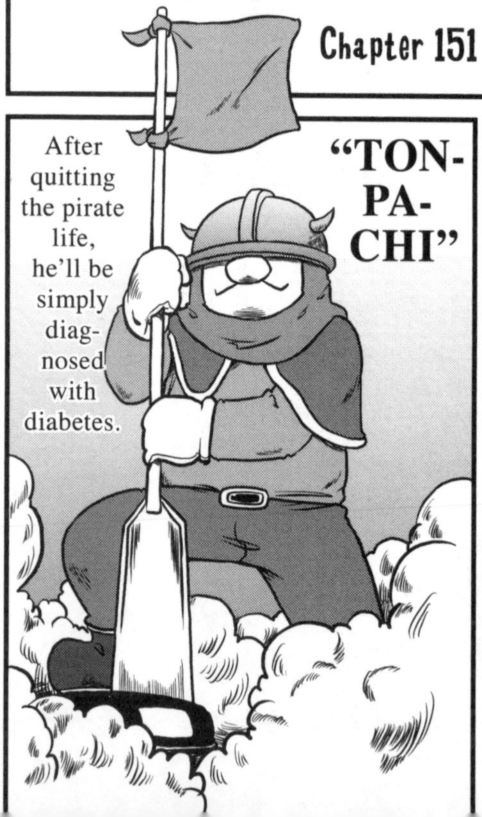
"TON-PA-CHI"
After quitting the pirate life, he'll be simply diag-nosed with diabetes.

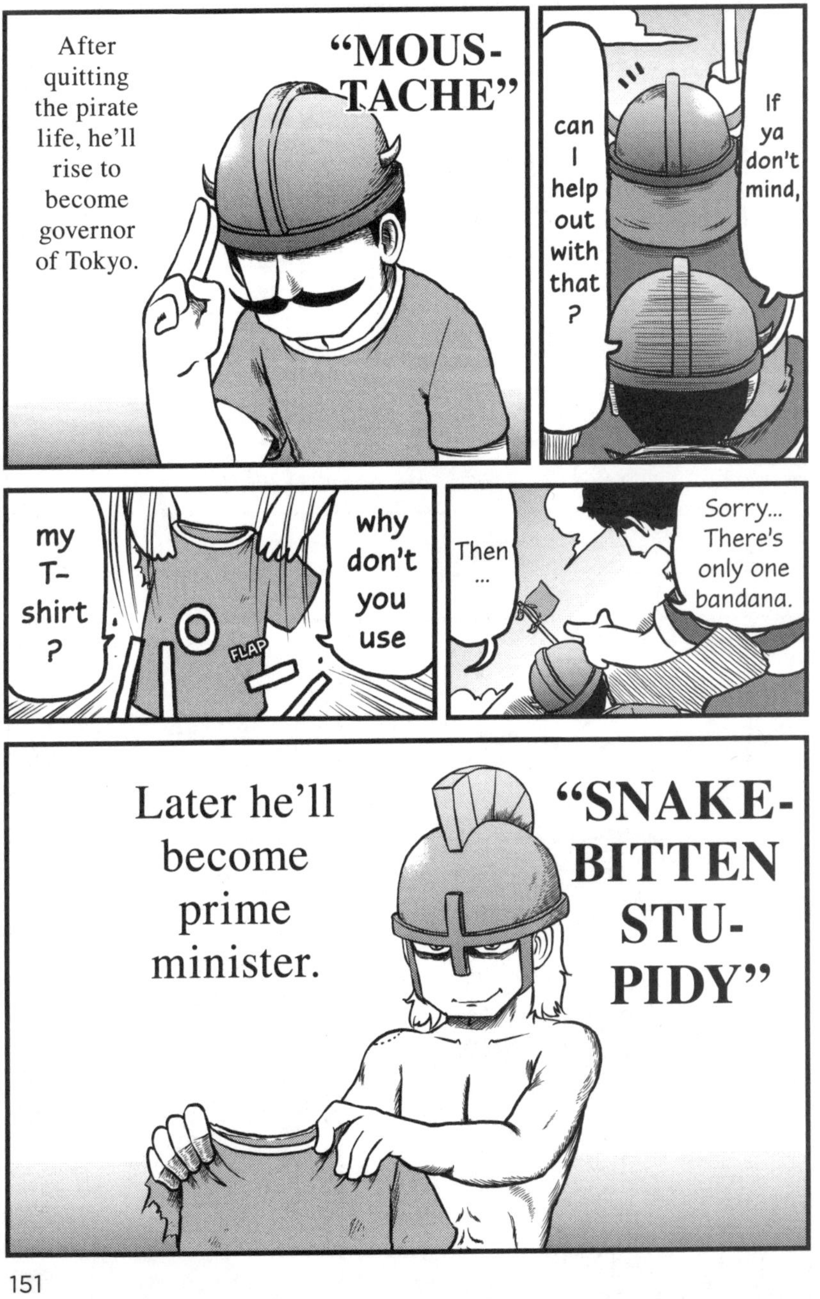
If ya don't mind,
can I help out with that?
"MOUSTACHE"
After quitting the pirate life, he'll rise to become governor of Tokyo.
Sorry... There's only one bandana.
Then...
why don't you use
FLAP
my T-shirt?
"SNAKE-BITTEN STUPIDY"
Later he'll become prime minister.

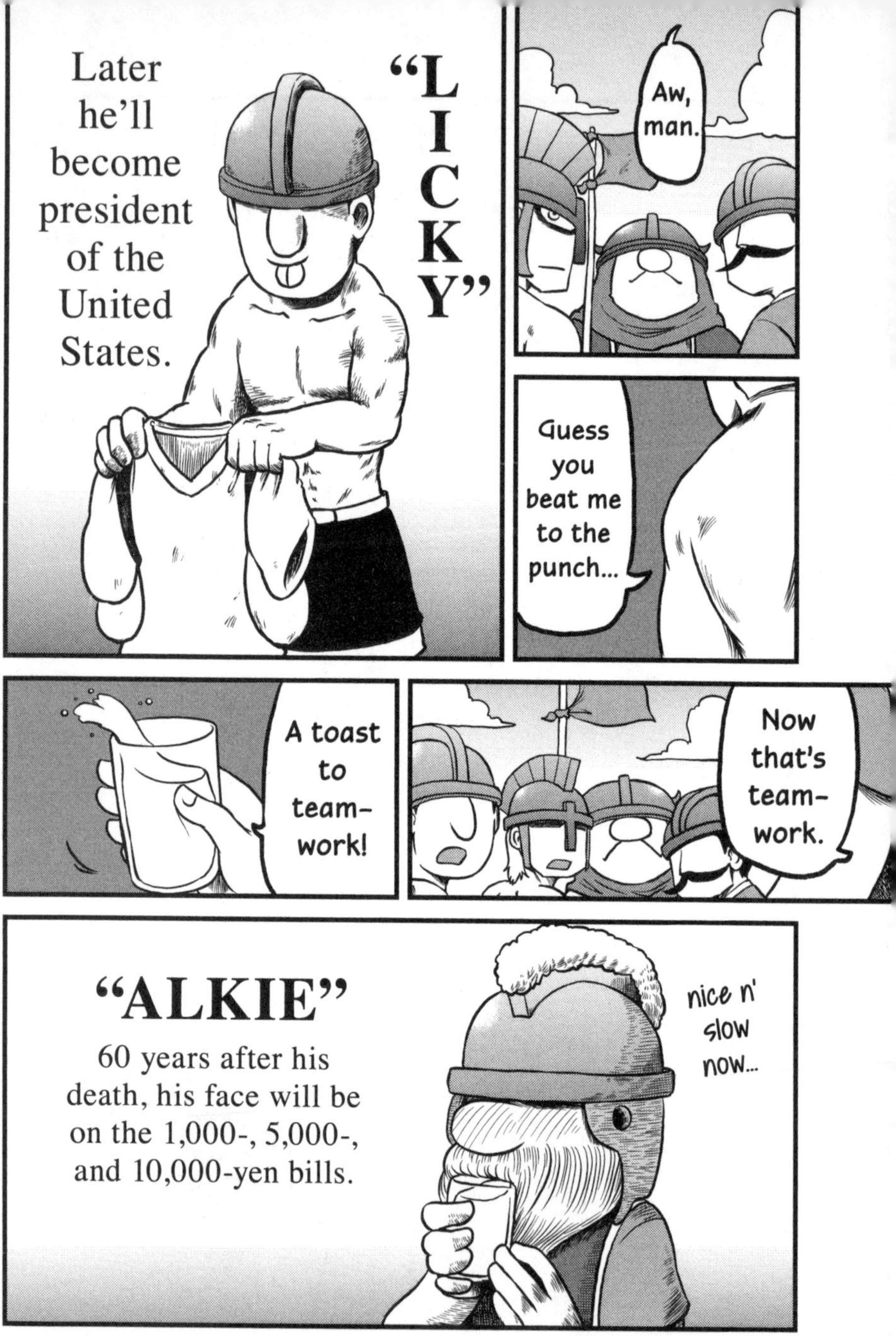
Aw, man.
Guess you beat me to the punch...
"LICKY"
Later he'll become president of the United States.
Now that's team-work.
A toast to team-work!
nice n' slow now...
"ALKIE"
60 years after his death, his face will be on the 1,000-, 5,000-, and 10,000-yen bills.

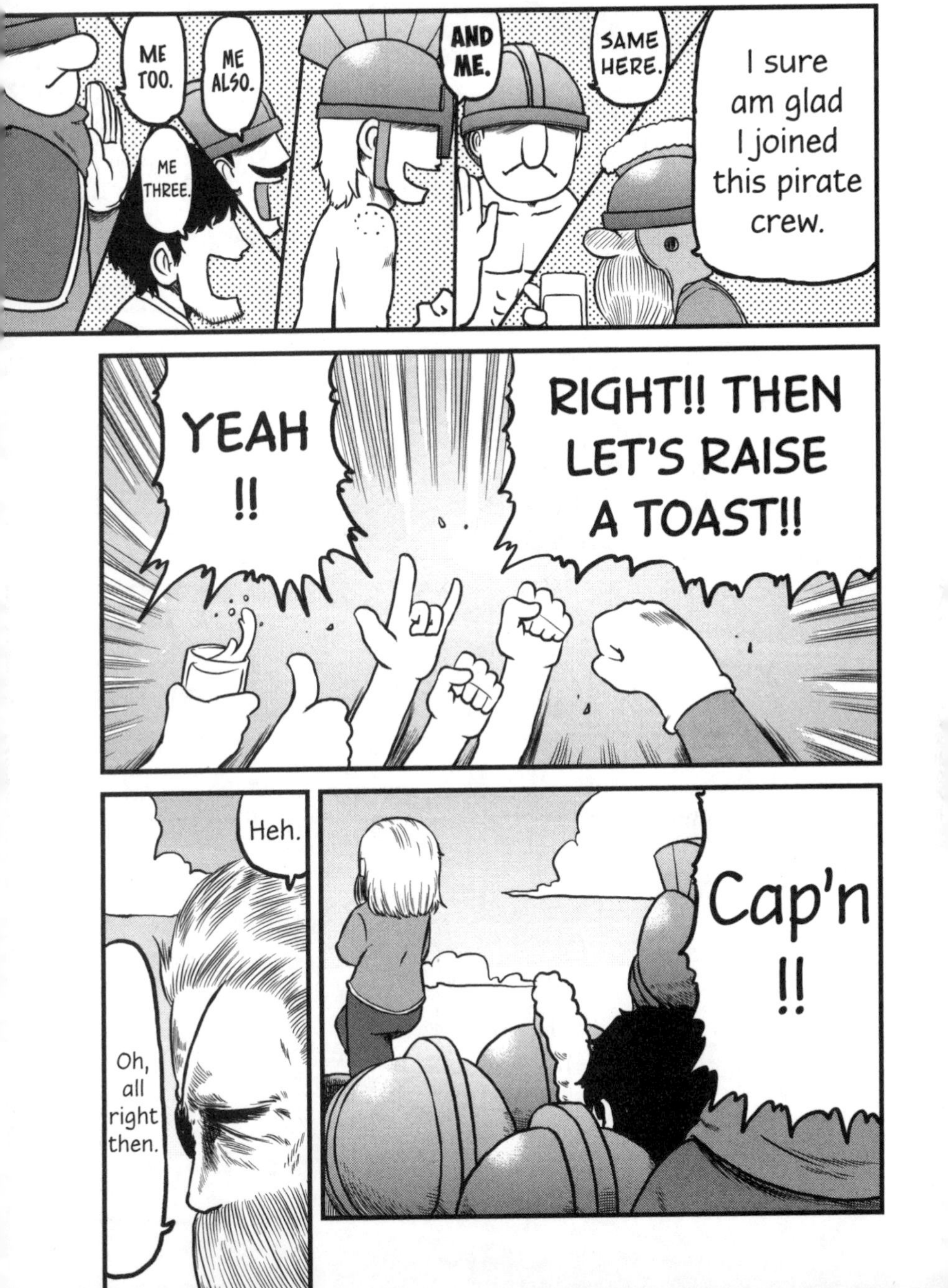
I sure am glad I joined this pirate crew.
SAME HERE.
AND ME.
ME ALSO.
ME TOO.
ME THREE.
RIGHT!! THEN LET'S RAISE A TOAST!!
YEAH !!
Cap'n !!
Heh.
Oh, all right then.

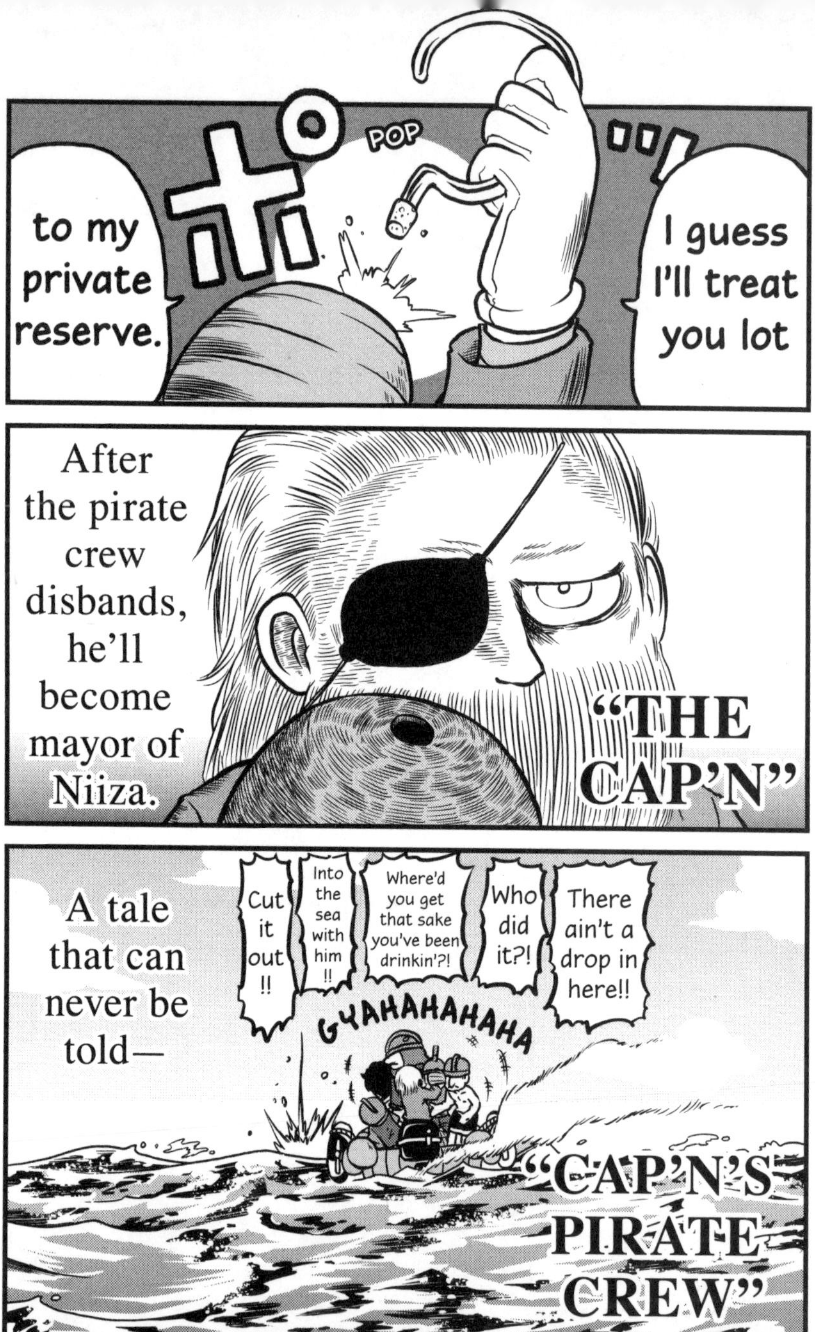
POP
I guess I'll treat you lot
to my private reserve.
After the pirate crew disbands, he'll become mayor of Niiza.
"THE CAP'N"
There ain't a drop in here!!
Who did it?!
Where'd you get that sake you've been drinkin'?!
Into the sea with him!!
Cut it out!!
GYAHAHAHAHAHA
A tale that can never be told—
"CAP'N'S PIRATE CREW"

CITY

SIDE STORY

CITY

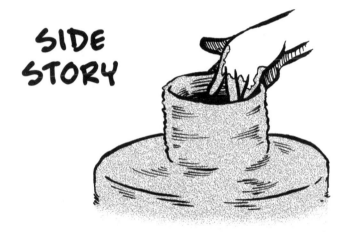

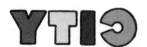

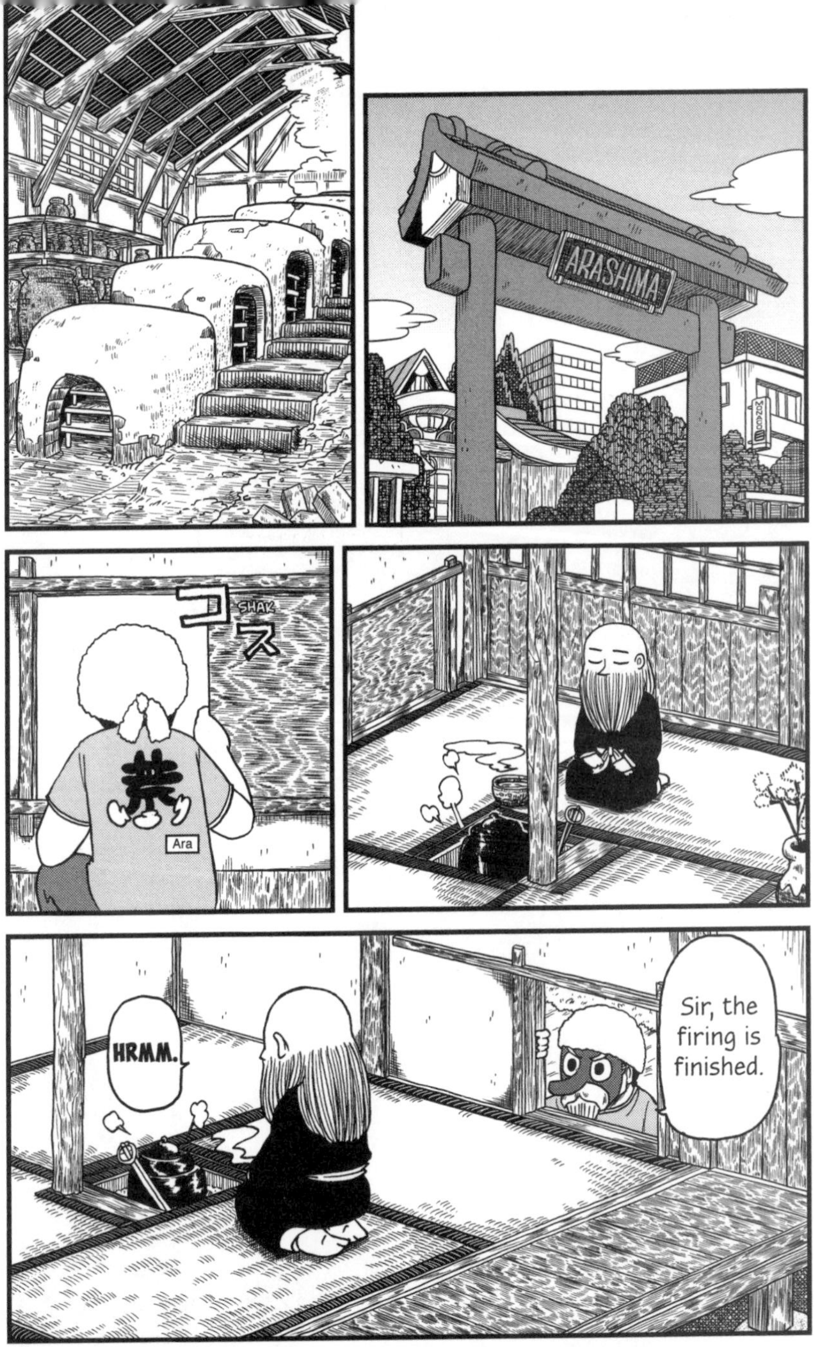
ARASHIMA
コス
SHAK
Ara
Sir, the firing is finished.
HRMM.

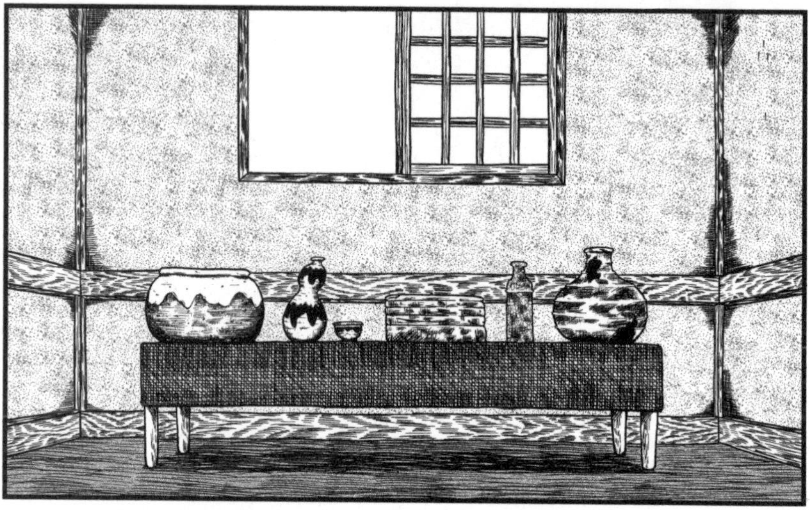

Chapter 152 ◇ Living National Treasure Souun Arashima

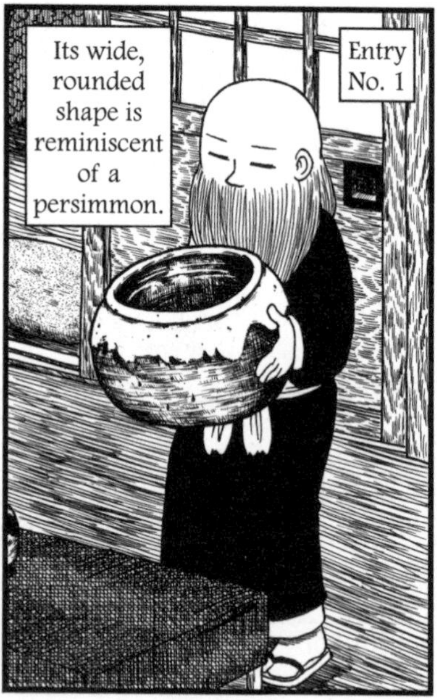
Entry No. 1
Its wide, rounded shape is reminiscent of a persimmon.

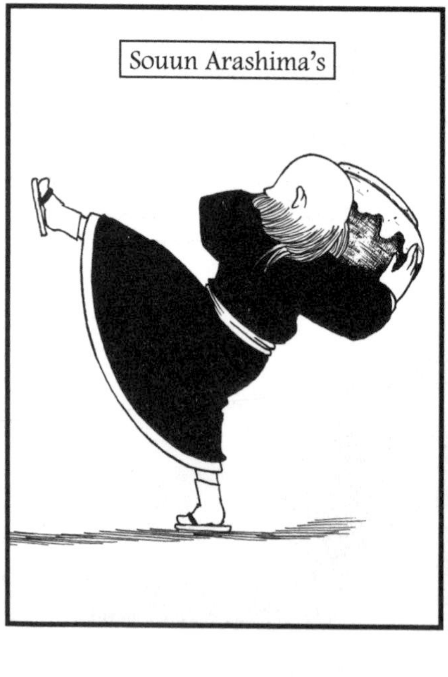
Souun Arashima's

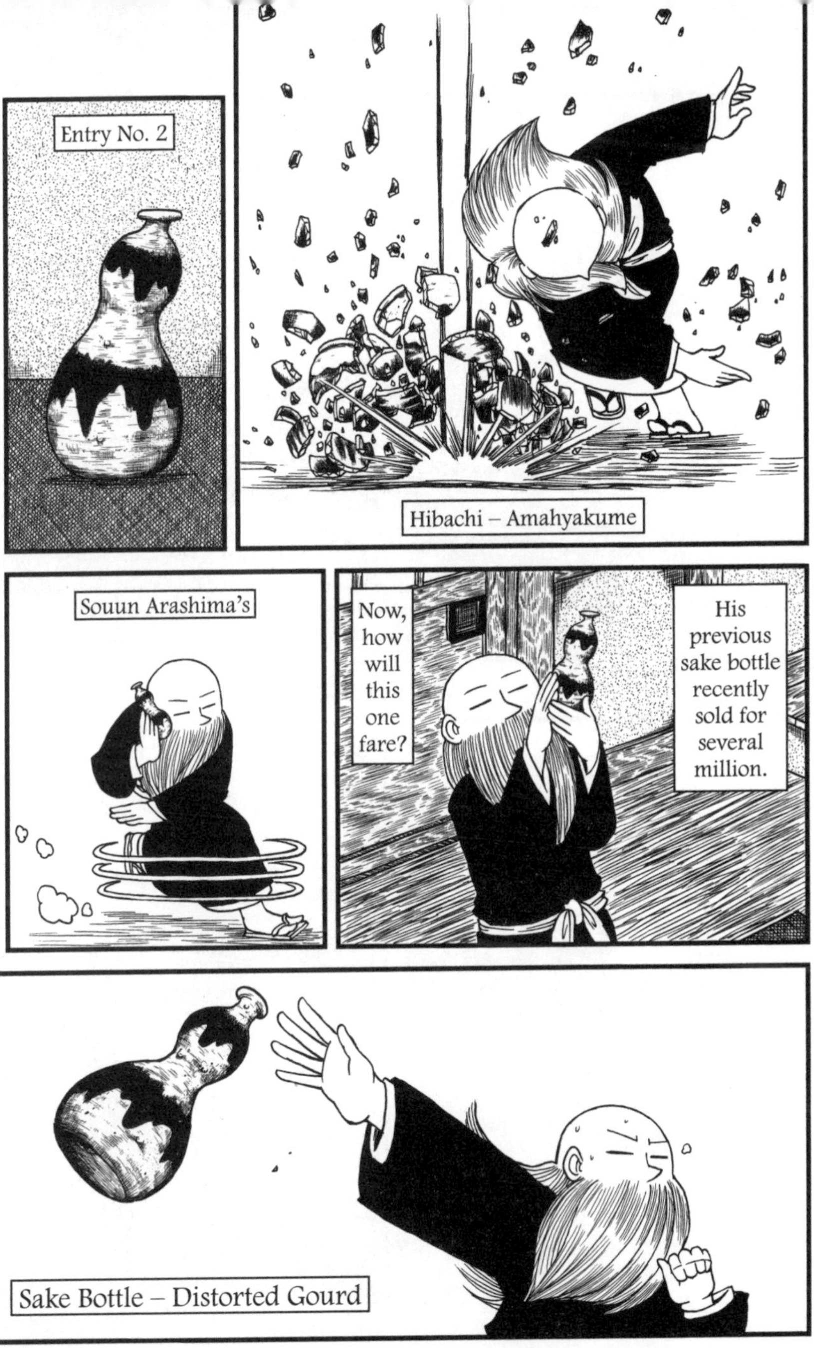
Hibachi – Amahyakume
Entry No. 2
His previous sake bottle recently sold for several million.
Now, how will this one fare?
Souun Arashima's
Sake Bottle – Distorted Gourd

Sake Cup (Set)

&

Entry No. 3

Birthed by "Vase Master Arashima"

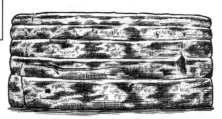

Souun Arashima's

and highly favored by the Rothschild family.

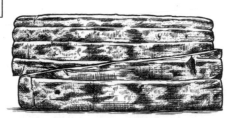

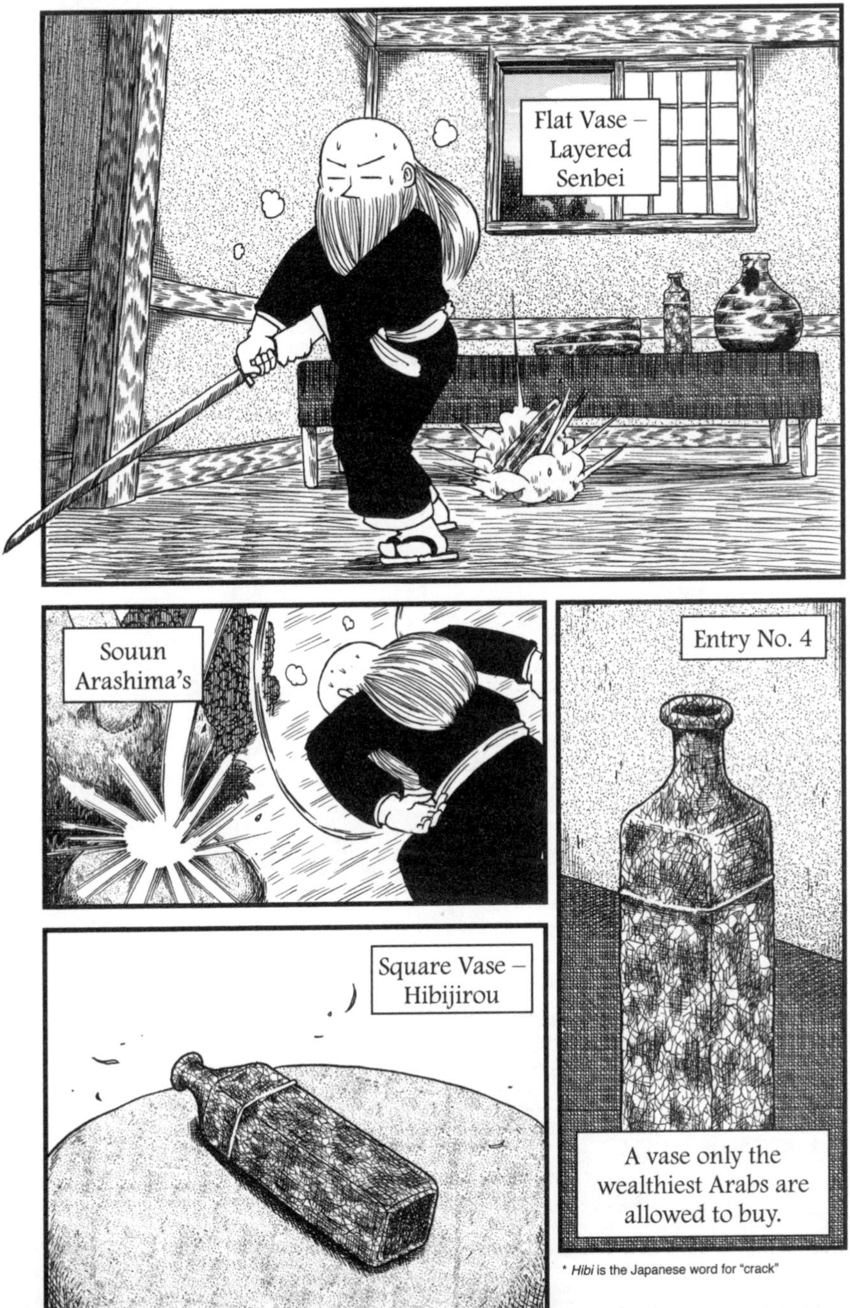
Flat Vase – Layered Senbei
Entry No. 4
A vase only the wealthiest Arabs are allowed to buy.
Souun Arashima's
Square Vase – Hibijirou

* *Hibi* is the Japanese word for "crack"

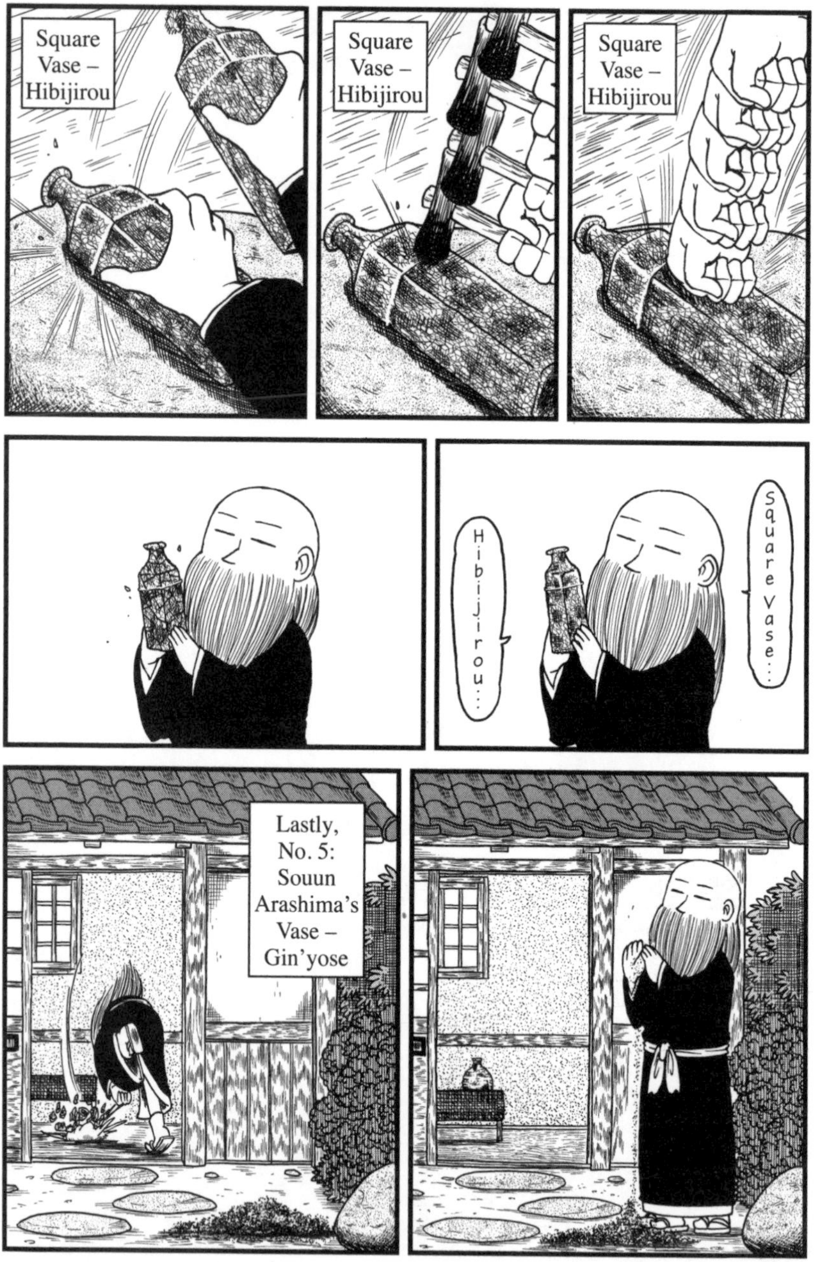
Square Vase – Hibijirou
Square Vase – Hibijirou
Square Vase – Hibijirou
Square Vase…
Hibijirou…
Lastly, No. 5: Souun Arashima’s Vase – Gin’yose

NEXT

CITY

Recent Author Photo

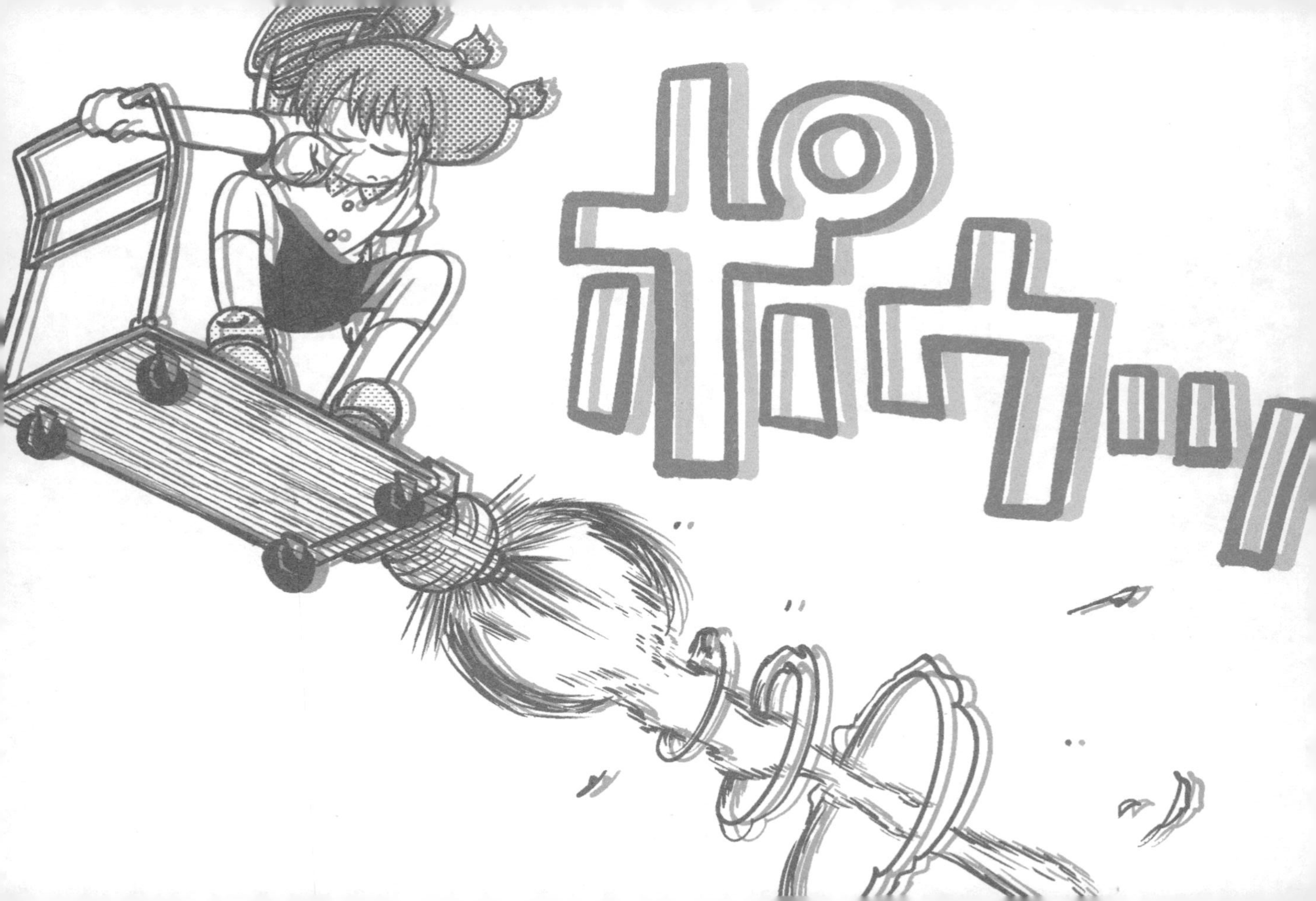
ポワウ…ッ

CITY
11

define "ordinary"

in this just-surreal-enough take on the "school genre" of manga, a group of friends (which includes a robot built by a child professor) grapples with all sorts of unexpected situations in their daily lives as high schoolers.

the gags, jokes, puns and random haiku keep this series off-kilter even as the characters grow and change. check out this new take on a storied genre and meet the new ordinary.

all volumes available now!

nichijou

my ordinary life

keiichi arawi

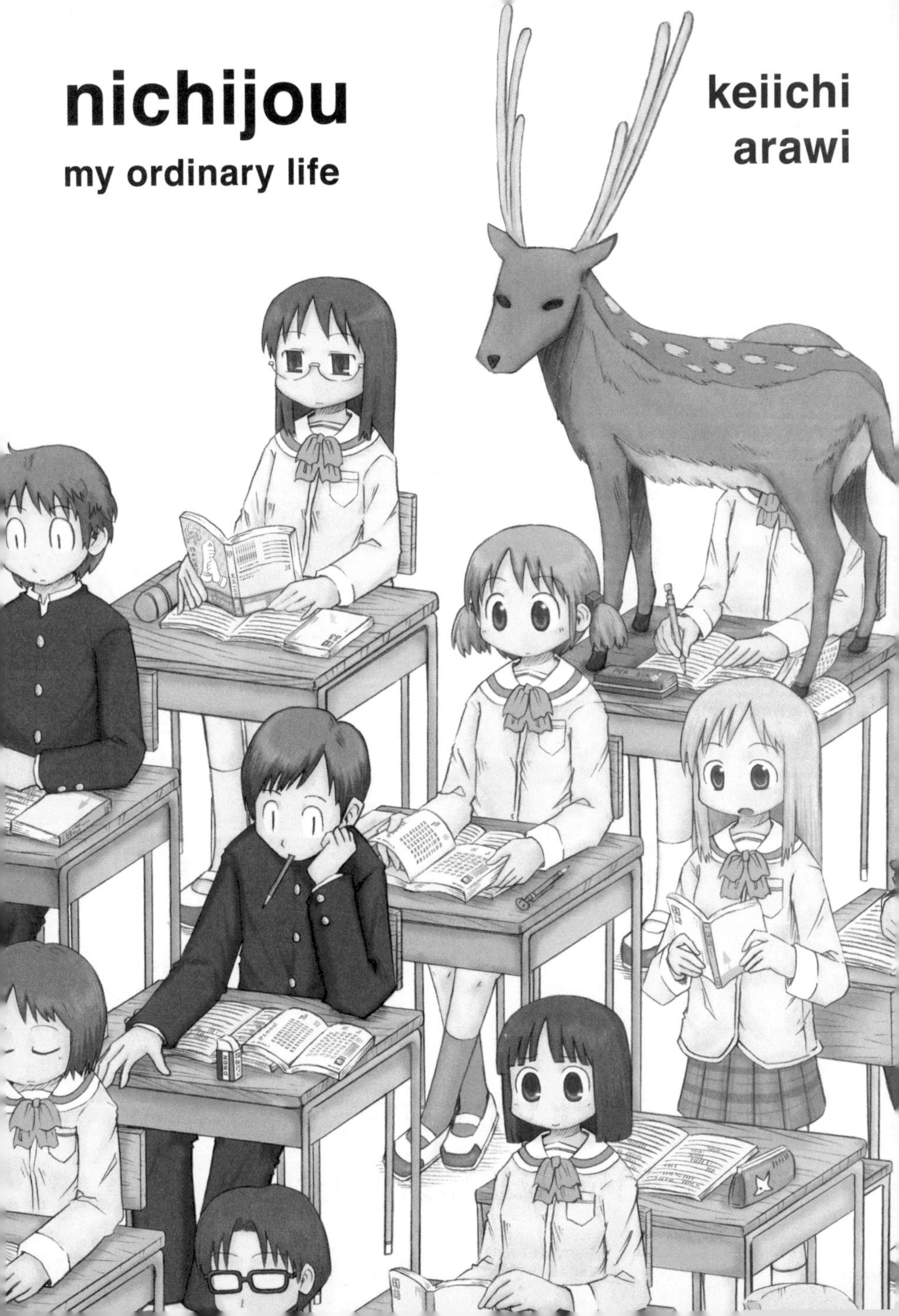

The follow-up to the hit manga series *nichijou*, *Helvetica Standard* is a full-color anthology of Keiichi Arawi's comic art and design work. Funny and heartwarming, *Helvetica Standard* is a humorous look at modern day Japanese design in comic form.

Helvetica Standard is a deep dive into the artistic and creative world of Keiichi Arawi. Part comic, part diary, part art and design book, *Helvetica Standard* is a deconstruction of the world of *nichijou*.

Both Parts Available Now!

Keiichi
Arawi

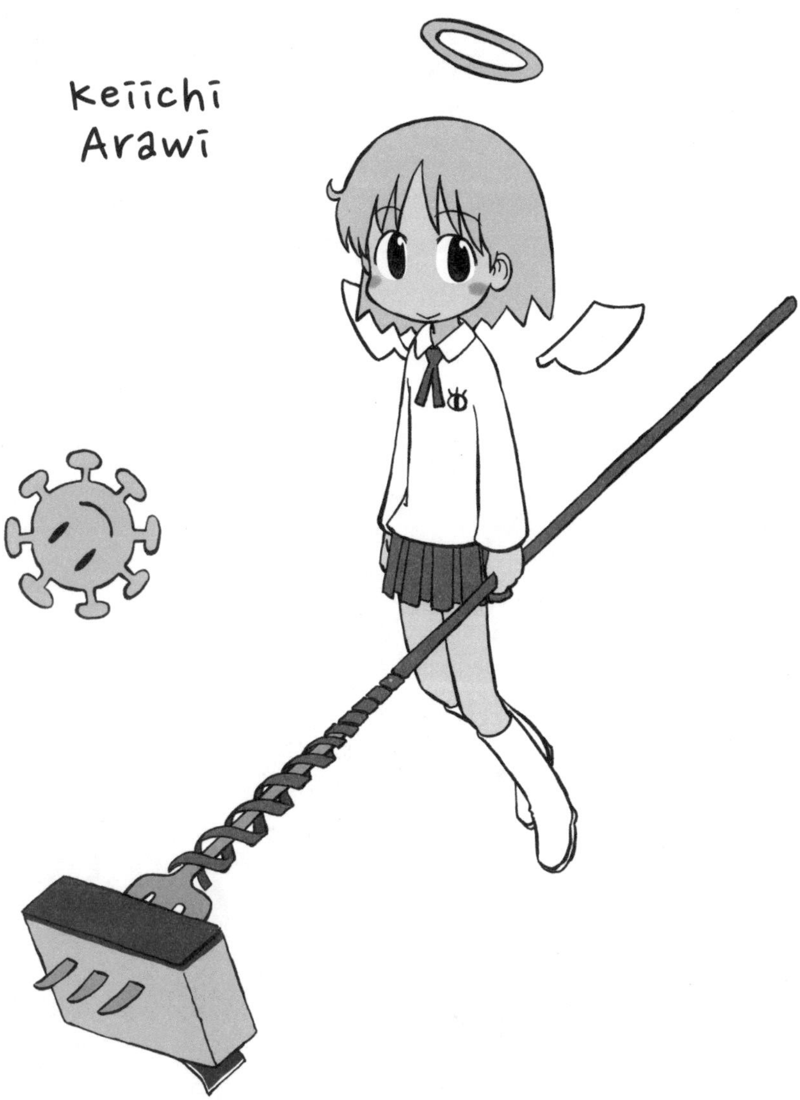

Helvetica Standard

CITY 11

A Vertical Comics Edition

Editor: Daniel Joseph
Translation: Jenny McKeon
Production: Grace Lu
Hiroko Mizuno

First published in Japan in 2020 by Kodansha, Ltd., Tokyo
Publication rights for this English edition arranged through Kodansha, Ltd., Tokyo
English language version produced by Vertical Comics,
an imprint of Kodansha USA Publishing, LLC

Translation provided by Vertical Comics, 2021
Published by Kodansha USA Publishing, LLC, New York

Originally published in Japanese as *CITY 11* by Kodansha, Ltd.
CITY first serialized in *Morning,* Kodansha, Ltd., 2016-

ISBN: 978-1-647290-06-1

Manufactured in Canada

First Edition

Kodansha USA Publishing, LLC
451 Park Avenue South
7th Floor
New York, NY 10016
www.kodansha.us

Vertical books are distributed through Penguin-Random House Publisher Services.